The PEAR Installer Manifesto

Revolutionizing PHP Application Development and Deployment

The creator of the latest innovations in this powerful code management and deployment system shows you how to unleash its hidden power across your complete PHP development lifecycle.

Gregory Beaver

D1737612

BIRMINGHAM - MUMBAI

The PEAR Installer Manifesto
Revolutionizing PHP Application Development and Deployment

First published: October 2006

Production Reference: 1201006

Published by Packt Publishing Ltd.
32 Lincoln Road
Olton
Birmingham, B27 6PA, UK.

ISBN 1-904811-19-1

www.packtpub.com

Cover Image by www.visionwt.com

Credits

Author

Gregory Beaver

Reviewers

Sebastian Bergmann

Lukas Kahwe Smith

Development Editor

Douglas Paterson

Technical Editors

Divya Menon

Saurabh Singh

Editorial Manager

Dipali Chittar

Indexer

Mithil Kulkarni

Proofreader

Chris Smith

Layouts and Illustrations

Shantanu Zagade

Cover Designer

Shantanu Zagade

About the Author

Gregory Beaver has been one of the most active contributors to open-source PHP development since 2001. As the primary developer of important infrastructure software such as phpDocumentor, the PEAR installer, PHP_Archive, PHP_LexerGenerator, and PHP_ParserGenerator as well as co-lead of the Phar PHP extension, Gregory has helped to ease the development needs of PHP developers around the world.

After he transformed phpDocumentor from a small project into the most advanced auto-documentation tools for PHP, phpDocumentor was voted second best PHP tool in Germany-based *PHP Magazin's* 2003 Reader's Choice awards list for best PHP application, and voted third best PEAR package (`http://tinyurl.com/bn7pb`). Currently, he is working to refactor the PEAR installer for PHP 6, as well as helping to lead the PEAR community forward. Gregory blogs about his programming escapades and other news on his blog, Lot 49 (`http://greg.chiaraquartet.net`). Gregory also leads a mysterious double life as the cellist of the internationally renowned Chiara String Quartet (`http://www.chiaraquartet.net`) with whom he tours the world. He lives in Lincoln, Nebraska where he is a full-time lecturer/artist-in-residence at the University of Nebraska-Lincoln Hixson-Lied College of Fine Arts.

To Julie, who does not love PHP, but loves me anyways.

About the Reviewers

Sebastian Bergmann is a long-time contributor to various PHP projects, including PHP itself. He is currently working at eZ systems AS in Skien, Norway on the Workflow Management component for the eZ platform. As the developer of PHPUnit, he also helps with testing the eZ components. In his free time he likes to hack on Open Source software and to take photographs, preferably while travelling the world.

Lukas Kahwe Smith has been developing PHP since 2000 and joined the PEAR repository in 2001. Since then he has developed and maintained several PEAR packages, most notably MDB2 and LiveUser and has influenced the organization of the project itself as a founding member of the PEAR Group steering committee and QA core team. Aside from several magazine publications, he is a well-known speaker at various international PHP conferences.

Table of Contents

Preface

Chances are, you've seen the acronym **PEAR** at some point in your use of PHP, whether it was in passing or when installing and using a package from `pear.php.net`. If you've investigated, you've probably heard of popular software provided by PEAR, such as the DB database abstraction package, or the HTML_QuickForm package. What you may not realize is that PEAR is much more than just a collection of packages that you can use. PEAR also contains the most versatile installation program for PHP, the PEAR installer.

With the PEAR installer, you can do much more than just install packages from `pear.php.net`. You can install packages from other PEAR channels, distribute your own software projects using your own PEAR channel, and even maintain a complex web project, all using the PEAR installer. Surprised? Well read on, as this book reveals the intimate secrets of the PEAR installer and how it will revolutionize your everyday development with the PHP programming language!

What This Book Covers

Chapter 1 introduces you to the PEAR installer. We begin with a look at the traditional unzip-and-go method of distributing PHP software and compare its advantages and disadvantages to the PEAR installer's package-based method of distributing PHP software. You will see the innovation of PEAR channels, take a peek inside how the PEAR installer installs files from packages, and learn how it knows where to install them. Finally, you will see the many ways to acquire the PEAR installer and even how to install PEAR remotely onto a web host that does not provide shell access.

Chapter 2 is a must-read for all PHP developers, as it explains the basic workings of `package.xml`, the heart of the PEAR installer. `package.xml` is used to control almost everything the PEAR installer can do. You will learn about the importance of versioning in controlling the quality of packages installed, the importance of dependencies, and how the PEAR installer manages this important link between libraries and applications. You will also learn how `package.xml` organizes package metadata such as the package name, authors, release notes, and changelog, and has critical installation data such as files, dependencies, and versioning organized.

Chapter 3 goes further in depth for developers who want to take advantage of the full application-support features introduced in `package.xml` version 2.0.

Chapter 4 takes a break from looking at the details of the PEAR installer, and dives into using the PEAR installer to develop and to maintain a complicated and rapidly evolving website.

Chapter 5 covers PEAR channels. Channels are designed to make it easy to install packages from any location, but difficult to compromise your system in the process, following a basic security principle: always design things so that the easiest way to do them is the most secure.

Channels open up `pear.php.net`'s monopoly over the PEAR installer to the entire Internet. Custom-built packages distributed through your channel can even be sold and made available to specific users while co-existing peacefully with publicly available open-source packages.

Chapter 6 teaches you how to embed the PEAR installer to create a plug-in manager. The chapter creates a fake blog application that provides the ability to seamlessly query a remote PEAR channel server designed to distribute templates. Using the internal classes of the PEAR installer, our blog web application intelligently installs and upgrades templates with all of the sophistication expected from the PEAR installer.

Conventions

In this book, you will find a number of styles of text that distinguish between different kinds of information. Here are some examples of these styles, and an explanation of their meaning.

There are three styles for code. Code words in text are shown as follows: "Next, you need to create a configuration file for the remote machine using the `config-create` command."

A block of code will be set as follows:

```
<file name="blah.php" role="php">
  <tasks:replace from="@DATABASE-URL@" to="database_url"
  type="pear-config" />
</file>
```

When we wish to draw your attention to a particular part of a code block, the relevant lines or items will be made bold:

```
if (is_object($infoplugin)) {
        $bag  = new serendipity_property_bag;
        $infoplugin->introspect($bag);
    if ($bag->get('version') == $data['version']) {
      $installable = false;
    } elseif (version_compare($bag->get('version'),
    $data['version'], '<')) {
      $data['upgradable'] = true;
        $data['upgrade_version'] = $data['version'];
        $data['version'] = $bag->get('version');
```

Any command-line input and output is written as follows:

```
$ pear -c pear.ini remote-install -o DB_DataObject
```

New terms and **important words** are introduced in a bold-type font. Words that you see on the screen, in menus or dialog boxes for example, appear in our text like this: "clicking the **Next** button moves you to the next screen".

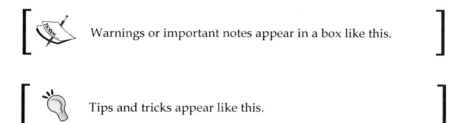

Warnings or important notes appear in a box like this.

Tips and tricks appear like this.

Reader Feedback

Feedback from our readers is always welcome. Let us know what you think about this book, what you liked or may have disliked. Reader feedback is important for us to develop titles that you really get the most out of.

To send us general feedback, simply drop an email to feedback@packtpub.com, making sure to mention the book title in the subject of your message.

If there is a book that you need and would like to see us publish, please send us a note in the **SUGGEST A TITLE** form on www.packtpub.com or email suggest@packtpub.com.

If there is a topic that you have expertise in and you are interested in either writing or contributing to a book, see our author guide on www.packtpub.com/authors.

Customer Support

Now that you are the proud owner of a Packt book, we have a number of things to help you to get the most from your purchase.

Downloading the Example Code for the Book

Visit http://www.packtpub.com/support, and select this book from the list of titles to download any example code or extra resources for this book. The files available for download will then be displayed.

The downloadable files contain instructions on how to use them.

Errata

Although we have taken every care to ensure the accuracy of our contents, mistakes do happen. If you find a mistake in one of our books—maybe a mistake in text or code—we would be grateful if you would report this to us. By doing this you can save other readers from frustration, and help to improve subsequent versions of this book. If you find any errata, report them by visiting http://www.packtpub.com/support, selecting your book, clicking on the **Submit Errata** link, and entering the details of your errata. Once your errata have been verified, your submission will be accepted and the errata added to the list of existing errata. The existing errata can be viewed by selecting your title from http://www.packtpub.com/support.

Questions

You can contact us at questions@packtpub.com if you are having a problem with some aspect of the book, and we will do our best to address it.

1
Acquiring PEAR: What is it and How do I Get It?

Chances are, you've seen the acronym PEAR at some point in your use of PHP, whether it was in passing or when installing and using a package from pear.php.net. If you've investigated, you might have probably heard of popular software provided by PEAR, such as the DB database abstraction package, or the HTML_QuickForm package. What you may not realize is that PEAR is much more than just a collection of packages that you can use. PEAR also contains the most versatile installation program for PHP, the PEAR installer. With the PEAR installer, you can do much more than just install packages from pear.php.net. You can install packages from other PEAR channels, distribute your own software projects using your own PEAR channel, and even maintain a complex intranet web project, all using the PEAR installer. Surprised? Read on, this book will reveal the intimate secrets of the PEAR installer and how it will revolutionize your everyday development with the PHP programming language.

The primary purpose of PEAR is to support code reuse. **PEAR** stands for the **PHP Extension and Application Repository**. PEAR provides both an advanced installer and a code repository at http://pear.php.net. Unlike competing PHP code repositories that you may be familiar with such as http://www.phpclasses.org or general purpose development sites like http://www.sourceforge.net, all PEAR code is organized into discrete reusable components called packages. A **package** consists of a group of files and a descriptor file called package.xml that contains meta-data about the package's contents, such as the package version, any special dependencies, and textual information such as the package description and authors.

Although most packages contain PHP code, there is no special restriction on the contents of a package. Some packages, such as http://pear.php.net/HTML_AJAX provide JavaScript files as well as PHP files. One of the example packages mentioned in Chapter 4 bundles only MP3 music files. Literally anything you can save as a file can be distributed in a PEAR package.

The software that transforms a package from an inert grouping of files into a dynamic software package is called the **PEAR installer** and is itself a PEAR package, located at http://pear.php.net/PEAR. In other words, the PEAR installer can be used to upgrade itself. It is truly a very powerful application.

Traditionally, PHP software has been distributed with a passive installation approach, following these typical steps:

1. Download a .zip or a .tar.gz containing all the files of the application
2. Decompress the files into a folder in your website's document root
3. Read the *Readme* and *Install* files
4. Do various post-installation tasks, creating files, checking requirements
5. Test it
6. Often, changes are required at the system-level changes (adding extensions to php.ini, changing php.ini settings, upgrading PHP itself)

For lack of a better name, we'll call this the *"unzip-and-go"* system of PHP software distribution. Although this in fact works very well for small, single-developer low-traffic websites, it contains a hidden cost that is not immediately apparent. There is one single fact about the unzip-and-go software installation system that limits its ultimate usefulness:

 Upgrading unzip-and-go installations is very hard

In today's fast-paced development world, one of the weaknesses of the Internet is security. Quite often, serious security vulnerabilities are discovered in software that requires an immediate upgrade to fix. When using a complete unzip-and-go software application, upgrading involves a large degree of risk. First of all, once the upgrade is complete, if the software is broken, reverting the upgrade requires either restoring from a backup or re-installing the old software. Reverting to an earlier package version with the PEAR installer is a one-line command and is very straightforward.

Why is Upgrading Necessary at all if the Code is Working?

Just a month before writing this chapter, our hosting provider's website was compromised. Due to a number of unfortunate events, I was completely locked out of our server for an unacceptable period of time and we lost business as a result of the delay in receiving important emails.

The cause of this compromise was—an innocent installation of an outdated copy of a CVS viewing program. The program contained an arbitrary PHP execution vulnerability, and the systems administrator had not upgraded to the latest version because it was tremendously difficult to upgrade the viewing software.

Had this same software been distributed as a PEAR package, upgrading would have been a one-line command as follows:

```
$ pear upgrade PackageName
```

The lost business would have never been a problem then. In today's world, upgrading software is in fact critical to the long-term success of any website, no matter how large or small.

The advantages of using the PEAR installer over a simple unzip-and-go solution are most apparent when projects grow in complexity. Let's look at a short list of the advantages:

- File conflicts are not possible

- Problems caused by incompatible PHP versions/PHP extensions/PHP code are all handled by advanced dependency resolution

- Distributing application development between different sites is simple due to the revolutionary new PEAR channels feature introduced in PEAR version 1.4.0 (Chapter 5 is devoted to exploration of PEAR channels)

- All installation configurations can be handled in a standardized and consistent way for all packages—once you learn how to handle one PEAR package; all the others are handled in the same way.

- Versioning of code allows clear fault resolution as well as the ability to revert changes that break code.

Before using the PEAR installer, it is important to understand the disadvantages of using the PEAR installer over unzip-and-go:

- The PEAR installer itself must be installed on the development machine and preferably on the server (although this is no longer required thanks to the PEAR_RemoteInstaller package, discussed in section 1.3.3.1, Synchronizing to a server with no shell access using PEAR_RemoteInstaller).

- If you are distributing your own packages, you need a full understanding of the `package.xml` description file, and possibly an understanding of PEAR channels in order to set one up yourself.

- Depending on relative file locations is not always possible through traditional means. This is due to the flexibility of PEAR configuration. Rather than relying upon `dirname(__FILE__)`, a PEAR-specific way must be used, such as file replacement tasks (discussed in Chapter 2).

- Additional configuration outside of `php.ini` may be needed in `pear.conf/pear.ini` (most of this configuration is handled when the PEAR installer is installed).

The most significant barrier to using PEAR has traditionally been the effort it takes to install the PEAR installer itself, and this has been the focus of recent efforts to improve the installer's installation process. There is a great deal of possibility in recent innovations made possible by PHP version 5.1.0 or newer, as evidenced by work made possible by the PHP_Archive PEAR package (`http://pear.php.net/PHP_Archive`) and its sibling, the phar PECL extension (`http://pecl.php.net/phar`). These packages enable the distribution of an application in a single file that greatly enhances the capabilities of an installer.

A Democratic Innovation for PHP: PEAR Channels

The most important innovation of the PEAR installer is PEAR channels, something that no other package distribution mechanism supports. PEAR channels are a simple way to easily install packages from multiple sources over the Internet.

Through the use of PEAR channels, applications can reliably depend on code from several unrelated sources. Some of the more prominent channels are:

- `pear.php.net`: PEAR itself is a channel
- `pecl.php.net`: PECL is for PHP extensions what PEAR is to regular PHP packages
- `gnope.org`: PHP-GTK2 channel

- `pear.chiaraquartet.net`: The first PEAR channel outside the `php.net` domain

- `components.ez.no`: eZ components PEAR channel

- `pearified.com`: source of PEAR-packaged Smarty, phpMyAdmin and others

Also of interest are channel aggregators like:

- `http://www.pearadise.com`: Tobias Schlitt's PEAR channel aggregator

- `http://www.pearified.com`: The channel aggregator portion of the pearified channel

- `http://www.upear.com`: Another aggregator

Each PEAR channel distributes code fitting a wide variety of needs.

What is PEAR? A Code Repository or an Installer?

PEAR has a tendency to confuse people as the name is used interchangeably for the PEAR installer and for the PEAR repository at `http://pear.php.net`. This confusion naturally arises from the fact that the front page of `pear.php.net` says **"PEAR is a framework and distribution system for reusable PHP components"** but the PEAR installer's package name is "PEAR". In fact, PEAR is both a code repository and an installer; the two are linked inextricably by the fact that much of PEAR's strength is the ability to update a local installation from packages on a remote server over the Internet.

PEAR Package Repository and PEAR Channel

The PEAR package repository at `pear.php.net` is the official PEAR channel, and is the oldest PEAR channel, predating the concept of PEAR channels by five years. Many popular packages are distributed via `pear.php.net` such as **HTML_QuickForm**, **DB_DataObject**, **MDB2**, and **PhpDocumentor**. Most of the time, when people refer to "PEAR" in the abstract, one of the packages distributed at `pear.php.net` is what they are talking about.

The package repository at `pear.php.net` was established in 1999 by Stig Bakken and a few others to help fill in the gaps in PHP. PEAR's first usable release coincided with approximately PHP version 4.0.6. At this time, PEAR was designed as a framework, providing several base classes and an installer to manage them. The PEAR package provided two of the base classes, `PEAR` and `System`. The PEAR class, located in file

`PEAR.php` was designed to provide basic error handling and a few other add-ons beyond what is available in PHP's internal `trigger_error()` error handling.

Several basic packages were designed to handle common tasks, such as DB for database-independent code, **HTML_Form** for **HTML Forms**, **Log** for basic logging, and this list expanded (to make a long story short) until the present day where there are 374 packages available from `pear.php.net` at the time of this chapter, and more on the way via pending proposals.

PEAR has had its share of woes since its rosy beginnings. PHP has evolved, and introduced several features that supersede the functionality provided by PEAR. For instance, the `Exception` class introduced in PHP 5.0.0 provides similar functionality to the `PEAR_Error class`, the PDO extension provides similar functionality to the DB package, and so on. In addition, as PEAR has grown, some problems in its initial design as a repository have surfaced and led to both minor and major crises.

Several good things have come out of these growing pains, including the efficient PEPr proposal system for proposing new packages, and a strong push towards both stability and innovation. Much of the push towards innovation is coming from external pressure due to the advent of new ideas from projects like SolarPHP, eZ components, Phing, Propel, Agavi, and the Zend Framework. However, one of the significant forces of innovation in PEAR is the PEAR installer itself, specifically with the new features found in version 1.4.0 and newer.

One of the crucial new features in the newer versions of the PEAR installer is PEAR channels. A **PEAR channel** is simply a server that provides packages like `pear.php.net`, and also provides special web services that enable the PEAR installer to communicate with the server; channels are covered in detail in Chapter 4.

PEAR Installer

Most books that discuss PEAR spend a great deal of time on using popular packages from the PEAR repository (`http://pear.php.net`) such as DB (`http://pear.php.net/DB`) or HTML_QuickForm (`http://pear.php.net/HTML_QuickForm`). This book takes a different route, instead focusing exclusively on the power surrounding the installation mechanism of the PEAR installer itself. When you see a reference to *PEAR* in this book, you should know that it is in fact a reference to the PEAR installer (`http://pear.php.net/PEAR`) and not to the repository at large.

The PEAR installer consists of four abstract task-oriented sections:

- `package.xml` parser and dependency processor
- File installation processor, configuration processor, and package registry

- User front end and command processor
- Remote server synchronization and downloading engine

Fortunately, as an end-user, you don't really need to know or care about any of these beyond the way that your application communicates with the installer and how people will actually use the installer to install your code.

First and foremost, you need to understand how PEAR actually installs its packages, as this is a little different from the old unzip-and-go philosophy. PEAR categorizes files into different types, and installs each file type differently. For instance, files of type php will be installed into a subdirectory of the user's configuration variable `php_dir`. So if the user has set `php_dir` to `/usr/local/lib/php/pear`, a file that is packaged in directory `Foo/Bar/Test.php` will be installed into `/usr/local/lib/php/pear/Foo/Bar/Test.php`. Files of type data will be installed into a subdirectory of the user's configuration variable `data_dir`, but unlike PHP files, data files are installed into their own private sub-directory based on the package name. If the user has set `data_dir` to be `/usr/local/lib/php/data` and the package is named "TestPackage", a file that is packaged in directory `Foo/Bar/Test.dat` will not be installed at `/usr/local/lib/php/data/Foo/Bar/Test.dat`, but instead be installed in `/usr/local/lib/php/data/TestPackage/Foo/Bar/Test.dat`! This and other details of PEAR's installation are covered in Chapter 2.

Next, you need to know a bit about how PEAR knows which files are in a package, what it needs in order to work (i.e. "This package only works in PHP 4.3.0 and newer, and needs any version of the DB_DataObject package, and only versions 1.2.3 of the Log package, recommending version 1.4.6 be installed"), or its dependencies. This information is also covered in Chapter 2, where we learn about the `package.xml` file format.

After reading Chapters 2 and 3, you should know enough about PEAR to manage the creation of your own packages for local installation, or to propose a new package to the official `pear.php.net` repository. Should you wish to distribute your packages for others to use, whether it be free, for private clients, or for sale, you will need to have an understanding of how PEAR channels work. Setting up a channel server is a relatively easy task. At the time of writing this chapter, there was one option available for setting up a channel, but several potential competing options are on the verge of completion. It's an exciting time to be involved in PHP! Setting up your own channel is covered in Chapter 5.

Of course, not everyone is distributing their code publicly. Most developers are busy designing their own websites either by themselves or in a team. The PEAR installer is a highly effective tool for managing a complete website when used in conjunction with a revision control system. Chapter 4 covers this topic in great detail.

In short, the PEAR installer is one of the most effective tools for managing a high-quality software library, high-quality application, or a high-quality website.

Installing the PEAR Installer

There are three methods of acquiring PEAR. The first way has been available since PHP 4.2.0, and simply involves installing PHP and either configuring --with-pear (on Unix) or running go-pear from within the PHP directory.

I'm Running Windows and my PHP doesn't have PEAR in it, Where is it?

If you are running PHP version 5.1 or older, to get a copy of PHP that bundles PEAR, you need to download the .zip file rather than the Windows installer (.msi). PHP 5.2.0 and newer has vastly improved the Windows Installer (.msi) distribution, and this is recommended to acquire PEAR. The installer (at least at this time) is not really useful at all, as it is never updated unless there is a critical error. As such, getting the truly useful elements of PHP requires using the .zip file. Never fear, PHP is pretty much an unzip-and-go language on Windows.

If I were less diplomatic, I might say something like "Don't even think about running PHP on Windows as a production server." However, I do feel it is important to say this: "In my opinion, running PHP on Windows as a production server is not worth the effort and expense." Although it can be done, the only reason it should ever be considered is if your boss will fire you on installing Unix. Or you work for a company that maintains the Windows operating system. In that case, you will be forgiven.

The second involves grabbing the go-pear script from http://pear.php.net/go-pear, and saving it as go-pear.php, then running this file. Last, there are a few unofficial sources for acquiring PEAR, the most notable being the Gnope installer that sets up PHP 5.1, PEAR, and PHP-GTK2 in one step.

PEAR Bundled with PHP

As mentioned above, if you are running Windows, installing PEAR is relatively simple. Running the go-pear command will run the installation script. In addition, as of PHP version 5.2.0, there is an excellent Windows Installer-based (.msi file extension) installation mechanism that bundles PEAR in its distribution, and is recommended. For earlier PHP versions, in order to obtain a bundled PEAR, you must download the .zip file distribution instead of the .msi Windows Installer-based installation mechanism.

If you are running Unix, you need to use at least this minimal configure line to set up PEAR:

```
$ ./configure --enable-cli --enable-tokenizer --with-pcre-regex --
enable-xml
```

To take full advantage of PEAR, it is a good idea to enable the zlib extension for accessing compressed PEAR packages as well:

```
$ ./configure --enable-cli --enable-tokenizer --with-pcre-regex --
enable-xml --with-zlib
```

When you install, be sure that you have full write access to the directory that PEAR will be installed in (usually /usr/local/lib, but configurable with the --prefix option; /lib is appended to the prefix). When you install PEAR, it will also install the needed packages Console_Getopt and Archive_Tar.

```
$ make install-pear
Installing PEAR Environment:        /usr/local/lib/php/
[PEAR] Archive_Tar    - installed : 1.3.1
[PEAR] Console_Getopt - installed : 1.2
pear/PEAR can optionally use package "pear/XML_RPC" (version >= 1.4.0)
[PEAR] PEAR           - installed : 1.4.9
Wrote PEAR system config file at: /usr/local/etc/pear.conf
You may want to add: /usr/local/lib/php to your php.ini include_path
```

After completing PEAR installation, as the last line of installation suggests, you will want to ensure that PEAR is in php.ini's include_path setting. The easiest way to determine this is to first find php.ini:

```
$ php -i |grep php[.]ini
Configuration File (php.ini) Path => /usr/local/lib
```

This example shows that php.ini is located at /usr/local/lib/php.ini. Open this file with your favorite editor, and either find the line that says "include_path=" or add a new one that is something like this:

```
    include_path=.:/usr/local/lib/php
```

Of course, substitute the suggested path from your specific installation (the last line of output) for /usr/local/lib/php.

What is this so-called "include_path"?

Oh dear — time to pull out the PHP manual again, to be specific, http://www.php.net/include. To summarize, the include statement and its cousins include_once, require and require_once all serve to dynamically include external PHP code. If you pass a full path like /path/to/my.php:

```
include '/path/to/PEAR.php';
```

then naturally /path/to/my.php will *replace* the include statement and be executed. If, however, you pass in a relative path like:

```
include 'PEAR.php';
```

This will instead search through the include_path and try to find a PEAR.php file. If the include_path is .:/usr/local/lib/php, then PHP will first try to find PEAR.php in the current directory (.), and if it is not found, then it will search for PEAR.php in /usr/local/lib/php/PEAR.php. This allows customization of library locations on the disk, which is precisely what PEAR attempts to accomplish.

If you are running Windows, the go-pear batch file will prompt you to choose a location to install PEAR, defaulting to either C:\php4 for version 4, C:\php5 for version 5.0, or the current directory for version 5.1 or newer. Unless you have a compelling reason to install PEAR elsewhere, it is a good idea to accept the default locations, as it will save some potential trouble later on. If you are installing PEAR from version 5.1.0 or newer, the installer will ask you if you are installing a local or a system installation.

```
Are you installing a system-wide PEAR or a local copy?

(system|local) [system] :
```

Simply hit *Return* to install a system-wide PEAR (in general, with installation of PEAR, if you don't know what it is asking you, always choose the default value). Next, it will ask you for a location to install your copy of PEAR:

```
Below is a suggested file layout for your new PEAR installation.  To
change individual locations, type the number in front of the
directory.  Type 'all' to change all of them or simply press Enter to
accept these locations.
```

```
1. Installation base ($prefix)    : C:\php51
2. Binaries directory             : C:\php51
3. PHP code directory ($php_dir)  : C:\php51\pear
4. Documentation directory        : C:\php51\pear\docs
5. Data directory                 : C:\php51\pear\data
6. Tests directory                : C:\php51\pear\tests
7. Name of configuration file     : C:\php5\pear.ini
8. Path to CLI php.exe            : C:\php51\.

1-8, 'all' or Enter to continue:
```

Change any values you wish to change by typing the number in front of the item and hit *Enter*. If you wish to change the installation base directory, type **1** and hit *Enter*. If you want to modify all of the values, type **all** and hit *Enter*. Once you are satisfied, hit *Enter* without typing anything to continue. At this point, it will install packages (which should look similar to what is displayed in Unix installation of PEAR) and finally ask if you would like to modify php.ini. If you choose to do this, it will automatically update the include_path setting in php.ini, and you will be good to go.

Installation for PHP Versions Older than 5.1.0

If you have a version of PHP older than 5.1.0 and wish to install PEAR, you should not use the bundled version of PEAR, but instead install PEAR via the go-pear script. To retrieve this script, browse to http://pear.php.net/go-pear in any web browser and save it to disk as go-pear.php, or if on Unix, then you have the wget command:

```
$ wget -O go-pear.php http://pear.php.net/go-pear
```

Once you have go-pear.php accessible, simply run it:

```
$ php go-pear.php
```

Why Just for PHP 5.1.0 and Older?

As I was asked once, "Why is it important to only use the `go-pear` script for PHP versions older than 5.1.0? Will this not also change over time when there is a new PEAR installer released with PHP 6.0.0?"

The reason for this has to do with how `go-pear` works. The `go-pear` script is a brilliant design that extracts key files directly from CVS based on their release tags and then downloads packages and installs them based on their latest stable version. Although brilliant, this is a dangerous approach that guarantees your installation will break if there is a problem in CVS.

The PEAR installer bundled with PHP version 5.1.0 and newer is in fact self-contained, does not contact the Internet at all, and is tested and guaranteed to work with that version of PHP. Once PEAR is installed, grabbing the latest version is both easy and safer than using `go-pear`:

```
pear upgrade PEAR
```

Output will be very similar to `go-pear` from bundled PHP, but will instead begin with:

```
$ php go-pear.php
Welcome to go-pear!

Go-pear will install the 'pear' command and all the files needed by
it.  This command is your tool for PEAR installation and maintenance.

Use 'php go-pear.php local' to install a local copy of PEAR.

Go-pear also lets you download and install the PEAR packages bundled
with PHP: DB, Net_Socket, Net_SMTP, Mail, XML_Parser, PHPUnit.

If you wish to abort, press Control-C now, or press Enter to continue:
```

Because `go-pear` requires internet access, the next question will be for a proxy. Be sure that if you are behind a firewall, you know whether you need to use a proxy:

```
HTTP proxy (http://user:password@proxy.myhost.com:port),
or Enter for none::
```

The next step of the installation process should look pretty familiar:

```
Below is a suggested file layout for your new PEAR installation. To
change individual locations, type the number in front of the directory.
Type 'all' to change all of them or simply press Enter to accept
these locations.

  1. Installation prefix          : C:\php51
  2. Binaries directory           : $prefix
  3. PHP code directory ($php_dir) : $prefix\pear
  4. Documentation base directory  : $php_dir\docs
  5. Data base directory           : $php_dir\data
  6. Tests base directory          : $php_dir\tests
  7. Temporary files directory     :
  8. php.exe path                  : C:\php51\php.exe

1-8, 'all' or Enter to continue:
```

After choosing location, `go-pear` will download the needed code, and install PEAR packages. It will also ask whether to install a few more packages, and at the end whether to modify `php.ini`.

If you are feeling adventurous, you might also simply try opening `go-pear.php` inside a web browser. This will install the web front end to PEAR, which is very nice but not as actively maintained as the **Command-Line Installer** (CLI).

Other Unofficial Sources

Before we continue, it is important to note that everything in this section is unofficial and therefore not supported by the folks over at `pear.php.net`. Any problems you encounter are the domain of the site from which you downloaded it! Ok, enough preambles.

Christian Weiske over at `http://www.gnope.org` has been working hard at both making PHP-GTK2 work in PHP 5.1 and making it easy to install PHP-GTK2 applications using PEAR. As such, he worked very closely with me to create a GTK2 front end to the PEAR installer, which is now available through PEAR at `http://pear.php.net/PEAR_Frontend_Gtk2`. This is the official PHP-GTK2 front end for PEAR. The front end requires that PEAR already be installed in order to use it.

However, Christian has taken it up a notch, and has written a Windows installer that provides the latest stable PHP 5.1, PEAR, and PHP-GTK2 that sets up everything for you. This is a great way to get started with PEAR, if you are new to the whole process. The current release is version 1.0, but this is an alpha release, so things may not work properly.

The first thing you should note is that if you have already set up PHP, the PATH environment variable in Windows may cause some conflicts with the existing PHP installation. In short, don't try to install both a regular copy of PHP and the gnope PHP unless you know what you are doing.

Installing gnope is really easy, just download the installer and run it. The prompts are just like any other Windows installation.

Synchronizing to a Server with no Shell Access Using PEAR_RemoteInstaller

Once you have successfully installed PEAR on a development machine, how do you properly install PEAR on the live server? For many developers, this is simply a matter of repeating the same steps on the live server that are performed on the development server. However, many developers out there have the misfortune of using a shared hosting provider who does not provide a shell, but does provide PHP. In the past, this essentially eliminated any possibility of successfully installing PEAR packages.

As of PEAR 1.4.0, this is no longer an issue, thanks to the PEAR_RemoteInstaller package (`http://pear.php.net/PEAR_RemoteInstaller`). This package provides special commands for synchronizing a customized PEAR server and the remote server. Unlike other solutions, the only tools required to implement this are PHP 5 on your development machine, and access to an FTP server.

To get started, install PEAR_RemoteInstaller onto your development machine:

```
$ pear install PEAR_RemoteInstaller
```

Publication Limitation

Note that at the time this book was written, the latest version of PEAR_RemoteInstaller was 0.3.0, stability alpha. To install, you will need to append –alpha or -0.3.0 as in:

```
$ pear install PEAR_RemoteInstaller-alpha
```

Or

```
$ pear install PEAR_RemoteInstaller-0.3.0
```

Next, you need to create a configuration file for the remote machine using the `config-create` command. However, before this is possible, it is important to know the full path to your host. The easiest system to determine this is to run this simple script on your web host:

```php
<?php
echo __FILE__;
?>
```

Save this as me.php, and upload it to your web host. When run, this will output something similar to:

```
/home/myuser/htdocs/me.php
```

Once you have this information, you can begin

```
$ pear config-create /home/myuser pear.ini
```

This will display something similar to:

```
CONFIGURATION (CHANNEL PEAR.PHP.NET):

=======================================
```

Auto-discover new Channels	auto_discover	<not set>
Default Channel	default_channel	pear.php.net
HTTP Proxy Server Address	http_proxy	<not set>
PEAR server [DEPRECATED]	master_server	<not set>
Default Channel Mirror	preferred_mirror	<not set>
Remote Configuration File	remote_config	<not set>
PEAR executables directory	bin_dir	/home/myuser/pear
PEAR documentation directory	doc_dir	/home/myuser/pear/docs
PHP extension directory	ext_dir	/home/myuser/pear/ext
PEAR directory	php_dir	/home/myuser/pear/php
PEAR Installer cache directory	cache_dir	/home/myuser/pear/cache
PEAR data directory	data_dir	/home/myuser/pear/data
PHP CLI/CGI binary	php_bin	C:\php5\php.exe
PEAR test directory	test_dir	/home/myuser/pear/tests
Cache TimeToLive	cache_ttl	<not set>
Preferred Package State	preferred_state	<not set>
Unix file mask	umask	<not set>
Debug Log Level	verbose	<not set>
PEAR password (for maintainers)	password	<not set>
Signature Handling Program	sig_bin	<not set>
Signature Key Directory	sig_keydir	<not set>
Signature Key Id	sig_keyid	<not set>
Package Signature Type	sig_type	<not set>

PEAR username (for maintainers)	username	<not set>
User Configuration File	Filename	C:\test\pear.ini
System Configuration File	Filename	#no#system#config#

Successfully created default configuration file "C:\test\pear.ini"

Once you have the `pear.ini` file, upload it to your remote web host and save it in the `/home/myuser` directory (the default directory of your FTP login). Next, we need to create our local working copy of PEAR:

```
$ mkdir remote
```

```
$ cd remote
```

If you are running Windows:

```
$ pear config-create -w C:\remote\ pear.ini
```

Otherwise (assuming you are running as user `foo` on your development machine):

```
$ pear config-create /home/foo pear.ini
```

Next, determine the kind of FTP connection you use. You'll need to know your username and password for accessing FTP, and the host name. For our example, we will use `myuser` and `password` as the user/password combination, and `yourwebsite.example.com` as the host.

If you use regular FTP, you will want to do:

```
$ pear -c pear.ini config-set remote_config ftp://myuser:password@
yourwebsite.example.com/
```

If you use FTPS, you will want to do:

```
$ pear -c pear.ini config-set remote_config ftps://myuser:password@
yourwebsite.example.com/
```

If you use SFTP, you will want to do:

```
$ pear -c pear.ini config-set remote_config ssh2.sftp://myuser:password@
yourwebsite.example.com/
```

In order to use SFTP, you need to install the SSH2 extension from `pecl.php.net` (`http://pecl.php.net/ssh2`), an excellent extension written by Sara Golemon. On Unix, this is simple; SSH2 can be installed via:

```
$ pecl install ssh2
```

On Windows, `php_ssh2.dll` should be distributed with your distribution of PHP 5. If not, you can grab a copy from `http://pecl4win.php.net`.

Once we reach this stage, the next step is to try installing a package. Let's install Savant3, an excellent template engine for PHP 5+ that utilizes the elegance of PHP itself as a templating language.

```
$ pear -c pear.ini channel-discover savant.pearified.com
$ pear -c pear.ini remote-install savant/Savant3
```

If everything works, you will see:

remote install OK: savant.pearified.com/Savant3-3.0.0

At this point, fire up your FTP browser and you'll see that the files were uploaded to /home/myuser/pear/php/Savant3.php and to the /home/myuser/pear/php/ Savant3 directory.

Errors about alpha/beta

If installation fails with a notice about preferred state, try appending -alpha as in:

```
$ pear -c pear.ini remote-install savant/
Savant3-alpha
```

This will work because it instructs the installer to temporarily ignore your preferred_state configuration variable and to instead download the latest alpha or more stable version. In other words, with a preferred_state of stable, if Savant3 version 3.2.0 stable is available, it will be installed. However, if version 3.2.1 alpha is available, a newer version, it will not be installed because its stability is too low. However, by appending -alpha, the installer is instructed to instead grab the newest version 3.2.1 and install that version.

You may be thinking, how does this differ from just extracting the files and uploading them manually? The answer becomes apparent when managing more complex packages like DB_DataObject or LiveUser. Both of these packages have dependencies that must be installed in order to work. Although it is possible to manually install them and upload, it is very easy to forget a dependency. Worse, the entire process has to be repeated upon upgrade.

Installing DB_DataObject with its dependency on PEAR, Validate, and DB is as simple as:

```
$ pear -c pear.ini remote-install -o DB_DataObject
```

The same is true of upgrading:

```
$ pear -c pear.ini remote-upgrade -o DB_DataObject
```

Uninstalling is also simple, and responds to the full strength of the PEAR installer's dependency validation:

```
$ pear -c pear.ini remote-uninstall DB_DataObject
```

The rsync Method

If you are developing a complex website for a customer who has money, it may be best to develop on an identical machine with identical software and hardware configuration. Set up the entire website locally, and synchronize it with the remote website using `rsync`. This still works well with using source control and a PEAR-installable package, as development should be synced with discrete package versions.

Summary

In this chapter, we learned about the split personality of PEAR as code repository at `pear.php.net` and as the PEAR installer. We investigated the predominant unzip-and-go method of distributing PHP software and compared its advantages and disadvantages to the PEAR installer's package-based method of distributing PHP software. After a quick look into the exciting new innovation of PEAR channels, we took a peek inside the basics of how the PEAR installer installs files from packages and how it knows where to install them. Finally, we learned the many ways to acquire the PEAR installer and even how to install PEAR remotely onto a web host that does not provide shell access.

2
Mastering PHP Software Management with the PEAR Installer

In this chapter, we learn how to turn PHP software into distributable PEAR packages. In September 2005, version 1.4.0 of the PEAR installer was released. This release was a milestone, marking the transformation of PEAR from a niche-market tool for installing small libraries distributed by `pear.php.net` to a full-fledged application installation tool. For the first time, it is possible to distribute large-scale applications, and even complete web-based database-intensive applications can be installed and configured in one step.

The PEAR installer now can be used to install traditional web-based applications like phpMyAdmin and non-PEAR libraries like the popular Smarty template engine (both happen to be installable through the `http://pearified.com` PEAR channel). Two of the primary design goals of the PEAR installer are to:

- Make it possible to distribute application development across multiple development teams (i.e. stop re-inventing the wheel)
- Prevent conflicting packages from overwriting each other

All of this magic is made possible by the `package.xml` file format. `package.xml` is the heart and soul of the PEAR installer, and in order to take full advantage of PEAR's power, you need to understand its structure. Contained in `package.xml` is a list of files to be installed, information used by the PEAR installer to distinguish between different packages and releases, and information that is useful to humans, such as a description of what the package is and a changelog. This file is in fact all the PEAR installer needs to properly install software. The PEAR installer also uses the information in `package.xml` to create an installable archive in either `.tar` format or compressed `.tar` (`.tgz`) using the `pear package` command.

The PEAR installer is not limited to installation of local files, and in fact is designed to communicate over the Internet with **PEAR channel servers**. What is a channel server? A channel server provides downloadable releases for each package, and web service interfaces to meta-information about those packages and releases through XML-RPC, REST, or SOAP. Channels are discussed in depth in Chapter 5. Now that PEAR 1.4.0+ and packages like Chiara_PEAR_Server (`http://pear.chiaraquartet.net/index.php?package=Chiara_PEAR_Server`) are available, it is simple to set up your own PEAR channel server and distribute libraries and applications with all of the sophistication you've come to expect from the `pear` command.

CLI versus Web/Gtk2 Installer

Some of you reading this have probably installed the Web front end (PEAR_Frontend_Web package from `pear.php.net`) or the Gtk2 front end (PEAR_Frontend_Gtk2 package from `pear.php.net`). If so, then you have probably noticed that installing packages from other channels is even simpler, as the end user simply needs to choose the channel to install from, and all packages are listed with the most recent version and available upgrades.

We will be working with the command-line (CLI) front end to the PEAR installer in the next few chapters, as a much greater level of sophistication is available than what is possible through the Web front end, which is designed more for end users of PEAR packages than it is for developers of PEAR packages. At the time of writing this chapter, the Gtk2 front end is far more sophisticated than the Web installer, and is worth using if you are running PHP 5.1.0 or newer.

For example, if your server is `pear.example.com`, and you release a package named `Foo`, the only thing your users need to type in order to install your package is:

```
$ pear channel-discover pear.example.com
$ pear install pear.example.com/Foo
```

However, the most dynamic and important feature of the PEAR installer is the sophisticated way in which it handles dependencies on other packages, on PHP version, on PHP extensions, and on the system architecture. Through very simple syntax in `package.xml`, incredibly complex dependency scenarios can be easily and securely managed.

Before we can get started with the actual work of creating our own packages, it is important to understand the core concepts behind the design of the PEAR installer and how you will need to shape your software design to best utilize its strengths.

Distributing Libraries and Applications

The most important thing to understand is how the PEAR installer actually installs files. Most PHP developers distribute their applications as unzip-and-go archives. As such, we tend to assume that files will be in the exact same relative locations on the end user's machine that they are on our development machine. PEAR, however, is designed to be far more flexible than this.

For instance, it is common for shared web hosts to install a global copy of PEAR, but users can also install local copies and use the `include_path` from `php.ini` to choose local packages when available and global ones when they are not. In order to make this flexibility possible, PEAR groups and installs files by their type or file *role*.

Each file role has a corresponding configuration entry that defines the location at which all files of that file role will be installed. For instance, the php file role has a configuration variable named `php_dir` that defines the directory into which all PHP files are installed, the data file role has a configuration variable named `data_dir`, and so on.

This is a radical break from the traditional unzip-and-go philosophy, as it allows users to configure the installation locations in any way they desire on their own machine. This also means that the use of clever constructs to locate installed files such as `dirname(__FILE__)` are dangerous ways to code in a PEAR package. Fortunately, there are other clever ways around this that are even more flexible and secure.

PEAR Configuration

To retrieve all configuration variables and their values, use the `config-show` command. Configuration variables that correspond to file roles generally have `_dir` in their name, such as `doc_dir`, and `php_dir`.

This also changes the development process slightly: instead of testing by running code right out of the development directory, the code should first be installed via its `package.xml` file and tested as the PEAR equivalent of unzip-and-go. For this reason, the most common `pear` command to be used is:

```
$ pear up -f package.xml
```

or

```
$ pear upgrade --force package.xml
```

This command allows the "upgrade" from (for instance) PEAR version 1.5.0a1 to PEAR version 1.5.0a1 when a bug has been fixed or a new feature has been added. This command in actuality facilitates rapid development by allowing one to quickly replace the existing files within a version after having made changes without requiring a bump in version number. In other words, if we had to change the version every time a minor change was made on a development machine, this would be onerous. The --force option circumvents this problem.

Although managing installations using PEAR may seem to be more complicated on the surface, a quick investigation of *useful* unzip-and-go packages show that many unzip-and-go packages actually require a large amount of manual configuration that could easily be supplanted by the automated features of the PEAR installer. In short, once you get used to it, you'll wonder how you ever developed in PHP without using the PEAR installer to manage your packages.

Differences between Libraries and Applications from the Installer's Point of View

The acronym **PEAR** means P*HP* E*xtension and* A*pplication* R*epository*, but until PEAR version 1.4.0, support for applications was minimal. Most PEAR packages are libraries designed to be integrated into other external applications. The initial design of the PEAR installer supported this model very effectively, but did not provide all of the customization that applications need in order to be installed and configured effectively. One of the primary motivations for the new features introduced in PEAR version 1.4.0 was better support for application installation.

In spite of the obvious differences in functionality between libraries and complete applications, from the installer's point of view, libraries and applications don't need to be handled very differently. Both are distributed using package.xml, both are stored in the registry in the same way, and the same rules of versioning and dependencies are applied. In fact, this is one of PEAR installer's greatest strengths, in that it both follows the **KISS (Keep It Simple, Stupid)** principle and leaves application design to the way package.xml is used. Consequently, a thorough understanding of the design of package.xml is necessary to use its capabilities to the fullest for any application or library package.

New features designed to simplify application development include:

- Customizable file roles
- Customizable file tasks
- More advanced dependency possibilities and pre-download dependency resolution
- The ability to bundle several packages into a single tarball
- Static dependencies based on a single release rather than an abstract package

After reading this list, if your head is spinning or you're seeing spots resembling question marks, fear not—all of these features will be simply and extensively explored in the next few sections.

Before we launch into the new features, lets take a closer look at some basic principles that provide the foundation for best use of the new features.

Using Versioning and Dependencies to Help Track and Eliminate Bugs

Versioning and dependencies are two features that every enterprise-level distribution system must support at a very high level. With both simple dependencies and advanced versioning features, the PEAR installer makes depending on external packages safer and easier than ever before.

Versioning

The most basic foundation of the PEAR installer is the concept of versioning. Versioning should be familiar to all of us in the form of "Software package version X.Y.Z" such as "PHP version 5.1.4". The basic idea is that older versions of software have a lower number. In other words, PHP version 4.0.6 is older than PHP version 4.1.1beta1, which is older than PHP version 4.1.1.

How does versioning help track and eliminate bugs? Imagine this scenario:

You are working on a Wiki, and allowing users to grab the source from your FTP site at any time and use it themselves. One of them finds a bug and reports, "It is doing this weird thing where it tries to delete all of my files." The user can't remember when he or she downloaded the source, as he or she had to restore from a backup and the file modification time has been reset. At this point, the only way to figure out the problem and whether it still exists in the current source is to grab the user project and compare it to the current source line by line. At best, this is tedious and at worst completely impossible.

Taking a fluid, ever-changing software project and making releases at specific times and assigning them a version number makes it much simpler for an end user to report a bug. The end user can simply say "Version 1.2.3 of your software package does this weird thing where it tries to delete all of my files" and you as the developer can ask the user to try the latest version, or the current development copy, making bug fixing much simpler.

In addition, it is possible to maintain two branches of the same code, a stable version, and an unstable version with innovative new features. There are many subtle ways of using versioning to provide more information about a software release. For instance, the Linux kernel versioning system is described in detail at `http://en.wikipedia.org/wiki/Linux_kernel#Version_Numbering`. In this case, one of the decimal places is used to denote the stability of the kernel, such that it is possible to have version 1.2.9 released after 1.3.0.

The PEAR installer takes a more explicit approach to versioning. Rather than providing stability information inside the version number, a separate field in `package.xml`, `<stability>`, is used to designate the stability of the code. This does not preclude the use of Linux-style versioning, or any other versioning scheme, as long as the basic premise (1.3.0 is always newer than 1.2.9) still holds.

Versioning Time versus Absolute Time

PEAR's simple versioning rules can actually be kind of confusing in the real world. The PEAR installer doesn't particularly care when a version was released in real-world time but about its stability and version number.

This can mean that, for instance, PEAR 1.3.6 (stable) released on August 18, 2005 is older than PEAR 1.4.0a1 (alpha) released on February 26, 2005 because 1.3.6 is less than 1.4.0. Absolute time has nothing to do with versioning time.

The end user can tell the PEAR installer through a configuration variable called `preferred_state` how stable packages must be in order to be installed. In our hypothetical example, if this variable is set to `stable` or to `beta`, then PEAR 1.3.6 would be installed instead of 1.4.0a1; otherwise for values less stable than beta (`alpha`, `devel`, and `snapshot`) version 1.4.0a1 would be installed, even though version 1.3.6 was released months later, because 1.4.0 is always *newer* than 1.3.6 in *versioning time*.

PEAR Packaging and Strict Version Validation

The PEAR package repository at `pear.php.net` uses a strict versioning protocol. All package versions are of format X.Y.Z, as in "1.3.0". The first digit (X) is used to describe the **Applications Program Interface (API)** version, the second digit (Y) is used to describe the feature set version, and the third digit (Z) is used to describe the bugfix revision level. As examples, here are some version numbers and their meaning:

Sample PEAR version numbers and their meanings	
Version Number	**Meaning**
1.0.0	Stable API version 1.0, initial stable release of package
0.4.5	Unstable (developing) API, 4th feature set design, 5th bugfix release of this feature set
2.4.0	Stable API version 2.0, 4th feature set design, initial release of this new feature set
1.3.4	Stable API version 1.0, 3rd set of new features since the initial stable release, 4th bugfix release of this feature set

At installation time, this information is irrelevant: The PEAR installer will install anything it is given, including version numbering schemes like 24.25094.39.430 or 23.4.0-r1 and so on. However, the validation used when packaging up a package via:

```
$ pear package
```

is much stricter than that used when downloading a PEAR package. In order to assist developers trying to meet the PEAR package repository's strict coding standards, there are a set of validation routines within the PEAR package located in `PEAR/Validate.php` that check a number of important aspects of the PEAR coding standards, and emit warnings for anything that does not comply. For instance, version 1.0.0 must be stable (and not `devel`, `alpha`, or `beta` stability), and so the following snippet from a `package.xml` will cause a warning:

```
<version>
 <release>1.0.0</release>
 <api>1.0.0</api>
</version>
<stability>
 <release>beta</release>
 <api>beta</api>
</stability>
```

Specifically, it would look something like this:

```
$ pear package
```

```
Warning: Channel validator warning: field "version" - version 1.0.0
probably should not be alpha or beta
```

Although this is extremely helpful for anyone who wishes to adhere to PEAR's strict coding standards, in some cases this warning is not helpful, but is instead annoying or distracting. For instance, a private project may wish to use the Linux versioning scheme. Fortunately, there is a way to control the way custom validation routines are handled at the packaging, download, or installation phases of the PEAR installer. By extending the PEAR_Validate class located in PEAR/Validate.php, a special validator can be created using object-oriented inheritance. To activate it, the validator must be associated with a channel. Although this process will be discussed in detail in Chapter 5, here is a simple example.

The developers of PHP extensions at pecl.php.net have a much looser version validation system, and there is a wide variation of versioning accepted, from a two-digit 1.0 to the 7.5.00.26 used by the maxdb package (http://pecl.php.net/maxdb) to mirror versioning used by MySQL's MaxDB database. As such, pecl.php.net is a separate channel from pear.php.net, and in its channel definition file channel.xml (also discussed in depth in Chapter 5) defines a channel validator:

```
<validatepackage version="1.0">PEAR_Validator_PECL</validatepackage>
```

This particular channel validator is distributed with the PEAR installer in the file PEAR/Validator/PECL.php. This file is both the perfect example of a customized channel validator and the simplest, so here it is, in all of its glory:

```php
<?php
/**
 * Channel Validator for the pecl.php.net channel
 *
 * PHP 4 and PHP 5
 *
 * @category   pear
 * @package    PEAR
 * @author     Greg Beaver <cellog@php.net>
 * @copyright  1997-2005 The PHP Group
 * @license    http://www.php.net/license/3_0.txt  PHP License 3.0
 * @version    CVS: $Id: PECL.php,v 1.3 2005/08/21 03:31:48 cellog
Exp $
 * @link       http://pear.php.net/package/PEAR
 * @since      File available since Release 1.4.0a5
 */
/**
 * This is the parent class for all validators
 */
require_once 'PEAR/Validate.php';
```

```php
/**
 * Channel Validator for the pecl.php.net channel
 * @category   pear
 * @package    PEAR
 * @author     Greg Beaver <cellog@php.net>
 * @copyright  1997-2005 The PHP Group
 * @license    http://www.php.net/license/3_0.txt  PHP License 3.0
 * @version    Release: @package_version@
 * @link       http://pear.php.net/package/PEAR
 * @since      Class available since Release 1.4.0a5
 */
class PEAR_Validator_PECL extends PEAR_Validate
{
    function validateVersion()
    {
        if ($this->_state == PEAR_VALIDATE_PACKAGING) {
            $version = $this->_packagexml->getVersion();
            $versioncomponents = explode('.', $version);
            $last = array_pop($versioncomponents);
            if (substr($last, 1, 2) == 'rc') {
                $this->_addFailure('version',
                'Release Candidate versions must have ' .
                'upper-case RC, not lower-case rc');
                return false;
            }
        }
        return true;
    }

    function validatePackageName()
    {
        $ret = parent::validatePackageName();
        if ($this->_packagexml->getPackageType() == 'extsrc') {
            if (strtolower($this->_packagexml->getPackage()) !=
              strtolower($this->_packagexml->getProvidesExtension())) {
                $this->_addWarning('providesextension',
                'package name "' .
                $this->_packagexml->getPackage() . '"
                is different from extension name "' .
                $this->_packagexml->getProvidesExtension());
            }
        }
        return $ret;
    }
}
?>
```

This class simply overrides the strict version validation of its parent, and then adds in a PECL-specific check to see if an extension package is claiming to distribute a differently-named extension from the package name. In addition, it checks for a release candidate with (lower-case) `rc` in the version, as PHP's `version_compare()` function (`http://www.php.net/version_compare`) treats this very differently from versions containing (upper-case) `RC`.

Why are pear.php.net and pecl.php.net Separate Channels?

In earlier PEAR versions, the `pear` command was used to install both PEAR packages and **PHP Extension Community Library (PECL)** packages. This was changed in version 1.4.0 for a number of reasons. First of all, the developers at `pear.php.net` are developing packages written in PHP. Developers at `pecl.php.net` are developing packages written in C that are compiled to shared `.dll` or `.so` files as internal components (extensions) of PHP itself. There are intrinsic differences in the way PEAR-style packages are installed and maintained compared to the PECL-style packages.

One of these differences is the importance given to proper versioning. PECL and PHP extensions can't co-exist with conflicting extensions; only one can run at a time. PEAR packages do not have this restriction, as several different versions of a PEAR package can co-exist and be loaded interchangeably through the `include_path`, so versioning becomes much more important.

In addition, because of file locking, an extension that is loaded into memory cannot be uninstalled, making upgrading PHP extensions impossible unless `php.ini` is not used.

There are a number of other small reasons that all added up to the need for a split, such as confusion over the function of packages (is this a PHP extension or a script written in PHP?) and so now we have both the `pear` and the new `pecl` command for managing PECL-packages.

Enterprise-Level Dependency Management

Dependencies are a natural evolution in software design. If your forum package attempts to separate business logic from display by using a template engine, it is far better to focus your energies on developing the forum functionality than it is to design a new template engine. Not only have the authors of existing template engines spent more time working on and thinking about template engines, their template engine has been used by thousands of other developers just like you. All of the common and most of the unusual problems have been encountered and solved. In the event that you do find a new problem, you can report it to the maintainers, or even exercise the full strength of open source and fix the problem yourself and give the solution back to the maintainers.

On the other hand, this requires putting trust in the maintainers of the template engine. By using the template engine, you implicitly trust the maintainers to effectively manage it, to fix all bugs discovered, and to prevent introducing new bugs into future releases. You also trust the maintainers to continue maintaining the package and to respond to issues you encounter.

PEAR developers have been around long enough to know that at its worst, this trust can be naïve or stupid, as software is still maintained by humans who have the capacity to screw up. Fortunately, because of this knowledge, `package.xml` provides complete control over the "trust" of a dependency.

Dependencies in package.xml

For more details on how dependencies work in `package.xml`, see the section *External Dependencies*

The simplest dependency tells the installer that a package must be used but that we don't need to check for versioning issues: it is enough that it is installed. In `package.xml 2.0`, this dependency looks something like:

```
<package>
 <name>Dependency</name>
 <channel>pear.php.net</channel>
</package>
```

A slightly more restrictive dependency might tell the installer to only install versions newer than a minimum of version 1.2.0:

```
<package>
 <name>Dependency</name>
 <channel>pear.php.net</channel>
 <min>1.2.0</min>
</package>
```

Going further, it may be the case that there were a few bungled releases. We can tell the installer to ignore specific releases 1.2.0 and 1.4.2, but that every other version newer than 1.2.0 is OK to install:

```
<package>
 <name>Dependency</name>
 <channel>pear.php.net</channel>
 <min>1.2.0</min>
 <exclude>1.2.0</exclude>
 <exclude>1.4.2</exclude>
</package>
```

Finally, we can also tell the installer that we want to strongly recommend version 1.4.5, and to never upgrade unless we say it is OK:

```
<package>
 <name>Dependency</name>
 <channel>pear.php.net</channel>
 <min>1.2.0</min>
 <recommended>1.4.5</recommended>
 <exclude>1.2.0</exclude>
 <exclude>1.4.2</exclude>
</package>
```

In this last case, we are given a tremendous amount of control over the dependency. The end user cannot accidentally break our package by upgrading to a newer release of a dependency unless the maintainers of the dependency have worked with you on your package and certified its compatibility with another tag, <compatible>, or you do another release of your package that recommends the newer version.

The differing levels of trust afforded by dependencies in package.xml mean you can securely depend on other packages, but this is only the beginning of PEAR's dependency features. The other common problem solved by the use of dependencies is basic incompatibilities with the end user's computer, operating system, PHP version, or enabled extensions in php.ini. PEAR provides dependency tags for each one of these situations. In addition, optional features or plug-ins can be implemented through optional dependencies or dependency groups. The list of possibilities is staggering, and yet the syntax in package.xml is simple and very easy to learn.

Distribution and Upgrades for the End User

From the end user's perspective, one of the most complex tasks faced when using an unzip-and-go package is upgrading. In the closed-source world, newer versions of a package break something that used to work with the old package as a means of forcing their users to upgrade, which sometimes requires significant work.

In the open-source world, many developers continue to follow this model by introducing exciting new features that mean you can no longer use the old version. The actual upgrade process usually means overwriting the current version with the new files, possibly with new configuration needed. In addition, it opens up the scary prospect of completely breaking a live site, prompting the need for some kind of backup system.

By using the PEAR installer, all of these fears and dangers are a thing of the past. It is simple to upgrade to a new version by using:

```
$ pear upgrade Package
```

It is just as simple to downgrade to a previous version of the package:

```
$ pear upgrade --force Package-1.2.3
```

This makes the task of maintaining a live site both easy and secure — a rare and wonderful combination. Note that this example assumes the old version of the package is 1.2.3.

In addition, upgrading or installing dependencies is just as easy. Required dependencies are always downloaded and installed for packages that make use of package.xml 2.0, and for packages that use package.xml 1.0, dependencies can be automatically downloaded and installed with the --onlyreqdeps (only required dependencies) option like this:

```
$ pear upgrade --onlyreqdeps Package
```

Optional dependencies can also be automatically installed using the --alldeps (all dependencies) option:

```
$ pear upgrade --alldeps Package
```

In addition, creating feature groups, or grouping several related packages into a single dependency, is easily accomplished with dependency groups, meaning users can install feature groups like PEAR's web installer feature like so:

```
$ pear install PEAR#webinstaller
```

When configuring a package, there is often a large amount of work that needs to be performed to configure file locations, set up databases, and so on. PEAR provides some simple ways to automate configuration, and also provides ways to standardize any level of complex setup through post-installation scripts.

If you're anything like me, thinking of all the possibilities built into the PEAR installer makes your heart race faster with anticipation. Even if you're not quite that geeky, I'm sure you will find that the power of the PEAR installer will make your programming life easier.

An Overview of package.xml Structure

`package.xml` contains all of the information the PEAR installer needs to install and configure PEAR packages. By leveraging standards such as XML and XSchema to document package structure (`http://pear.php.net/dtd/package1.xsd` and `http://pear.php.net/dtd/package2.xsd` have full definitions of `package.xml 1.0` and `package.xml 2.0` respectively), PEAR opens up future programming possibilities that would not be available otherwise. For instance, using XSchema allows future extensibility of `package.xml` using XML namespaces to provide custom functionality.

When discussing `package.xml`, it is important to understand both the commonality and the differences between `package.xml 1.0` and `package.xml 2.0`. The `package.xml 2.0` is a superset of `package.xml 1.0`. In other words, it is possible to represent every single possible `package.xml` version 1.0 as a `package.xml 2.0`, but there is a large set of `package.xml 2.0` that cannot be reduced to unique `package.xml 1.0`.

The best way to get acquainted with the structure of `package.xml 1.0` is to peruse the CVS of the PEAR repository at `cvs.php.net`. Each subdirectory contains a `package.xml` file. If that `package.xml` file begins with `<package version="1.0"`... then it is a `package.xml 1.0`. Many packages are already taking advantage of `package.xml 2.0`, using a file named `package2.xml`. Also useful is to investigate the PECL repository at `http://cvs.php.net/pecl/` and see how PHP extension developers are using `package.xml`.

To explore the equivalent `package.xml 2.0`, there is a convenient PEAR command that can be used to convert a `package.xml 1.0` into a `package.xml 2.0`. This command is invoked as follows:

```
$ pear convert
```

This will parse a file in the current directory named `package.xml` and spit out a file named `package2.xml` in the new format.

In addition, full up-to-date documentation on `package.xml` is always available in the PEAR manual at `http://pear.php.net/manual/`.

For the purposes of this book, we will be primarily discussing `package.xml 2.0`, and only mentioning 1.0 to remark on important conceptual changes for those who are familiar with the old format.

Here is a sample `package.xml` file. This one is taken from the PEAR package itself, and demonstrates a number of `package.xml`'s features that will be explored in the sections to come. Feel free to skim this example and then refer back to it later on. For now, just absorb the basic structure and the specifics will make sense when you read about them later on in this text.

```
<?xml version="1.0" encoding="UTF-8"?>
<package version="2.0" xmlns="http://pear.php.net/dtd/package-2.0"
xmlns:tasks="http://pear.php.net/dtd/tasks-1.0"
xmlns:xsi="http://www.w3.org/2001/XMLSchema-instance"
xsi:schemaLocation="http://pear.php.net/dtd/tasks-1.0
http://pear.php.net/dtd/tasks-1.0.xsd
http://pear.php.net/dtd/package-2.0
http://pear.php.net/dtd/package-2.0.xsd">
 <name>PEAR</name>
 <channel>pear.php.net</channel>
 <summary>PEAR Base System</summary>
 <description>The PEAR package contains:
 * the PEAR installer, for creating, distributing
   and installing packages
 * the beta-quality PEAR_Exception PHP5 error handling mechanism
 * the beta-quality PEAR_ErrorStack advanced error handling class
 * the PEAR_Error error handling mechanism
 * the OS_Guess class for retrieving info about the OS
   where PHP is running on
 * the System class for quick handling of common operations
   with files and directories
 * the PEAR base class
 </description>
 <lead>
  <name>Greg Beaver</name>
  <user>cellog</user>
  <email>cellog@php.net</email>
  <active>yes</active>
 </lead>
 <lead>
  <name>Stig Bakken</name>
  <user>ssb</user>
  <email>stig@php.net</email>
  <active>yes</active>
 </lead>
 <lead>
  <name>Tomas V.V.Cox</name>
  <user>cox</user>
  <email>cox@idecnet.com</email>
  <active>yes</active>
 </lead>
 <lead>
  <name>Pierre-Alain Joye</name>
  <user>pajoye</user>
```

```
  <email>pajoye@pearfr.org</email>
  <active>yes</active>
 </lead>
 <helper>
  <name>Martin Jansen</name>
  <user>mj</user>
  <email>mj@php.net</email>
  <active>no</active>
 </helper>
 <date>2005-10-09</date>
 <version>
  <release>1.4.2</release>
  <api>1.4.0</api>
 </version>
 <stability>
  <release>stable</release>
  <api>stable</api>
 </stability>
 <license uri="http://www.php.net/license">PHP License</license>
 <notes>
  This is a major milestone release for PEAR.
  In addition to several killer features,
  every single element of PEAR has a regression test,
  and so stability is much higher than any previous PEAR release,
  even with the beta label.

  New features in a nutshell:
  * full support for channels
  * pre-download dependency validation
  * new package.xml 2.0 format allows tremendous flexibility
  * while maintaining BC support for optional dependency groups
  * and limited support for sub-packaging robust dependency support
  * full dependency validation on uninstall
  * remote install for hosts with only ftp access -
  * no more problems with restricted host installation
  * full support for mirroring
  * support for bundling several packages into a single tarball
  * support for static dependencies on a uri-based package
  * support for custom file roles and installation tasks
 </notes>
 <contents>
  <dir name="/">
   <dir name="OS">
    <file name="Guess.php" role="php">
     <tasks:replace from="@package_version@" to="version"
```

```
type="package-info" />
    </file>
  </dir> <!-- /OS -->
  <dir name="PEAR">
   <dir name="ChannelFile">
    <file name="Parser.php" role="php">
     <tasks:replace from="@package_version@" to="version"
type="package-info" />
    </file>
   </dir> <!-- /PEAR/ChannelFile -->
   <dir name="Command">
    <file name="Auth-init.php" role="php"/>
    <file name="Auth.php" role="php">
     <tasks:replace from="@package_version@" to="version"
type="package-info" />
    </file>
    <file name="Build-init.php" role="php"/>
    <file name="Build.php" role="php">
     <tasks:replace from="@package_version@" to="version"
type="package-info" />
    </file>
[snip...]
  </dir> <!-- /PEAR -->
  <dir name="scripts" baseinstalldir="/">
   <file name="pear.bat" role="script">
    <tasks:replace from="@bin_dir@" to="bin_dir" type="pear-config"
/>
    <tasks:replace from="@php_bin@" to="php_bin" type="pear-config"
/>
    <tasks:replace from="@include_path@" to="php_dir" type="pear-
config" />
    <tasks:windowseol/>
   </file>
   <file name="peardev.bat" role="script">
    <tasks:replace from="@bin_dir@" to="bin_dir" type="pear-config"
/>
    <tasks:replace from="@php_bin@" to="php_bin" type="pear-config"
/>
    <tasks:replace from="@include_path@" to="php_dir"
    type="pear-config" />
    <tasks:windowseol/>
   </file>
   <file name="pecl.bat" role="script">
    <tasks:replace from="@bin_dir@" to="bin_dir" type="pear-config"
```

```
/>
   <tasks:replace from="@php_bin@" to="php_bin" type="pear-config"
/>
   <tasks:replace from="@include_path@" to="php_dir"
   type="pear-config" />
   <tasks:windowseol/>
  </file>
  <file name="pear.sh" role="script">
   <tasks:replace from="@php_bin@" to="php_bin" type="pear-config"
/>
   <tasks:replace from="@php_dir@" to="php_dir" type="pear-config"
/>
   <tasks:replace from="@pear_version@" to="version"
   type="package-info" />
   <tasks:replace from="@include_path@" to="php_dir"
   type="pear-config" />
   <tasks:unixeol/>
  </file>
[snip...]
 </dir> <!-- /scripts -->
 <file name="package.dtd" role="data" />
 <file name="PEAR.php" role="php">
  <tasks:replace from="@package_version@" to="version"
type="package-info" />
 </file>
 <file name="System.php" role="php">
  <tasks:replace from="@package_version@" to="version"
type="package-info" />
 </file>
 <file name="template.spec" role="data" />
 </dir> <!-- / -->
</contents>
<dependencies>
 <required>
  <php>
   <min>4.2</min>
  </php>
  <pearinstaller>
   <min>1.4.0a12</min>
  </pearinstaller>
  <package>
   <name>Archive_Tar</name>
   <channel>pear.php.net</channel>
   <min>1.1</min>
   <recommended>1.3.1</recommended>
```

```
  <exclude>1.3.0</exclude>
 </package>
 <package>
  <name>Console_Getopt</name>
  <channel>pear.php.net</channel>
  <min>1.2</min>
  <recommended>1.2</recommended>
 </package>
 <package>
  <name>XML_RPC</name>
  <channel>pear.php.net</channel>
  <min>1.4.0</min>
  <recommended>1.4.1</recommended>
 </package>
 <package>
  <name>PEAR_Frontend_Web</name>
  <channel>pear.php.net</channel>
  <max>0.5.0</max>
  <exclude>0.5.0</exclude>
  <conflicts/>
 </package>
 <package>
  <name>PEAR_Frontend_Gtk</name>
  <channel>pear.php.net</channel>
  <max>0.4.0</max>
  <exclude>0.4.0</exclude>
  <conflicts/>
 </package>
 <extension>
  <name>xml</name>
 </extension>
 <extension>
  <name>pcre</name>
 </extension>
</required>
<group name="remoteinstall" hint="adds the ability to install
packages to a remote ftp server">
 <subpackage>
  <name>PEAR_RemoteInstaller</name>
  <channel>pear.php.net</channel>
  <min>0.1.0</min>
  <recommended>0.1.0</recommended>
 </subpackage>
</group>
```

```
    <group name="webinstaller" hint="PEAR's web-based installer">
     <package>
      <name>PEAR_Frontend_Web</name>
      <channel>pear.php.net</channel>
      <min>0.5.0</min>
     </package>
    </group>
    <group name="gtkinstaller" hint="PEAR's PHP-GTK-based installer">
     <package>
      <name>PEAR_Frontend_Gtk</name>
      <channel>pear.php.net</channel>
      <min>0.4.0</min>
     </package>
    </group>
   </dependencies>
   <phprelease>
    <installconditions>
     <os>
      <name>windows</name>
     </os>
    </installconditions>
    <filelist>
     <install as="pear.bat" name="scripts/pear.bat" />
     <install as="peardev.bat" name="scripts/peardev.bat" />
     <install as="pecl.bat" name="scripts/pecl.bat" />
     <install as="pearcmd.php" name="scripts/pearcmd.php" />
     <install as="peclcmd.php" name="scripts/peclcmd.php" />
     <ignore name="scripts/peardev.sh" />
     <ignore name="scripts/pear.sh" />
     <ignore name="scripts/pecl.sh" />
    </filelist>
   </phprelease>
   <phprelease>
    <filelist>
     <install as="pear" name="scripts/pear.sh" />
     <install as="peardev" name="scripts/peardev.sh" />
     <install as="pecl" name="scripts/pecl.sh" />
     <install as="pearcmd.php" name="scripts/pearcmd.php" />
     <install as="peclcmd.php" name="scripts/peclcmd.php" />
     <ignore name="scripts/pear.bat" />
     <ignore name="scripts/peardev.bat" />
     <ignore name="scripts/pecl.bat" />
    </filelist>
   </phprelease>
```

```
<changelog>
 <release>
  <version>
   <release>1.3.6</release>
   <api>1.3.0</api>
  </version>
  <stability>
   <release>stable</release>
   <api>stable</api>
  </stability>
  <date>2005-08-18</date>
  <license>PHP License</license>
  <notes>
* Bump XML_RPC dependency to 1.4.0
* return by reference from PEAR::raiseError()
  </notes>
 </release>
 <release>
  <version>
   <release>1.4.0a1</release>
   <api>1.4.0</api>
  </version>
  <stability>
   <release>alpha</release>
   <api>alpha</api>
  </stability>
  <date>2005-02-26</date>
  <license uri="http://www.php.net/license/3_0.txt">PHP
License</license>
  <notes>
 This is a major milestone release for PEAR.  In addition to several
killer features,
 every single element of PEAR has a regression test, and so
stability is much higher
 than any previous PEAR release, even with the alpha label.

 New features in a nutshell:
 * full support for channels
 * pre-download dependency validation
 * new package.xml 2.0 format allows tremendous flexibility while
maintaining BC
 * support for optional dependency groups and limited support for
sub-packaging
 * robust dependency support
```

```
      * full dependency validation on uninstall
      * support for binary PECL packages
      * remote install for hosts with only ftp access -
      * no more problems
with
        restricted host installation
      * full support for mirroring
      * support for bundling several packages into a single tarball
      * support for static dependencies on a url-based package

      Specific changes from 1.3.5:
      * Implement request #1789: SSL support for xml-rpc and download
      * Everything above here that you just read
       </notes>
      </release>
    [snip...]
    </changelog>
    </package>
```

Tags Shared between package.xml 1.0 and 2.0

If you have a basic understanding of `package.xml 1.0` and just want to see what has changed in `package.xml 2.0`, it is best to skim the next few sections. Differences are always presented at the beginning of each section, followed by an in-depth exploration of the reasoning behind the changes.

Before launching into the advanced new features of `package.xml 2.0`, it is important to explore the tags and attributes that have been carried over from `package.xml 1.0` that both formats have in common. Most tags are unchanged. A few have either added information or changed their name slightly, and others have been completely redesigned. Let's get started.

Package Metadata

Both `package.xml` versions provide similar package metadata. Some basic information that must be present in any package includes:

- Package name/channel
- Maintainers (authors)
- Package description
- Package summary (one-line description)

Most of this information remains unchanged from release to release. For instance, the package name and channel are constant. The package description and summary will change rarely. The maintainers may change more frequently, depending on the community, so even though this is grouped under package metadata, it is probably reasonable to think of this as release-based information.

Package Name/Channel

These two fields are at the beginning of a `package.xml`, and form the heart of the PEAR installer's package differentiation. These are like the primary key in a database table: a unique combination of package/channel = a unique package. Note that the `<channel>` and `<uri>` tags are only present in `package.xml 2.0`.

```
<name>Packagename</name>
<channel>channel.example.com</channel> -or-
<uri>http://www.example.com/Packagename-1.2.3</uri>
```

Channels and package.xml 1.0

As you learned earlier, the concept of channels is introduced in `package.xml 2.0`. How does `package.xml 1.0` define the channel when it is not a part of its specification?

PEAR handles this problem in a simple way: all packages packaged using `package.xml 1.0` are installed as if they had a `<channel>pear.php.net</channel>` tag inserted right after the package name declaration. Note that `pecl.php.net` packages that used `package.xml 1.0` are allowed to migrate to the `pecl.php.net` channel when they upgrade to using a `package.xml 2.0`, but all other packages must start over with a new channel.

The package name is declared using the `<name>` tag, and must begin with a letter, and otherwise contain only letters, numbers and the underscore character, unless the channel-specific validator allows another format for the package name. Channel-specific validators are covered in depth in Chapter 5. If you are simply creating a package, you need not know anything about channel-specific validators. If your package satisfies the requirements for a package, when you run:

```
$ pear package
```

Your package will be created without errors. Otherwise, packaging will fail, and one or more error messages will be presented describing the reasons for failure.

The `<channel>` tag cannot co-exist with the `<uri>` tag. A package that uses the `<uri>` tag is in fact automatically part of the pseudo-channel __uri, a channel that does not have a server or protocols associated with it. The __uri channel is in fact a true magic channel that only serves to act as a namespace preventing URI-based packages from conflicting with packages from other channels.

For instance, consider a package whose `package.xml` begins with:

```
<name>Packagename</name>
<uri>http://pear.php.net/Packagename-1.2.3</uri>
```

This package is *not* the same as a package whose `package.xml` begins with the following code even if the version number of the package is `1.2.3`.

```
<name>Packagename</name>
<channel>pear.php.net</channel>
```

URI-based packages are strictly release-based. The `<uri>` tag must be an absolute, real-world URI that can be used to access the package. However, the URI should not include a `.tgz` or `.tar` file extension, but both should be present. In our example above, both `http://pear.php.net/Packagename-1.2.3.tgz` and `http://pear.php.net/Packagename-1.2.3.tar` should exist and be identical except for the use of zlib compression on the `.tgz`.

Maintainers (Authors)

The list of maintainers in `package.xml` should serve the same function that a traditional AUTHORS file serves. However, this list of authors is more than just useful information. The `<user>` tag is used by a channel server to match up package maintainers with the release of a package, allowing non-channel administrators to upload releases of software packages that they maintain. If you are maintaining a package that is released through `pear.php.net`, for instance, the `<user>` tag must contain your PEAR username. For non-channel releases, the contents of these tags are informational only, and let end users of your package know how to contact you.

The `<role>` tag in `package.xml 1.0` may only contain the values lead, developer, contributor, or helper. This proves to be impossible to validate using XSchema, and so to make things easier, `package.xml 2.0` has taken the contents of the `<role>` tag and extracted them out to new tags `<lead>`, `<developer>`, `<contributor>`, and `<helper>`. In addition, the `<maintainers>` and `<maintainer>` tag have been removed to simplify parsing.

For `package.xml 1.0`:

```
<maintainers>
 <maintainer>
```

```
 <user>pearserverhandle</user>
 <role>lead</role>
 <name>Dorkus McForkus</name>
 <email>dorkus@example.com</email>
</maintainer>
<maintainer>
 <user>pearserverhelper</user>
 <role>helper</role>
 <name>Horgie Borgie</name>
 <email>borgie@example.com</email>
</maintainer>
</maintainers>
```

For `package.xml 2.0`:

```
<lead>
 <name>Dorkus McForkus</name>
 <user>pearserverhandle</user>
 <email>dorkus@example.com</email>
 <active>yes</active>
</lead>
<helper>
 <name>Horgie Borgie</name>
 <user>pearserverhelper</user>
 <email>borgie@example.com</email>
 <active>no</active>
</helper>
```

Package Description and Summary

The example summary/description pair below shows how the `<summary>` and `<description>` tags should be used in both `package.xml 1.0` and `package.xml 2.0`. These tags are strictly informational, and are not used by the installation portions of the PEAR installer. If a package is served through a channel, commands like `list-all` will display the summary. The description is displayed when a user types commands like `info` or `remote-info` to display information about a particular package or release.

Be sure that these tags are clear, concise, and understandable. Too often, I have seen summaries like `GBRL` for a package named `File_GBRL` — define your acronyms if they are not commonly known!

```
<summary>Provides an interface to the BORG collective</summary>
<description>
 The Net_BORG package uses PHP to interface with the neural
```

```
Implants found in the face of all BORG.  Both an object-oriented
and a functional interface is available.  Both will be used.
Resistance is futile.
</description>
```

Basic Release Metadata

The rest of `package.xml` is generally release-specific data, with a few exceptions. Release-specific data is more apt to change than things like the name of a package. Specifically, the areas of release-specific information documented in `package.xml` are:

- Package version
- Package stability
- External dependencies
- Release notes
- Release license
- Changelog
- File list, or contents of the package

In `package.xml 1.0`, this data was enclosed in a redundant `<release>` tag. This tag has been removed in version 2.0.

Package Version

The package version is very important, as this is the primary mechanism used by the installer to determine the relative age of different releases. Versions are sequential, meaning version 1.3.6 is older than version 1.4.0b1, even if version 1.3.6 was released a month after 1.4.0b1.

```
<version>1.2.3</version>
```

For `package.xml 2.0`:

```
<version>
 <release>1.2.3</release>
 <api>1.0.0</api>
</version>
```

The API version of a release is strictly for informational purposes. This can, however, be used in a `replace` task as follows:

```
<file name="Foo.php" role="php">
 <tasks:replace from="apiversion" to="@API-VER@" type="package-info"/>
</file>
```

This reduces redundancy in maintaining versioning inside files. In fact, providing API version through an API method is a very good idea. In my packages, I usually provide this code:

```
/**
 * Get the current API version
 * @return string
 */
function APIVersion()
{
    Return '@API-VER@';
}
```

Upon packaging, the Foo.php file containing the above code would look like this:

```
/**
 * Get the current API version
 * @return string
 */
function APIVersion()
{
    Return '1.0.0';
}
```

In other words, all instances of the @API-VER@ token will be replaced with the contents of the <api> version tag. Replacement file tasks are used to perform this magic.

Package Stability

In package.xml 1.0, the <state> tag was used to describe the stability of code. In package.xml 2.0, the <release> tag inside <stability> is used to describe the stability of code.

```
<state>beta</state>
```

For package.xml 2.0:

```
<stability>
 <release>beta</release>
 <api>stable</api>
</stability>
```

The PEAR installer uses the release stability in conjunction with an end user's preferred_state configuration variable to determine whether a release is stable enough to install. If the user wishes to install the Foo package, and these releases are available:

Version	Stability
1.0.1	stable
1.1.0a1	alpha
1.0.0	stable
0.9.0	beta
0.8.0	alpha

The installer will choose versions to install based on the user's `preferred_state` setting.

preferred_state value	Foo version that would be installed
stable	1.0.1
beta	1.0.1
alpha	1.1.0a1

Note that for a `preferred_state` of `beta`, when there is a choice of a newer version 1.0.1 (`stable`) and older version 0.9.0 (`beta`), the installer will choose the latest, most stable version—version 1.0.1. For a `preferred_state` of `alpha`, the installer will choose the newer and less stable version 1.1.0a1 (`alpha`) over the older version 1.0.1 (`stable`), even though version 1.0.1 was released *after* version 1.1.0a1.

The list of legal stabilities for release stability in order of diminishing stability is:

- `stable`: code should be working in all situations.
- `beta`: code should be working in all situations, and is feature-complete, but needs real-world testing.
- `alpha`: code is in a state of flux, features may change at any time, stability is uncertain.
- `devel`: code is not yet feature-complete, and may not work in most situations.
- `snapshot`: this is a current copy of development code from source during live development in between normal releases.

API stability serves the same informational purpose as API version. It is not used by the installer, but can be used to track the rate of change of an API. An API marked stable should in fact never change except for adding new features—users need to be able to depend upon a stable API in order for package dependencies to work. This is a key feature of enterprise-level dependencies.

The list of legal stabilities for API differs slightly in that an API snapshot is not allowed. API stability should be thought of as:

- `stable`: API is set, and will not break backward compatibility.
- `beta`: API is probably set, and will only change to fix serious bugs in design that are encountered during testing.
- `alpha`: API is fluid, and may change, breaking any existing features, as well as adding new ones.
- `devel`: API is extremely unstable, and may change dramatically at any time.

External Dependencies

There are two kinds of dependencies that the PEAR installer recognizes: *required* and *optional* dependencies. In addition, there are two classes of dependencies, those that restrict installation, and those that describe other resources (packages/extensions) used by the primary package. Restrictive dependencies are defined by the `<php>`, `<pearinstaller>`, `<arch>`, `<extension>`, and `<os>` dependencies. Resource-based dependencies are defined by the `<package>`, `<subpackage>`, and `<extension>` dependencies.

Although the `package.xml 1.0` DTD defined several dependency types, only three were ever implemented:

- `pkg`: dependencies on packages
- `ext`: dependencies on extensions
- `php`: dependencies on PHP versions

The structure of dependencies in `package.xml 1.0` was quite simple:

```
<deps>
 <dep type="php" rel="ge" version="4.2.0"/>
 <dep type="pkg" rel="has">PackageName</dep>
 <dep type="pkg" rel="ge" version="1.0">PackageName2</dep>
 <dep type="pkg" rel="ge" version="1.0"
     optional="yes">PackageName3</dep>
 <dep type="ext" rel="not">ExtensionName</dep>
</deps>
```

The legal values of the `rel` attribute are:

- `has`: the dependency must exist
- `not`: the dependency must not be present

- `gt`: in conjunction with `version` attribute, the dependency must have version > the required version.

- `ge`: in conjunction with `version` attribute, the dependency must have version >= the required version

- `eq`: in conjunction with `version` attribute, the dependency must have version == the required version.

- `lt`: in conjunction with `version` attribute, the dependency must have version < the required version.

- `le`: in conjunction with `version` attribute, the dependency must have version <= the required version.

- `ne`: in conjunction with `version` attribute, the dependency must have version != the required version. (PEAR version 1.3.6 only.)

How is Version Comparison Done?

The PHP function `version_compare()` is used to determine whether a version-based dependency validates. Documentation for `version_compare()` is at `http://www.php.net/version_compare`.

Only after a great deal of experience did the serious design flaws of this approach reveal themselves:

- *XML validation with tools like xmllint cannot reveal invalid dependencies.* Consider the following dependency `<dep type="php" rel="has" version="4.3.0"/>`. This dependency is not valid because `rel="has"` ignores the version attribute, and so the dependency validation will not be performed—every PEAR installation has PHP installed by definition.

- *Trust level of dependency upgrades cannot be controlled.* The PEAR package depends upon the Console_Getopt package. At one point, the maintainer of Console_Getopt *fixed* a bug that suddenly caused PEAR to stop working upon upgrade. A good deal of scrambling resulted in a fix, but the event highlighted the fatal flaw in the design of the PEAR installer pre-version 1.4.0: dependencies upon packages are inherently unsafe. There is no way to restrict trust of dependencies. The `rel="eq"` attribute does not have the desired effect because this prevents upgrading safely for any reason, effectively freezing development. In addition, flaws in the validation of dependencies meant that even upgrading to a newer package version is forbidden.

  If the current version has a dependency tag of `<dep type="pkg" rel="eq" version="1.0">Deppackage</dep>`, the PEAR installer would look at the dependencies for the new version with `<dep type="pkg" rel="eq" version ="1.1">Deppackage</dep>` then look on disk to see that `Deppackage` version 1.0 was installed, and fail to upgrade. Even if both the main package and `Deppackage` were passed in, upgrade of `Deppackage` would fail because the installed version of the main package requires version 1.0 of `Deppackage`.

- *Dependencies on PECL extension-based packages cannot work.* A `<dep type="ext" rel="has">peclextension</dep>` will only check for an extension in memory. Most PECL extensions can either be built directly into PHP (non-shared), distributed with PHP as a shared module, or downloaded and installed. If a PECL extension is built into PHP, distributed as a shared module, or installed via PECL, the `type="ext"` dependency will work just fine. Unfortunately, in order to upgrade the extension using the PEAR installer, `php.ini` must be disabled otherwise file locking will prevent overwriting the extension when it is in use by the current PHP process. Newer extensions such as PDO have drivers that depend on the PDO extension being present for installation. If `php.ini` is disabled, there is no way to detect extensions to validate dependencies!

Simplifying XML Validation of package.xml

In order to make it possible to validate dependencies with external tools, the structure needed to be redesigned. Generally, using tags in preference to attributes and particularly in preference to attribute values is the approach used in `package. xml 2.0`. The dependency examples from `package.xml 1.0` can be represented in `package.xml 2.0` with:

```
<dependencies>
 <required>
  <php>
   <min>4.2.0</min>
  </php>
  <pearinstaller>
   <min>1.4.1</min>
  </pearinstaller>
  <package>
   <name>Packagename</name>
   <channel>pear.php.net</channel>
  </package>
  <package>
   <name>PackageName2</name>
   <channel>pear.php.net</channel>
   <min>1.0</min>
  </package>
  <package>
```

```
   <name>ExtensionName</name>
   <channel>pecl.php.net</channel>
   <providesextension>ExtensionName</providesextension>
   <conflicts/>
  </package>
 </required>
 <optional>
  <package>
   <name>PackageName3</name>
   <channel>pear.php.net</channel>
   <min>1.0</min>
   <exclude>1.0</exclude>
  </package>
 </optional>
</dependencies>
```

Note that attributes `optional="yes"` and the implied `optional="no"` have both been extracted out of the `<dep>` tag into the tags `<required>` and `<optional>`. In addition, the `type` attribute has been extracted out into the tags `<package>`, `<php>`, and the previously undefined `<pearinstaller>` tag. Finally, both the `rel` and the `version` attributes have been completely replaced with a new set of tags.

In `package.xml 1.0`, in order to define a version set for a single dependency, multiple `<dep>` tags were needed:

```
<dep type="pkg" rel="ge" version="1.2.3">PackageName</dep>
<dep type="pkg" rel="ne" version="1.3.0">PackageName</dep>
<dep type="pkg" rel="lt" version="2.0.0">PackageName</dep>
```

This can be compared to the `package.xml 2.0` equivalent:

```
<package>
 <name>PackageName</name>
 <channel>pear.php.net</channel>
 <min>1.2.3</min>
 <max>2.0.0</max>
 <exclude>1.3.0</exclude>
 <exclude>2.0.0</exclude>
</package>
```

In fact, this change promotes much simpler debugging of dependency problems in complex `package.xml` file. The above dependency easily translates into English as "Package PackageName from channel `pear.php.net`, minimum version 1.2.3, maximum version 2.0.0, excluding versions 1.3.0 and 2.0.0." Not only is it easier to detect errors using tools like `xmllint`, it is much easier to comprehend complex versioning of dependencies.

The `rel`/`version` duo has been effectively made obsolete by the combination of `<min>`/`<max>`/`<exclude>` tags. These three tags can be thought of as newer implementations of `rel`'s `ge`, `le`, and `ne`:

- `<min>1.2.0</min>` = `<dep rel="ge" version="1.2.0">`
- `<max>1.2.0</max>` = `<dep rel="le" version="1.2.0">`
- `<exclude>1.2.0</exclude>` = `<dep rel="ne" version="1.2.0">`

With these three tags, we can effectively and simply define any version set in a single dependency, without needing to think in terms of mathematical comparison operators.

Managing Trust of Dependencies

The PEAR installer is extremely lithe, making upgrading to newer versions of packages so simple; until PEAR version 1.4.0 its greatest strength was also its greatest weakness. The ability to easily upgrade packages, as well as the ability to perform batch-automated upgrades with commands like `upgrade-all` and `download-all` followed by `upgrade` is one of the key selling points of the installer. However, this ease is built upon an implicit trust in the quality of newer versions. By depending on packages with a simple `<dep type="pkg" rel="ge" version="X.Y.Z">`, this gives a carte blanche to the developers of the dependent package. If a dependent package's developer introduces a break with previous releases, whether through carelessness or lack of sympathy for your code, your end users are in trouble. For this reason, bundling dependencies directly in the code has become a favored means of distributing applications. This, however, negates the primary benefit of the PEAR installer — the ability to quickly and easily upgrade in case of the discovery of serious bugs like functionality failures, or worse, subtle security vulnerabilities that open up a site to external attack. This also puts the burden of maintaining the bundled dependencies directly upon the application maintainer, reducing the efficiency of distributed development and all of its contingent benefits.

`package.xml` 2.0 solves this dilemma simply and elegantly through the introduction of a new dependency concept: recommended version. This dependency can be taken from PEAR's `package.xml`:

```
<package>
 <name>Console_Getopt</name>
 <channel>pear.php.net</channel>
 <min>1.2</min>
</package>
```

This instructs the installer to upgrade `Console_Getopt` at will to any release of `Console_Getopt`, version `1.2` or newer. By changing the dependency to:

```
<package>
 <name>Console_Getopt</name>
 <channel>pear.php.net</channel>
 <min>1.2</min>
 <recommended>1.2</recommended>
</package>
```

This changes everything. Now, the installer will not automatically upgrade to version 1.3.0 upon release, unless the `--force` or `--loose` option is passed, or a `<compatible>` tag is present in the release of `Console_Getopt`.

The syntax of `<compatible>` is simple:

```
<compatible>
 <name>ParentPackage</name>
 <channel>pear.example.com</channel>
 <min>1.0.0</min>
 <max>1.3.0</max>
 <exclude>1.1.2</exclude> [optional]
</compatible>
```

As in dependencies, `<min>`/`<max>`/`<exclude>` is used to define a set of versions that the package is guaranteed to be compatible with. Unlike dependencies, the `<max>` tag is required to limit the set of versions. In addition, the set of versions must be limited to actual existing releases that have been tested.

In theory, it is still possible for lazy developers to implement a `<compatible>` tag that is every bit as dangerous as the old `rel="ge"`-based technique of dependency management, but this is both unlikely due to the principle of developer inertia and easy to catch and correct for the developer whose application depends on the dependency.

The Principle of Developer Inertia

Developers, like electrons, will choose the path of least resistance to achieve their goals. Make it difficult to write bad code and easy to write good code, and developers will write good code.

Reliably Depending on PECL Packages

Reliably depending on PECL packages has become possible due to two innovations:

1. The split of the `pear` script into two scripts: `pear` and `pecl`
2. The introduction of the `<providesextension>` tag

The primary difference between the `pear` and `pecl` commands can be summarized as: "Use `pear` to manage packages written in PHP like those at `pear.php.net`, and use `pecl` to manage packages extending PHP like those at `pecl.php.net`." Technically, the `pecl` command disables `php.ini`, and defaults to the `pecl.php.net` channel, but otherwise it is identical to the `pear` command. Disabling `php.ini` makes it possible to upgrade extensions that are inside `php.ini` without unloading them.

The `<providesextension>` tag is used in dependencies as follows:

```
<package>
 <name>PDO</name>
 <channel>pecl.php.net</channel>
 <min>1.0</min>
 <providesextension>PDO</providesextension>
</package>
```

This simple addition instructs the installer to treat the package dependency on `PDO` as if it were a combination of these two dependencies:

```
<extension>
 <name>PDO</name>
 <min>1.0</min>
</extension>
<package>
 <name>PDO</name>
 <channel>pecl.php.net</channel>
 <min>1.0</min>
</package>
```

The installer will first check to see if the `PDO` extension is present in memory, version 1.0 or newer, and if it is not, it will check the package registry to see if `pecl.php.net/PDO` version 1.0 or newer is installed. This allows, for instance, installation of production extensions for an Apache-based PEAR installation using a CLI-based PEAR installer without requiring the CLI-based installer to load each extension into its `php.ini`. In addition, it allows extensions like `PDO_mysql` to depend on `PDO` without requiring the `PDO` extension to be loaded in memory, greatly simplifying the end user experience.

Release Notes

In both `package.xml 1.0` and `package.xml 2.0`, release notes are defined by the `<notes>` tag. The format of this tag is any text.

```
<notes>
 Minor bugfix release

 These bugs are fixed:
 * Bug #1234: stupid politicians elected to office
 * Bug #2345: I guess we voted for them didn't we
</notes>
```

Release License

The text of the `<license>` tag is not validated—anything may be entered there.

```
<license>BSD license</license>
```

In `package.xml 2.0` there are optional attributes `uri` and `filesource` for linking a license to an online version and also to a specific license file within the package itself.

```
<license uri="http://www.opensource.org/licenses/bsd-license.php">BSD
license</license>
```

Changelog

The format of changelog in `package.xml 1.0` matches the format of a `<release>` tag with the exception that `<filelist>` is not allowed. The changelog is purely information for human purposes, and is not processed at all by the installer. The format for a changelog in `package.xml 2.0` is very similar to that of `package.xml 1.0`, and is best illustrated by an example:

```
<release>
 <version>
  <release>1.3.6</release>
  <api>1.3.0</api>
 </version>
 <stability>
  <release>stable</release>
  <api>stable</api>
 </stability>
 <date>2005-08-18</date>
 <license uri="http://www.php.net/license">PHP License</license>
 <notes>
```

```
    * Bump XML_RPC dependency to 1.4.0
    * return by reference from PEAR::raiseError()
     </notes>
    </release>
```

Like the release section of `package.xml`, the tags `<version>`, `<stability>`, `<date>`, `<license>`, and `<notes>` are all present. This is identical to `package.xml 1.0`. The only difference is the format of the `<version>`, `<stability>`, and `<license>` tags, which match the changes made in `package.xml 2.0`.

File List, or Contents of the Package

The primary purpose of PEAR, and by consequence, `package.xml` is to distribute files containing programming code. This is ultimately controlled by the list of files that are in a package, as defined by `<filelist>` or `<contents>`.

For `package.xml 1.0`:

```
    <filelist>
     <dir name="OS">
      <file role="php" name="Guess.php">
       <replace from="@package_version@" to="version" type="package-
   info" />
      </file>
     </dir>
     <dir name="PEAR">
      <dir name="ChannelFile" baseinstalldir="Foo">
       <file name="Parser.php" role="php">
        <replace from="@package_version@" to="version" type="package-
   info" />
       </file>
      </dir>
      <file role="data" name="Foo.dat"/>
     </dir>
     <file role="doc" name="linux-Howto.doc" install-as="README"
   platform="!windows"/>
     <file role="doc" name="windows-Howto.doc" install-as="README"
   platform="windows"/>
    </filelist>
```

For `package.xml 2.0`:

```
   <contents>
    <dir name="/">
     <dir name="OS">
      <file name="Guess.php" role="php">
```

```
            <tasks:replace from="@package_version@" to="version"
                        type="package-info"/>
        </file>
      </dir>
      <dir name="PEAR">
       <dir name="ChannelFile" baseinstalldir="Foo">
        <file name="Parser.php" role="php">
         <tasks:replace from="@package_version@" to="version"
                        type="package-info"/>
        </file>
       </dir>
       <file role="data" name="Foo.dat"/>
      </dir>
      <file role="doc" name="linux-Howto.doc"/>
      <file role="doc" name="windows-Howto.doc"/>
     </dir>
   </contents>
```

This tag is the heart of `package.xml` file. Once our trusty package has weathered dependency tests, this is the section of `package.xml` that is actually used during installation.

The file listing inside a `package.xml` is used to define the directory structure inside a release. It must reflect exactly the relative locations of files as they were on the computer of the developer. In other words, if the `package.xml` is in directory `/home/frank/mypackage/`, and a file in `package.xml` is located at `/home/frank /mypackage/foo/test.php`, it must be listed as:

```
<file role="php" name="foo/test.php"/>
```

Or, alternately as:

```
<dir name="foo">
 <file role="php" name="test.php"/>
</dir>
```

Either alternative will yield the same result. At installation time, PEAR will automatically convert all recursive directory trees like the second example into a single flat branch like the first example.

New Tags in package.xml

`package.xml 2.0` introduced the new tags `<phprelease>`, `<extsrcrelease>`, and `<extbinrelease>` to differentiate between the different kinds of packages the PEAR installer handles. `package.xml 2.1` introduces `<zendextsrcrelease>` and

`<zendextbinrelease>` in order to differentiate between regular PHP extensions and Zend extensions like `xdebug` (`http://pecl.php.net/xdebug`).

You may have noticed that the primary tag in `package.xml 1.0` is named `<filelist>`, whereas the primary tag in `package.xml 2.0` is named `<contents>`. This change came about as a result of a simple feature request. When PEAR 1.3.3 was popular, the need to customize installations grew; more and more attributes and information were crammed into the `<file>` tag. The `platform` attribute tells the installer that a file should only be installed on a particular platform, such as UNIX or Windows. This is used in the PEAR package in order to install the `pear` command using a `schell` script on UNIX, and using a `.bat` batch file on Windows. The feature request that came in was to implement an additional `platform="!windows"` hack that would tell the installer to install the file on every platform except Windows. This introduces a number of problems. As package complexity grows, and more systems are supported, it may be necessary to specify a limited list of systems a file can be installed on, or different names to install the file as required on different systems. Implementation of this would require a sophisticated mapping between the `install-as` and the `platform` attributes, something that was not anticipated by the designers of `package.xml 1.0`, and something that would introduce a miserable mess into a single file tag. Imagine encountering this nightmare and trying to debug it:

```
<file name="Foo.scr" role="script" install-
as="windows=Foo.bat;Darwim=Fooscr;unix=Foo;"
platform="windows;!Solaris;unix"/>
```

Do you see the typo buried deep in the install-as attribute?

One day while working on the problem caused by the spectre of such horribly complex features, it struck me that attributes like the `platform` attribute were actually kludgy ways of implementing dependencies for a specific file. Suddenly, the answer was clear. Far better than extending the attribute's meaning would be abstracting the information into separate release tags. Each release tag would have a file list and installation conditions that would define which one should be used on an end user's computer. For instance, instead of:

```
<file role="doc" name="linux-Howto.doc" install-as="README"
    platform="!windows"/>
<file role="doc" name="windows-Howto.doc" install-as="README"
    platform="windows"/>
```

We would have:

```
<file role="doc" name="linux-Howto.doc"/>
<file role="doc" name="windows-Howto.doc"/>
...
<phprelease>
```

```
<installconditions>
 <os>windows</os>
</installconditions>
<filelist>
 <install name="windows-Howto.doc" as="README"/>
 <ignore name="linux-Howto.doc"/>
</filelist>
</phprelease>
<phprelease>
 <filelist>
  <install name="linux-Howto.doc" as="README"/>
  <ignore name="windows-Howto.doc"/>
 </filelist>
</phprelease>
```

However, the most obvious benefit comes from the horrible "Darwin" example. This would translate from:

```
<file name="Foo.scr" role="script" install-
as="windows=Foo.bat;Darwim=Fooscr;unix=Foo;"
platform="windows;!Solaris;unix"/>
```

to:

```
<file name="Foo.scr" role="script"/>
...
<phprelease>
 <installconditions>
  <os>windows</os>
 </installconditions>
 <filelist>
  <install name="Foo.scr" as="Foo.bat"/>
 </filelist>
</phprelease>
<phprelease>
 <installconditions>
  <os>Darwim</os>
 </installconditions>
 <filelist>
  <install name="Foo.scr" as="Fooscr"/>
 </filelist>
</phprelease>
<phprelease>
 <installconditions>
  <arch>Solaris</arch>
```

```
 </installconditions>
 <filelist>
  <ignore name="Foo.scr"/>
 </filelist>
</phprelease>
<phprelease>
 <installconditions>
  <os>unix</os>
 </installconditions>
 <filelist>
  <install name="Foo.scr" as="Foo"/>
 </filelist>
</phprelease>
```

Here, the potential for simple validation is obvious: the `<os>` install condition is limited to a few known possibilities such as windows, unix, linux, Darwin, and so on. The OS "Darwim" would simply refuse to validate. In addition, the complexity of how Foo.scr is handled is grouped by OS rather than stuffed into a couple of attributes with error-prone non-XML syntax.

File/Directory Attributes: name, role, and baseinstalldir

The `<file>` and `<dir>` tags have a number of options available to them. Both tags require a name attribute, defining the name of the element as located on disk. Unlike an operating system, package.xml does not allow empty directories. All `<dir>` tags must contain at least one `<file>` tag. As described in the previous section, there are two ways to describe the location of a file in package.xml, either with a complete relative path separated by the UNIX path separator /:

```
<file role="php" name="foo/test.php"/>
```

Or, alternately as:

```
<dir name="foo">
 <file role="php" name="test.php"/>
</dir>
```

All files must have a **role** attribute. This attribute tells the installer how to handle a file. The default list of allowed file roles is:

Default File Roles	
Role	**Description**
php	PHP script files, like "PEAR.php"
data	Data files used by the script (read-only)
doc	Documentation files
test	Test scripts, unit test files
script	Executable script files (pear.bat, pear.sh)
ext	PHP Extension binaries (php_mysql.dll)
src	PHP Extension source files (mysql.c)

Each file role has a configuration value associated with it. For instance, on my Windows XP system, here is what I see when I list configuration values:

```
C:\>pear config-show
CONFIGURATION (CHANNEL PEAR.PHP.NET):
=====================================
Auto-discover new Channels  auto_discover <not set>
Default Channel    default_channel pear.php.net
HTTP Proxy Server Address  http_proxy  <not set>
PEAR server [DEPRECATED]  master_server pear.php.net
Default Channel Mirror   preferred_mirror pear.php.net
Remote Configuration File  remote_config <not set>
PEAR executables directory  bin_dir   C:\php4
PEAR documentation directory doc_dir   C:\php4\PEAR\docs
PHP extension directory  ext_dir   C:\php4\extensions
PEAR directory     php_dir   C:\php4\PEAR
PEAR Installer cache directory cache_dir  C:\DOCUME~1\GREGBE~1\LOCALS~1\
Temp\pear\cache
PEAR data directory    data_dir   C:\php4\PEAR\data
PHP CLI/CGI binary   php_bin   C:\php-4.3.8\cli\php.exe
PEAR test directory   test_dir   C:\php4\PEAR\tests
Cache TimeToLive    cache_ttl 3600
Preferred Package State  preferred_state stable
Unix file mask     umask   0
Debug Log Level    verbose  1
PEAR password (for    password  <not set> maintainers)
Signature Handling Program sig_bin   c:\gnupg\gpg.exe
Signature Key Directory sig_keydir C:\php4\pearkeys
Signature Key Id    sig_keyid <not set>
Package Signature Type  sig_type  gpg
PEAR username (for    username  <not set> maintainers)
User Configuration File  Filename  C:\php4\pear.ini
System Configuration File  Filename  C:\php4\pearsys.ini
```

In some cases, especially for subpackages like HTML_QuickForm_Controller (http://pear.php.net/package/HTML_QuickForm_Controller), all files should be installed into a subdirectory (HTML/QuickForm/Controller in our example). In order to reflect this installation path in our file, we would need to prepend all files with the full path, like so:

```
<file role="php" name="HTML/QuickForm/Controller.php"/>
<file role="php" name="HTML/QuickForm/Controller/Action.php"/>
```

Or, alternately use `<dir>` tags as follows:

```
<dir name="HTML">
 <dir name="QuickForm">
  <dir name="Controller">
   <file role="php" name="Action.php"/>
  </dir>
  <file role="php" name="Controller.php"/>
 </dir>
</dir>
```

In addition, our actual development path would need to reflect this. This does not fit the "make everything easy for lazy developers" development paradigm very well, and so PEAR provides the `baseinstalldir` attribute to simplify things. Now, all we need is:

```
<file role="php" baseinstalldir="HTML/QuickForm" name=" Controller.
php"/>
<file role="php" baseinstalldir="HTML/QuickForm" name=" Controller/
Action.php"/>
```

Or, the far more common:

```
<dir name="/" baseinstalldir="HTML/QuickForm">
 <dir name="Controller">
  <file role="php" name="Action.php"/>
 </dir>
 <file role="php" name="Controller.php"/>
</dir>
```

Path Locations on the Development Machine

Note that as a developer, in order for this to work, the actual paths on disk must match the `<dir>/<file>` tags. In our example above, the files should be in:

```
Controller/Action.php
Controller.php
package.xml
```

Rather than:

```
HTML/QuickForm/Controller/Action.php
HTML/QuickForm/Controller.php
package.xml
```

Otherwise the PEAR installer will be unable to find the files.

Generally speaking, if a file is listed in `package.xml` as:

```
<file role="php" name="Path/To/Foo.php"/>
```

And `php_dir` is `C:\php4\PEAR`, the file will be installed into `C:\php4\PEAR\Path\To\Foo.php`. This is not always advantageous, especially for things like scripts. PEAR, for instance, places all of its scripts in the `scripts/` subdirectory for easier organization. However, this would mean that if `bin_dir` is `C:\php4`,

```
<file role="script" name="scripts/pear.bat"/>
```

will be installed into `C:\php4\scripts\pear.bat`, which may not necessarily be in the path. To change the base installation directory in PEAR 1.4.x, you need to use an `<install>` tag inside a release tag, In addition, it is possible to perform text transformations on the contents of files.

Summary

In this chapter, we discovered the basics of how the PEAR installer's internals work through the lens of `package.xml`'s structure. First, we explored the basic design philosophies of the PEAR installer, and how PEAR packages differ from the old-fashioned unzip-and-go approach. We learned about PEAR's configuration options, and the versatile ways in which PEAR deals with libraries versus applications.

Next, we explored the importance of versioning in controlling the quality of packages installed, and the importance of dependencies, and how the PEAR installer manages this important link between libraries and applications. Then, we explored how easy it is to upgrade when using the PEAR installer, as compared to upgrading traditional unzip-and-go applications.

After this, we dove headfirst into the structure of `package.xml`, learning how package metadata such as the package name, authors, release notes, and changelog are organized. This was coupled with a look at how critical installation data such as files, dependencies, and versioning is organized.

The next chapter will examine advanced topics, specifically how `package.xml 2.0` introduces better application support, and how to leverage these new features in your own packages.

3

Leveraging Full Application Support with the PEAR Installer

In the last chapter we learned a great deal about the internals of `package.xml`. In this chapter, we are stepping up the intensity a notch, and exploring the exciting new features that enable us to easily distribute PHP applications and manage their installation and post-installation customization.

If you've ever wanted to make it easy to customize an installation of your PHP application across multiple platforms, PHP versions, and user setups, then this is the chapter for you.

package.xml Version 2.0: Your Sexy New Friend

The title of this section says it all. `package.xml 2.0` is a major improvement over `package.xml 1.0`. The implementations of several important new features in the PEAR installer such as custom file roles/tasks, enterprise-level dependencies, and channels are reflected by new tags in `package.xml 2.0`. In addition, the structure is designed to be easily validated using other tools.

PEAR Channels: A Revolution in PHP Installation

The smallest addition to `package.xml 2.0` is the `<channel>` tag. Don't be fooled though, channels are the most significant new feature implemented in the PEAR installer. Channels are to PEAR what dependencies are to team development. By opening up the ease of the PEAR installer to sites other than `pear.php.net`, a number of free choices have been made available to PHP users. For the first time, it is possible to design an application that depends upon packages from `pear.php.net`, `pear.example.com`, and any number of sites, and all of them can be automatically downloaded, installed, and easily upgraded on the end-user's computer with a single command. Although Chapter 5 discusses the minutiae of channels and the `channel.xml` channel definition file, it is good to have a basic understanding of how channels work when designing your packages.

There are two problems that channels effectively solve:

- Distributing application development across multiple development teams
- Preventing conflicting packages from overwriting each other

A user's PEAR installer can have knowledge of a channel, in this example, `channelserver.example.com` via:

```
$ pear channel-discover channelserver.example.com
```

Once the user's PEAR installer has this knowledge, packages from `channelserver.example.com`, like a hypothetical package named `Packagename` can be simply installed with:

```
$ pear install channelserver.example.com/Packagename
```

Users can also install packages that depend on `channelserver.example.com/Packagename`. This was impossible before the advent of PEAR channels.

When a user simply types the following command:

```
$ pear install Package
```

as they would with PEAR version 1.3.6 and older, the installer uses the `default_channel` configuration variable, which is usually `pear.php.net` or `pecl.php.net` (for the `pecl` command), and then acts as if the user had instead typed:

```
$ pear install pear.php.net/Package
```

In fact, every existing PEAR package Foo has now become `pear.php.net/Foo`, effectively acting as a namespace differentiating it from `channelserver.example.com/Foo`. This is the mechanism that channels use to prevent conflicting packages from overwriting each other. Since `pear.php.net/Foo` is not the same package as `channelserver.example.com/Foo`, it is not possible to *upgrade* from `pear.php.net/Foo` to `channelserver.example.com/Foo`. For this reason, it is time for an important concept:

 Even though *channel names* are *server names*, they also function as a classification naming scheme to differentiate packages from different sources.

To understand this, we need to study some of the history behind channels. In the original draft proposal describing channels, the name of a channel (as used in both installation and dependencies) and the server used to access the channel were different. For instance, the `pear.php.net` channel was originally named the PEAR channel, so that users would type:

```
$ pear install PEAR/Foo
```

After a few development releases of PEAR, it became clear that this was a bad idea for several reasons, one of them being the fact that if you didn't know where to locate a channel, it simply couldn't be located. So, by the first alpha version of PEAR, 1.4.0a1, the name of the channel became the same as the server name.

So Do We Always Have to Type pear.php.net/Package?

No, in fact the innovation that made it reasonable to use the server name as a channel's name was the idea of a channel alias. From the command line, we can type the following and PEAR would install `pear.php.net/Package`.

```
$ pear install pear/Package
```

In addition, if we wish, we can change this alias to anything we want by using the `channel-alias` command as shown:

```
$ pear channel-alias pear.php.net p
$ pear install p/Package
```

However, in `package.xml`'s `<channel>` and other tags, the full channel server name always must be used, aliases are never allowed.

The switch to using the server name as the channel name has another desirable consequence. Originally, it was possible to change the server associated with the channel transparently. This is a bad idea on many levels! Firstly, this meant that a malicious coder could quite easily override the conflict protections in the PEAR channel simply by changing the server that the PEAR channel uses to get package information. Secondly, by supplying identically-named packages to the ones available at pear.php.net with malevolent code hidden inside, it would even be possible to fool the user into using malicious code without their knowledge.

By using the server name as the channel name, this is no longer possible without an old-fashioned hacking attack against the original channel server, something that is bound to be noticed pretty quickly.

In short, the strength of channels lies not just in their ease of use for the end user and flexibility for the developer, but in the extensive security considerations that have gone into their design. As evidenced by recent security flaws in major PHP packages such as XML_RPC and phpBB, one cannot be too careful. At PEAR, security is deadly serious, and the developers have gone to great lengths to ensure that PEAR is hack-proof.

Application Support

So far, we have learned that the PEAR installer was designed to support libraries first, and then application support was added in PEAR version 1.4.0. Let's take a closer look at what that specifically means by examining four exciting new features: custom file roles, custom file tasks, post-installation scripts, and the ability to bundle several packages into a single archive.

In this section, we will explore the details of these features by creating a new custom file role chiaramdb2schema, a custom file task chiara-managedb, a post-install script to populate needed data, and a sample application. We'll then distribute the role and task in a single archive.

> Before we begin, you need to examine one vital point:
>
> What problem are you solving? Should you use a custom file role, custom file task, post-install script, or something else?

Custom file roles are designed to group related file classes together. If, for instance, you wish to install all web-based image files in a different way from web-based JavaScript files, custom file roles are the best way to do this.

Custom file tasks are designed to manipulate the contents of individual files prior to installation or prior to packaging. If you need to convert a generic template into a machine-specific file (such as a generic database creation SQL file into a MySQL-specific or Oracle-specific SQL file), custom tasks are a very good choice.

Post-installation scripts are designed to allow any other advanced configuration that the user must perform before the package will be ready for use.

Our sample file role and task are designed for a single-user situation. On a shared host, this must be done with a post-installation script, and so we will provide one to allow systems administrators to maintain multiple database installs of a package.

Naming Conventions for Custom File Roles/Tasks

It is a very good idea to use a custom prefix for all functionality that extends the PEAR Installer. In our examples, if we were to name the role sql instead of chiara_sql and the task updatedb instead of chiara_updatedb, there is a risk of conflicting with an official custom role or task distributed from pear.php. net. In particular, should any role or task be deemed useful enough to be implemented as a default part of the PEAR installer, users of your custom role/task would be unable to upgrade their PEAR installations unless they uninstalled the role and every package that depends on it.

Introduction to Custom File Roles

File roles are used to group related files together to handle installation. The standard file roles are php, data, doc, test, script, src, and ext. Each of these roles is handled differently by the installer. A file specified by a tag such as this one in a package named My_Package will be installed in My/Package/foo.php.

```
<file name="foo.php" role="php" baseinstalldir="My/Package"/>
```

However, the same tag with a role of data prompts the installer to act very differently. Instead of being installed in My/Package/foo.php, this file will be installed in My_Package/foo.php.

```
<file name="foo.php" role="data" baseinstalldir="My/Package"/>
```

The baseinstalldir attribute is ignored by the data, doc, and test roles, which are instead installed into <package name>/path/to/file as defined by the relative path in package.xml.

In addition, each role determines where to install files from a different `config` variable. The `role: configuration` variable mapping is as follows:

- php: `php_dir`
- data: `data_dir`
- doc: `doc_dir`
- test: `test_dir`
- script: `bin_dir`
- ext: `ext_dir`
- src: `<none>` (not installed)

Generally speaking, configuration variables are the same as the file role with `_dir` appended, with the exception of `role="script"`, which is to be appended with `bin_dir`. In addition, note that files with `role="src"` are not actually installed. Instead, these files are extracted and then compiled to create extension binaries, and then discarded. Each of these roles has a set of characteristics that differentiate it from other roles:

- Some are valid for PHP packages, others for extension packages
- Some are installed, others are not
- Installable roles have a configuration variable that determines where they should be installed
- Some honor the `baseinstalldir` attribute, others don't
- Some install into `<packagename>/path` and others don't
- Some represent PHP scripts
- Some represent executable files (like scripts)
- Some represent PHP extension binaries

These characteristics are all that is needed to define customized file roles. In fact, the existing file roles are defined using these traits and special objects. For instance, the code to define the PHP role is:

```php
<?php
/**
 * PEAR_Installer_Role_Php
 *
 * PHP versions 4 and 5
 *
 * LICENSE: This source file is subject to version 3.0 of the PHP
 * license
 * that is available through the world-wide-web at the following URI:
```

```
 * http://www.php.net/license/3_0.txt.  If you did not receive a copy
 * of the PHP License and are unable to obtain it through the web,
 * please send a note to license@php.net so we can mail you a copy
 * immediately.
 *
 * @category   pear
 * @package    PEAR
 * @author     Greg Beaver <cellog@php.net>
 * @copyright  1997-2005 The PHP Group
 * @license    http://www.php.net/license/3_0.txt   PHP License 3.0
 * @version    CVS: $Id: Php.php,v 1.5 2005/07/28 16:51:53 cellog Exp
$
 * @link       http://pear.php.net/package/PEAR
 * @since      File available since Release 1.4.0a1
 */

/**
 * @category   pear
 * @package    PEAR
 * @author     Greg Beaver <cellog@php.net>
 * @copyright  1997-2005 The PHP Group
 * @license    http://www.php.net/license/3_0.txt PHP License 3.0
 * @version    Release: @package_version@
 * @link       http://pear.php.net/package/PEAR
 * @since      Class available since Release 1.4.0a1
 */
class PEAR_Installer_Role_Php extends PEAR_Installer_Role_Common {}
?>
```

For most roles, this is the only code that needs to be defined! In addition to this PHP code, however, an XML file should be installed that documents the properties of a role. The XML file for the PHP role is as follows:

```
<role version="1.0">
 <releasetypes>php</releasetypes>
 <releasetypes>extsrc</releasetypes>
 <releasetypes>extbin</releasetypes>
 <installable>1</installable>
 <locationconfig>php_dir</locationconfig>
 <honorsbaseinstall>1</honorsbaseinstall>
 <unusualbaseinstall />
 <phpfile>1</phpfile>
 <executable />
 <phpextension />
 <config_vars />
</role>
```

The various tags are as follows:

- `<releasetypes>`: This tag works like an array, whose contents define which release types are allowed to contain this role. The list of possible release types is `php`, `extsrc`, `extbin`, or `bundle`.

- `<installable>`: This Boolean value determines whether a role is installed to disk or not.

- `<locationconfig>`: For installable roles, this string value determines which configuration variable to use for installing the file.

- `<honorsbaseinstall>`: This Boolean value (represented as 1 or an empty tag) determines whether `baseinstalldir` is used in calculating the final installation location.

- `<unusualbaseinstall>`: This Boolean value (represented as 1 or an empty tag) determines whether the package name is prepended to the installation path.

- `<phpfile>`: This Boolean value (represented as 1 or an empty tag) determines whether a file is treated as a PHP file (analyzed at packaging time for valid PHP/class names/function names).

- `<executable>`: This Boolean value (represented as 1 or an empty tag) determines whether a file is installed with the executable attribute on UNIX-based systems.

- `<phpextension>`: This Boolean value (represented as 1 or an empty tag) determines whether the installer will display a helpful error message if overwriting an existing extension binary fails due to file locking.

Creating PEAR_Installer_Role_Chiaramdb2schema Custom Role

First, it is important to understand how this role is used in `package.xml`. In order to implement a custom role, `package.xml` validation should be able to tell a user where to download and install it, as dependency validation occurs only after the `package.xml` file has been validated from a basic structural standpoint.

```
<package>
 <name>Role_Chiaramdb2schema</name>
 <channel>pear.chiaraquartet.net</channel>
</package>
```

As such, in addition to a package dependency `package.xml` should also contain the `<usesrole>` tag describing the name of a custom file role that is used, and the remote location of the package containing this role. For our example this will be as follows:

```
<usesrole>
 <role>chiaramdb2schema</role>
 <package>Role_Chiaramdb2schema</package>
 <channel>pear.chiaraquartet.net</channel>
</usesrole>
```

This tag will prompt the installer to first check if the `pear.chiaraquartet.net/Role_Chiaramdb2schemaql` package is installed. If not, the installer will issue a warning:

```
This package contains role "chiaramdb2schema" and requires package "pear.
chiaraquartet.net/Role_Chiaramdb2schema" to be used
```

Why Use <usesrole>/<usestask> in Addition to a Dependency?

The PEAR installer cannot successfully configure roles or tasks once installation has begun. They must be installed and configured prior to any attempt to install a package that uses them. For this reason, installation of custom roles or tasks must be performed in a separate process from the packages that use them.

To use a custom role inside the `<file>` tag is no different from any regular role.

```
<file name="dbcontents.xml" role="chiaramdb2schema"/>
```

All custom file roles are implemented in a single PHP file that is installed into the `PEAR/Installer/Role/` directory. So, for instance, the `data` role is located in `PEAR/Installer/Role/Data.php`. Unlike custom tasks, custom file roles cannot be in subdirectories, so prefixing should be done without underscores to match the PEAR naming conventions. In addition, every custom role must extend the `PEAR_Installer_Role_Common` class, which is found in `PEAR/Installer/Role/Common.php`.

Our custom file role uses the `data_dir` configuration variable to determine installation location, and so in terms of installation it acts exactly like the `data` role. However, it does a magical thing through this XML in the `Chiaramdb2schema.xml` file:

```
<config_vars>
 <chiaramdb2schema_driver>
  <type>string</type>
  <default />
  <doc>MDB2 database driver used to connect to the database</doc>
  <prompt>Database driver type.  This must be a valid MDB2 driver.
```

```
Example drivers are mysql, mysqli, pgsql, sqlite, and so on</prompt>
  <group>Database</group>
 </chiaramdb2schema_driver>
 <chiaramdb2schema_dsn>
  <type>string</type>
  <default />
  <doc>PEAR::MDB2 dsn string[s] for database connection, separated
by ;.
This must be of format:
[user@]host/dbname[;[Package[#schemafile]::]dsn2...]
One default database connection must be specified, and package-
specific databases
may be specified.  The driver type and password should be excluded.
Passwords
are set with the chiaramdb2schema_password config variable
</doc>
  <prompt>Database connection DSN[s] (no driver/password)</prompt>
  <group>Database</group>
 </chiaramdb2schema_dsn>
 <chiaramdb2schema_password>
  <type>string</type>
  <default />
  <doc>PEAR::MDB2 dsn password[s] for database connection.
This must be of format: password[:password...]
Each DSN in chiaramdb2schema_dsn must match with a password in this
list, or
none will be used.  To use no password, simply put another :: like
::::
</doc>
  <prompt>Database connection password[s]</prompt>
  <group>Database</group>
 </chiaramdb2schema_password>
</config_vars>
```

By defining the `<config_vars>` tag in this way, three entirely new configuration variables will be added to the PEAR configuration. They are manipulated in the same manner as any other configuration variable, and provide the information that will make our `chiaramdb2schema` role something special.

Our role takes advantage of the fact that MDB2-based schema files are a special sub-class of data files by directly extending the `PEAR_Installer_Role_Data` class. Here is the complete source code for our example role:

```
<?php
/**
```

```
 * Custom file role for MDB2_Schema-based database setup files
 *
 * This file contains the PEAR_Installer_Role_Chiaramdb2schema file
 * role
 *
 * PHP versions 4 and 5
 *
 * @package    Role_Chiaramdb2schema
 * @author     Greg Beaver <cellog@php.net>
 * @copyright  2005 Gregory Beaver
 * @license    http://www.opensource.org/licenses/bsd-license.php BSD
 * License
 * @version    Release: 0.2.0
 * @link
http://pear.chiaraquartet.net/index.php?package=Role_Chiaramdb2schema
 */
/**
 * Contains the PEAR_Installer_Role_Data class
 */
require_once 'PEAR/Installer/Role/Data.php';
/**
 * chiaramdb2schema Custom file role for MDB2_Schema-based database
 * setup files
 *
 * This file role provides the <var>chiaramdb2schema_driver</var>,
 * <var>chiaramdb2schema_dsn</var>, and
<var>chiaramdb2schema_password</var>
 * configuration variables for use by the chiara-managedb custom task
 * to set up and initialize database files
 *
 * PHP versions 4 and 5
 *
 * @package    Role_Chiaramdb2schema
 * @author     Greg Beaver <cellog@php.net>
 * @copyright  2005 Gregory Beaver
 * @license    http://www.opensource.org/licenses/bsd-license.php BSD
 * License
 * @version    Release: 0.2.0
 * @link
http://pear.chiaraquartet.net/index.php?package=Role_Chiaramdb2schema
 */
class PEAR_Installer_Role_Chiaramdb2schema extends
PEAR_Installer_Role_Data
{
}
?>
```

And the `Chiaramdb2schema.xml` file that accompanies this role:

```
<role version="1.0">
 <releasetypes>php</releasetypes>
 <releasetypes>extsrc</releasetypes>
 <releasetypes>extbin</releasetypes>
 <installable>1</installable>
 <locationconfig>data_dir</locationconfig>
 <honorsbaseinstall />
 <unusualbaseinstall />
 <phpfile />
 <executable />
 <phpextension />
 <config_vars>
  <chiaramdb2schema_driver>
   <type>string</type>
   <default />
   <doc>MDB2 database driver used to connect to the database</doc>
   <prompt>Database driver type.  This must be a valid MDB2 driver.
Example drivers are mysql, mysqli, pgsql, sqlite, and so on</prompt>
   <group>Database</group>
  </chiaramdb2schema_driver>
  <chiaramdb2schema_dsn>
   <type>string</type>
   <default />
   <doc>PEAR::MDB2 dsn string[s] for database connection, separated
by ;.
This must be of format:
[user@]host/dbname[;[Package[#schemafile]::]dsn2...]
One default database connection must be specified, and package-
specific databases
may be specified.  The driver type and password should be excluded.
Passwords
are set with the chiaramdb2schema_password config variable
</doc>
   <prompt>Database connection DSN[s] (no driver/password)</prompt>
   <group>Database</group>
  </chiaramdb2schema_dsn>
  <chiaramdb2schema_password>
   <type>string</type>
   <default />
   <doc>PEAR::MDB2 dsn password[s] for database connection.
This must be of format: password[:password...]
Each DSN in chiaramdb2schema_dsn must match with a password in this
list, or
```

```
none will be used.  To use no password, simply put another :: like
::::
</doc>
   <prompt>Database connection password[s]</prompt>
   <group>Database</group>
  </chiaramdb2schema_password>
 </config_vars>
</role>
```

That's it! Now that we've seen how to implement a simple role, let's examine the range of possibility built into the design of custom file roles.

Full Range of Possible Custom File Roles

Most custom file roles will only need to specify configuration variables and attributes as described in previous sections. However, sometimes this is not enough, and some unusual setup is required. The protected `setup()` method of the base class `PEAR_Installer_Role_Common` is provided specifically to allow file roles to perform any unusual setup functionality needed. The method signature is:

```
/**
 * Do any unusual setup here
 * @param PEAR_Installer
 * @param PEAR_PackageFile_v2
 * @param array file attributes
 * @param string file name
 */
function setup(&$installer, $pkg, $atts, $file)
```

The parameters are pretty straightforward:

- `PEAR_Installer $installer`: This allows any specialized installation tasks to be done through the public API of the `PEAR_Installer` class.
- `PEAR_PackageFile_v2 $pkg`: This allows retrieval of any information from the `package.xml` that may be useful to the custom role. Note that the `PEAR_PackageFile_v2` class's public API is read-only.
- `array $atts`: This is the file attribute as parsed from `package.xml`, in a format similar to the following:

```
array(
  'name' => 'Full/Path/To/File.php',
  'role' => 'customrolename',
  'baseinstalldir' => 'Whatever',
);
```

- `string $file`: This is the file name.

Note that the setup() method is called for every role just prior to any installation location calculations. In addition, the current PEAR_Config configuration object is available via the $this->config member.

Also important to explore is the manner in which custom file roles's configuration variables are defined.

The <config_vars> tag defines configuration variables. Each configuration variable is declared using a tag with its name. If you wish to create a simple configuration variable named foo, you would use this XML:

```
<config_vars>
 <foo>
  <type>string</type>
  <default />
  <doc>Foo configuration</doc>
  <prompt>Foo protocol login</prompt>
  <group>Auth</group>
 </foo>
</config_vars>
```

Legal configuration types are string, directory, file, set, and password. If you wish to limit possible input to specified values, you also need to define the set of valid values using the <valid_set> tag:

```
<config_vars>
 <foo>
  <type>set</type>
  <default />
  <doc>Foo configuration</doc>
  <valid_set>bar</valid_set>
  <valid_set>baz</valid_set>
  <valid_set>gronk</valid_set>
  <prompt>Foo protocol type</prompt>
  <group>Auth</group>
 </foo>
</config_vars>
```

Take a look in the PEAR/Config.php file for examples of existing configuration variable groups. This variable is for informational purposes, and can be anything you wish it to be.

The <default> tag, on the other hand, has a large range of possibilities. There are three kinds of values that can be accessed to set the default value of a configuration variable:

- Default values of existing configuration variables
- PHP constants
- Any text

In order to retrieve the default value of the `php_dir` configuration variable, you would use this tag:

```
<default><php_dir/></default>
```

Only built-in configuration variables may be accessed for their default values. To access a PHP constant like the `PHP_OS` constant, use this tag:

```
<default><constant>PHP_OS</constant></default>
```

Note that any constant defined in `PEAR/Common.php` or `PEAR/Config.php` will also be available for use as a default value. Finally, straight text may be used like so:

```
<default><text>hello world</text></default>
```

In order to combine several of these, simply use them in the desired sequence:

```
<default><php_dir/><constant>DIRECTORY_SEPARATOR</constant>
<text>foo</text></default>
```

If you wish to use multiple constants or multiple texts, append a number to the end of the tag name like so:

```
<default><text1>.</text1><constant>PATH_SEPARATOR</constant>
<text2>mychannel</text2></default>
```

Introduction to Custom File Tasks

There are three custom file tasks bundled with PEAR and one script task (post-install scripts are discussed in the next section). The tasks are as follows:

- `<tasks:replace/>`: Performs a basic `str_replace` on installed or packaged files. Possible replacement values are information from `package.xml`, information from PEAR's configuration such as the value of `php_dir`, or PHP constants like `PHP_OS`.
- `<tasks:windowseol/>`: This converts all line endings to Windows `"\r\n"` line endings.
- `<tasks:unixeol/>`: This converts all line endings to UNIX `"\n"` line endings

In this section, we will examine how these tasks are defined inside the PEAR code, and how to create your own custom file tasks.

File tasks are generally used to manipulate the contents of files prior to installation. However, this is only limited by your imagination. In our example, we will use a task to create and update a database's structure on upgrade using the `chiaramdb2schema` file role that we created earlier. This task is a very advanced task, performing sophisticated processing, and as such shows the versatility of such a system.

The only constraint on the XML content of custom tasks is that the task's namespace (normally `tasks`) must prefix each tag. Validation is controlled with the PHP code for each task. A custom file task must extend `PEAR_Task_Common`, and must reside in the `PEAR/Task/` subdirectory of PEAR. Unlike custom file roles, custom file tasks can support subdirectories directly by using underscores. In our example file task, `chiara-managedb`, the class name is `PEAR_Task_Chiara_Managedb`, and this is found in file `PEAR/Task/Chiara/Managedb.php`.

There are three kinds of custom file tasks: single, multiple, and script. Single tasks perform their operations on a single file, and are executed just prior to installation of the file. Multiple tasks operate on every file containing the task, and are executed after installation is completed. Script tasks are executed after installation using the `run-scripts` command, and are covered in detail in the next section on post-installation scripts. In addition, the order in which tasks appear in a file tag is important. The following possible but illogical task ordering will result in occurrences of `@blah@` within `foo.php` being replaced with the contents of the `data_dir` configuration variable.

```
<file name="foo.php" role="php">
 <tasks:replace from="@blah@" to="data_dir" type="pear-config"/>
 <tasks:replace from="@blah@" to="version" type="package-info"/>
</file>
```

However, the opposite ordering will result in occurrences of `@blah@` within `foo.php` being replaced with the contents of the `<version>` tag from `package.xml`.

```
<file name="foo.php" role="php">
 <tasks:replace from="@blah@" to="version" type="package-info"/>
 <tasks:replace from="@blah@" to="data_dir" type="pear-config"/>
</file>
```

In addition, single tasks can be executed when packaging. In other words, some tasks do not depend on the state of the client machine in order to execute. An example is the `replace` task. The `package-info` replacement only depends on the contents of the `package.xml` file, which is known at the time of `pear package`. The time at which a task is executed is referred to as the install phase of the task. Currently recognized install phases are install and package. A custom task can control its install phase with the `$phase` property. There are three constants defined:

- `PEAR_TASK_INSTALL`: Installation phase

- `PEAR_TASK_PACKAGE`: Packaging phase

- `PEAR_TASK_PACKAGEANDINSTALL`: Both installation and packaging phase

So, for instance, the phase declaration for the `windowseol` task is:

```
var $phase = PEAR_TASK_PACKAGEANDINSTALL;
```

The actual installation phase is set by the constructor of `PEAR_Task_Common`, and can be accessed through the `$installphase` property. The only legal values are `PEAR_TASK_INSTALL` and `PEAR_TASK_PACKAGE`. This member is used, for instance, to determine which replacements should occur. For instance, if `$this->installphase` is `PEAR_TASK_PACKAGE`, then `pear-config` and `php-const` replacements are not performed.

Perhaps the best introduction to custom file tasks is with some of the simpler tasks distributed in the PEAR package itself. The simplest tasks are the `<tasks:windowseol/>` and `<tasks:unixeol/>` tasks. These will process the contents of their file and convert line endings to Windows format, or to UNIX format. Here is the complete source code for the `windowseol` task:

```php
<?php
/**
 * <tasks:windowseol>
 *
 * PHP versions 4 and 5
 *
 * LICENSE: This source file is subject to version 3.0 of the PHP
 * license that is available through the world-wide-web at the
 * following URI:
 * http://www.php.net/license/3_0.txt.  If you did not receive a copy
 * of the PHP License and are unable to obtain it through the web,
 * please send a note to license@php.net so we can mail you a copy
 *                                                immediately.
 *
 * @category    pear
 * @package     PEAR
 * @author      Greg Beaver <cellog@php.net>
 * @copyright   1997-2005 The PHP Group
 * @license     http://www.php.net/license/3_0.txt   PHP License 3.0
 * @version     CVS: $Id: Windowseol.php,v 1.6 2005/10/02 06:29:39
 *              cellog Exp $
 * @link        http://pear.php.net/package/PEAR
 * @since       File available since Release 1.4.0a1
 */
```

```
/**
 * Base class
 */
require_once 'PEAR/Task/Common.php';
/**
 * Implements the windows line endings file task.
 * @category    pear
 * @package     PEAR
 * @author      Greg Beaver <cellog@php.net>
 * @copyright   1997-2005 The PHP Group
 * @license     http://www.php.net/license/3_0.txt   PHP License 3.0
 * @version     Release: @package_version@
 * @link        http://pear.php.net/package/PEAR
 * @since       Class available since Release 1.4.0a1
 */
class PEAR_Task_Windowseol extends PEAR_Task_Common
{
    var $type = 'simple';
    var $phase = PEAR_TASK_PACKAGE;
    var $_replacements;

    /**
     * Validate the raw xml at parsing-time.
     * @param PEAR_PackageFile_v2
     * @param array raw, parsed xml
     * @param PEAR_Config
     * @static
     */
    function validateXml($pkg, $xml, &$config, $fileXml)
    {
        if ($xml != '') {
            return array(PEAR_TASK_ERROR_INVALID,
                                        'no attributes allowed');
        }
        return true;
    }

    /**
     * Initialize a task instance with the parameters
     * @param array raw, parsed xml
     * @param unused
     */
    function init($xml, $attribs)
    {
```

```
    }

    /**
     * Replace all line endings with windows line endings
     *
     * See validateXml() source for the complete list of allowed
fields
     * @param PEAR_PackageFile_v1|PEAR_PackageFile_v2
     * @param string file contents
     * @param string the eventual final file location (informational
only)
     * @return string|false|PEAR_Error false to skip this file,
PEAR_Error to fail
     *       (use $this->throwError), otherwise return the new contents
     */
    function startSession($pkg, $contents, $dest)
    {
        $this->logger->log(3, "replacing all line endings with
        \\r\\n in $dest");
        return preg_replace("/\r\n|\n\r|\r|\n/", "\r\n", $contents);
    }
}
?>
```

As you can see, the primary operation performed is in the `startSession()` method. For most tasks, this is sufficient. Next, let's create our own custom file task!

Creating the PEAR_Task_Chiara_Managedb Custom Task

The first step in creating our task is to determine the desired purpose of the task. In our case, we can sum up the desired purpose with a problem that needs to be solved.

 THE PROBLEM: Installing and updating a database used by the package is a tedious process that should be automated.

More specifically, we need a solution that can perform these tasks:

- Create a database from scratch on a fresh installation of the package
- Update an existing database structure to reflect any changes in a new version of the package upon upgrading the package

- Operate with a large variety of databases, and easily manage migration to a different database at a future date
- Operate on different databases for different packages, as controlled by the user

In order to satisfy these constraints, we will be taking advantage of the MDB2_Schema package, available at `http://pear.php.net/MDB2_Schema`. This package provides a number of distinct advantages over any custom solution we could design from scratch:

- MDB2 supports a wide variety of database drivers.
- The XML schema format used to describe a database structure is database-independent, allowing users of any database MDB2 supports to use a package that uses this task.
- There is a wide user base and several active maintainers helping to ensure that the package performs as advertised.
- The `MDB2_Schema::updateDatabase()` method is capable of performing a sophisticated update of a database by comparing two schema files.

In addition, we will rely upon a less-than-optimal solution to satisfy the need for different databases per package: we will use a required format for the configuration variables provided by the `chiaramdb2schema` role.

In order to determine whether the task needs a unique database for the package, we will add an optional attribute named `unique` to the XML. As such, the three legal possibilities for our task in `package.xml` will be:

```
<tasks:chiara-managedb/>
<tasks:chiara-managedb unique="0"/>
<tasks:chiara-managedb unique="1"/>
```

> **PEAR 1.5.0a1 or Newer Is Needed to Run this Task**
>
> Unfortunately, a serious bug in PEAR versions prior to 1.5.0a1 prevents proper usage of this task, so if you want to try it, make sure you have the latest version of PEAR installed.

In addition, as we require the `chiaramdb2schema` role in order to be sure that our configuration variables are installed and ready to use, we will require that the task is contained with a file of role `chiaramdb2schema` like so:

```
<file name="blah.xml" role="chiaramdb2schema">
 <tasks:chiara-managedb/>
</file>
```

Here is the XML validation method for our task:

```
/**
 * Validate the raw xml at parsing-time.
 * @param PEAR_PackageFile_v2
 * @param array raw, parsed xml
 * @param PEAR_Config
 * @static
 */
function validateXml($pkg, $xml, &$config, $fileXml)
{
    if ($fileXml['role'] !='chiaramdb2schema') {
        return array(PEAR_TASK_ERROR_INVALID,
            'chiara_managedb task can only be ' .
                'used with files whose role is chiaramdb2schema.
                File is role "' .
            $fileXml['role'] . '"');
    }
    if (isset($xml['attribs'])) {
        if (!isset($xml['attribs']['unique'])) {
            return array(PEAR_TASK_ERROR_MISSING_ATTRIB, 'unique');
        }
        if (!in_array($xml['attribs']['unique'],
                                        array('0', '1'))) {
            return array
                    (PEAR_TASK_ERROR_WRONG_ATTRIB_VALUE, 'unique',
                    $xml['attribs']['unique'], array('0', '1'));
        }
    }
    return true;
}
```

When running the task, we will use the value of the unique attribute to control the database DSN (Data Source Name) used to connect to the database. As such, here is our initialization method:

```
/**
 * Initialize a task instance with the parameters
 * @param array raw, parsed xml
 * @param unused
 */
function init($xml, $attribs)
{
    if (isset($xml['attribs']['unique']) &&
        $xml['attribs']['unique']) {
```

```
            $this->_unique = true;
        } else {
            $this->_unique = false;
        }
    }
```

So far, this is pretty simple, isn't it? The next step is to determine which database to use, and how to connect. To do this, we will be using a combination of the `chiaramdb2schema_driver` configuration variable, the `chiaramdb2schema_dsn` variable, and the `chiara_mdb2schema_password` variable.

First of all, we will define a method to construct the data source name (DSN) from these configuration variables. Before analyzing the source, let's see it in all of its glory:

```
/**
 * parse the chiaramdb2schema_dsn config variable and the
 * password variable to determine an actual DSN that should be
 * used for this task.
 * @return string|PEAR_Error
 * @access private
 */
function _parseDSN($pkg)
{
    // get channel-specific configuration for this variable
    $driver = $this->config->get('chiaramdb2schema_driver',
        null, $pkg->getChannel());
    if (!$driver) {
        return PEAR::raiseError('Error: no driver set.  use
        "config-set ' . 'chiaramdb2schema_driver <drivertype>"
        before installing');
    }
    $allDSN = $this->config->get('chiaramdb2schema_dsn',
        null, $pkg->getChannel());
    if (!$allDSN) {
        return $this->throwError('Error: no dsn set.  use
        "config-set ' . 'chiaramdb2schema_dsn <dsn>"
        before installing');
    }
    $allPasswords = $this->config->get('chiaramdb2schema_password',
        null, $pkg->getChannel());
    $allDSN = explode(';', $allDSN);
    $badDSN = array();
    $allPasswords = explode(':', $allPasswords);
    for ($i = 0; $i < count($allDSN); $i++) {
        if ($i && strpos($allDSN[$i], '::')) {
            $allDSN[$i] = explode('::', $allDSN[$i]);
```

```php
        $password = (isset($allPasswords[$i]) &&
            $allPasswords[$i]) ? $allPasswords[$i] : '';
        if (!strpos($allDSN[$i][1], '@')) {
                    $password = '';
        } elseif ($password) {
            // insert password into DSN
            $a = explode('@', $allDSN[$i][1]);
            $allDSN[$i][1] = $a[0] . ':' . $password . '@';
            unset($a[0]);
            $allDSN[$i][1] .= implode('@', $a);
        }
    } elseif (!$i && !strpos($allDSN[0], '::')) {
        $password = (isset($allPasswords[0]) &&
            $allPasswords[0]) ? $allPasswords[0] : '';
        if (!strpos($allDSN[0], '@'))
                    {$password = '';
        } elseif ($password) {
            // insert password into DSN
            $a = explode('@', $allDSN[0]);
            $allDSN[0] = $a[0] . ':' . $password . '@';
            unset($a[0]);
            $allDSN[0] .= implode('@', $a);
        }
    } else {
        // invalid DSN
        $badDSN[$i] = $allDSN[$i];
        $allDSN[$i] = false;
    }
}
if ($this->_unique) {
    $lookfor = array($pkg->getPackage(),
        $pkg->getPackage() . '#' . $this->_file);
    foreach ($allDSN as $i => $dsn) {
        if (!$i) {
            continue;
        }
        if (strcasecmp($dsn[0], $lookfor[0]) === 0) {
            return $driver . '://' . $dsn[1];
        }
        if (strcasecmp($dsn[0], $lookfor[1]) === 0) {
            return $driver . '://' . $dsn[1];
        }
    }
    return $this->throwError('No valid DSNs for package "' .
```

```
        $pkg->getPackage() . '" were found in config variable
        chiaramdb2schema_dsn');
    } else {
        if (!$allDSN[0]) {
            return $this->throwError('invalid default DSN "' .
                $badDSN[0] . '" in config variable
                   chiaramdb2schema_dsn');
        }
        return $driver . '://' . $allDSN[0];
    }
}
```

First, the configuration variables are retrieved using the `$config` member, which is set in the constructor:

```
// get channel-specific configuration for this variable
$driver = $this->config->get('chiaramdb2schema_driver',
    null, $pkg->getChannel());
if (!$driver) {
    return PEAR::raiseError('Error: no driver set.  use
      "config-set ' . 'chiaramdb2schema_driver <drivertype>"
        before installing');
}
$allDSN = $this->config->get('chiaramdb2schema_dsn',
    null, $pkg->getChannel());
if (!$allDSN) {
    return $this->throwError('Error: no dsn set.  use
      "config-set ' . 'chiaramdb2schema_dsn <dsn>"
        before installing');
}
$allPasswords =
$this->config->get('chiaramdb2schema_password',
    null, $pkg->getChannel());
```

In order to make things simpler on the user's end, we will also attempt to retrieve configuration data for the package's channel, and then default to the `pear.php.net` channel configuration.

Next, we will split the DSN variable on its separator ";" and the Passwords variable on its separator ":". By iterating over the DSN variable, we can then insert the appropriate password for each DSN. For instance, for a DSN "user:pass@localhost/ databasename", the DSN will be stored as "user@localhost/databasename", so we will need to insert ":pass" right before the "@". In addition, the first DSN is the default DSN to be used if a non-package-specific DSN is found, so there is a special case for this DSN (which is found via `$allDSN[0]`).

```php
$allDSN = explode(';', $allDSN);
$badDSN = array();
$allPasswords = explode(':', $allPasswords);
for ($i = 0; $i < count($allDSN); $i++) {
    if ($i && strpos($allDSN[$i], '::')) {
        $allDSN[$i] = explode('::', $allDSN[$i]);
        $password = (isset($allPasswords[$i]) &&
            $allPasswords[$i]) ?
            $allPasswords[$i] : '';
        if (!strpos($allDSN[$i][1], '@')) {
            $password = '';
        } elseif ($password) {
            // insert password into DSN
            $a = explode('@', $allDSN[$i][1]);
            $allDSN[$i][1] = $a[0] . ':' . $password . '@';
            unset($a[0]);
            $allDSN[$i][1] .= implode('@', $a);
        }
    } elseif (!$i && !strpos($allDSN[0], '::')) {
        $password = (isset($allPasswords[0]) &&
            $allPasswords[0]) ?
            $allPasswords[0] : '';
        if (!strpos($allDSN[0], '@')) {
            $password = '';
        } elseif ($password) {
            // insert password into DSN
            $a = explode('@', $allDSN[0]);
            $allDSN[0] = $a[0] . ':' . $password . '@';
            unset($a[0]);
            $allDSN[0] .= implode('@', $a);
        }
    } else {
        // invalid DSN
        $badDSN[$i] = $allDSN[$i];
        $allDSN[$i] = false;
    }
}
```

Finally, we will determine whether the package requires a specific database connection string for the package using `$this->_unique`, which as you recall, was set in the `init()` method. Package-specific DSNs are prefixed with the package name as in "Packagename::user:password@localhost/databasename" or with a specific file within a package like "Packagename#file::user:password@localhost/databasename", so we will search through the parsed DSNs until we either find one or fail.

Finally, after determining which DSN to use, we need to prepend the kind of database that should be connected to. For instance, this could be MySQL, MySQLi, OCI, Firebird, pgSQL, and so on.

```php
if ($this->_unique) {
    $lookfor = array($pkg->getPackage(),
        $pkg->getPackage() . '#' . $this->_file);
    foreach ($allDSN as $i => $dsn) {
        if (!$i) {
            continue;
        }
        if (strcasecmp($dsn[0], $lookfor[0]) === 0) {
            return $driver . ':/' . $dsn[1];
        }
        if (strcasecmp($dsn[0], $lookfor[1]) === 0) {
            return $driver . ':/' . $dsn[1];
        }
    }
      return $this->throwError('No valid DSNs for package "' .
        $pkg->getPackage() .
        '" were found in config variable
        chiaramdb2schema_dsn');
} else {
    if (!$allDSN[0]) {
        return $this->throwError('invalid default DSN "' .
          $badDSN[0] . '" in config variable
          chiaramdb2schema_dsn');
    }
    return $driver . ':/' . $allDSN[0];
}
```

If you find your eyes glazing over, don't fear. What is important is to realize that at the end of the experience, the method will either return a PEAR_Error with a detailed error message, or a string like "**mysqli://user:pass@localhost/databasename**".

The final portion of our custom task is the startSession() method, which actually performs the task, as this is a task of type single.

```php
/**
 * Update the database.
 *
 * First, determine which DSN to use from the
 * chiaramdb2schema_dsn config variable
 * with {@link _parseDSN()}, then determine whether the database
 * already exists based
```

```
 * on the contents of a previous installation, and finally use
 * {@link MDB2_Schema::updateDatabase()}
 * to update the database itself
 *
 * PEAR_Error is returned on any problem.
 * See validateXml() source for the complete list of allowed fields
 * @param PEAR_PackageFile_v2
 * @param string file contents
 * @param string the eventual final file location
 * (informational only)
 * @return string|false|PEAR_Error false to skip this file,
 * PEAR_Error to fail
 *      (use $this->throwError), otherwise return the new contents
 */
function startSession($pkg, $contents, $dest)
{
    $this->_file = basename($dest);
    $dsn = $this->_parseDSN($pkg);
    if (PEAR::isError($dsn)) {
        return $dsn;
    }
    require_once 'MDB2/Schema.php';
    require_once 'System.php';
    $tmp = System::mktemp(array('foo.xml'));
    if (PEAR::isError($tmp)) {
        return $tmp;
    }
    $fp = fopen($tmp, 'wb');
    fwrite($fp, $contents);
    fclose($fp);
    $schema = &MDB2_Schema::factory($dsn);
    $reg = &$this->config->getRegistry();
    if ($installed && file_exists($dest)) {
        // update existing database
        $res = $schema->updateDatabase($tmp, $dest);
        if (PEAR::isError($res)) {
            return PEAR::raiseError($res->getMessage() .
              $res->getUserInfo());
        }
    } else {
        // create new database
        $res = $schema->updateDatabase($tmp);
        if (PEAR::isError($res)) {
            return PEAR::raiseError($res->getMessage() .
              $res->getUserInfo());
```

```
        }
    }
    // unmodified
    return $contents;
}
```

`MDB2_Schema::updateDatabase()` requires two schema files in order to upgrade a database. While upgrading the database, we will use the final installation destination `$dest` to determine whether we are replacing an existing schema file. If so, then this is passed to `updateDatabase()`. Otherwise, we will simply call `updateDatabase()` to create the new database structure.

Note that at this point, the contents of the file have *not* been written to disk yet, as the tasks are to operate on a file prior to installation. As such, we will write out the schema file to a temporary location created using the `System` class, which is bundled with the PEAR package.

The bulk of the task's work is performed by the `MDB2_Schema` class. After completing the task, the user's database is automatically configured on installation and upgrade.

The Full Range of Possible Custom File Tasks

The methods that are available to a custom task are:

- `true|array validXml($pkg, $xml, &$config, $fileXml)`: Validates task XML

- `void init($xml, $fileAttributes, $lastVersion)`: Initializes a task

- `true|PEAR_Error startSession($pkg, $contents, $dest)`: Starts (and generally finishes) task handling

- `true|PEAR_Error run($tasks)`: For tasks of type "multiple" only, processes all tasks and performs the needed actions

validXml($pkg, $xml, &$config, $fileXml)

This method is called for all three types of task during `package.xml` validation to validate the XML of a specific task. `$pkg` is a `PEAR_PackageFile_v2` object representing the `package.xml` containing the task. This is read-only, and should simply be used to retrieve information. `$xml` is the parsed contents of the file task, `$config` is a `PEAR_Config` object representing the current configuration, and `$fileXml` is the parsed contents of the file tag from `package.xml`.

Here is a simple mapping of some sample task XML and the contents of the `$xml` variable:

XML	Parsed Contents
`<tasks:something/>`	`''`
`<tasks:something att="blah"/>`	`array('attribs' => array('att' => 'blah'))`
`<tasks:something>blah</tasks:something>`	`'blah'`
`<tasks:something att="blah">blah2</tasks:something>`	`array('attribs' => array('att' => 'blah'), '_content' => 'blah2')`

`<tasks:something>`
`<tasks:subtag>hi</tasks:subtag>`
`</tasks:something>`
	`array('tasks:subtag' => 'hi')`

`<tasks:something>`
`<tasks:subtag>hi</tasks:subtag>`
`<tasks:subtag att="blah">again</tasks:subtag>`
`</tasks:something>`
	`array('tasks:subtag' => array(0 => 'hi', 1 => array('attribs' => array('att' => 'blah'), '_content' => 'again'))))`

The `$fileXml` parameter will consist of an array of this format containing all of the attributes defined in the `<file>` tag.

```
array('attribs' => array('name' => 'Filename', 'role' =>
'filerole',…));
```

Error should be returned as an array. The first index must be one of the following error codes:

- PEAR_TASK_ERROR_NOATTRIBS: The array should be returned as:
  `array(PEAR_TASK_ERROR_NOATTRIBS);`

- PEAR_TASK_ERROR_MISSING_ATTRIB: The array should be returned as:
  `array(PEAR_TASK_ERROR_MISSING_ATTRIB, 'attributename');`

- PEAR_TASK_ERROR_WRONG_ATTRIB_VALUE: The array should be returned as:
  `array(PEAR_TASK_ERROR_WRONG_ATTRIB_VALUE, 'attributename',`
  `'actualvalue', ['expectedvalue'|array('expectedvalue1',`
  `'expectedvalue2',…)]);`

- PEAR_TASK_ERROR_INVALID: The array should be returned as:
  `array(PEAR_TASK_ERROR_INVALID, 'unusual error message');`

init($xml, $fileAttributes, $lastVersion)

The `init()` method is called to initialize all non-script tasks, and can be used for any purpose. The three parameters are:

- `mixed $xml`: An array representing the task's XML from `package.xml`. This is the same format as the `$xml` parameter passed to `validXml()`.

- `array $fileAttributes`: An array representing the file attributes. This is in the same format as the `$fileXml` parameter to `validXml()`.

- `string|NULL $lastVersion`: The last installed version of the package if the package is being upgraded, or `NULL` if this package is being installed for the first time. This can be used for tasks that rely upon previously installed configuration to operate.

Any return value from `init()` is discarded.

startSession($pkg, $contents, $dest)

The `startSession()` method is called to execute a task, and is called after the `init()` method. It is important to note that this method is expected to return the exact contents of the file, as it should be installed to disk. No modification of files on disk should be performed. If there is any error running the task, a `PEAR_Error` object should be returned with a clear error message describing the problem, and containing information on the file that contains the task.

If the task determines that this file should not be installed, returning `FALSE` will prompt the installer to skip installation of this file. Note that only the literal `FALSE` will cause skipping of installation; an empty string, the number 0, and any other literal that can be used as a false condition will not affect installation.

After successful performance of a task, the complete file contents *must* be returned. The return value is used to write out the file contents to disk. For instance, the `windowseol` task returns the value of `$contents` after converting all new lines into `\r\n`.

The parameters passed to `startSession()` are:

- `PEAR_PackageFile_v2 $pkg`: The packagefile object representing the complete `package.xml` containing this task.

- `string $contents`: The complete contents of the file, which can be operated on and must be returned upon successful completion of the task.

- `string $dest`: The full path of the final installation location of the file. This is for informational use only.

run($tasks)

This method is only called for tasks of type multiple. The $tasks parameter is an array of each of the multiple tasks in `package.xml`. For instance, if `package.xml` contains tasks of type multiple `<tasks:foo/>` and `<tasks:bar/>`, the `run()` method will be called for all `foo` tasks and the $tasks parameter will contain an array of each `foo` task. Then, the same procedure will be repeated for the `bar` tasks.

The `run()` method is called after installation has been successfully completed, and as such, can manipulate the installed contents of a package.

Upon error, the `run()` method should return a `PEAR_Error` object with an error message containing detailed information on the cause of task failure. All other return values are ignored.

Post-Installation Scripts for Ultimate Customization

The third and final task type is post-installation scripts. These are the most powerful and customizable tasks, and can quite literally be used to perform any needed customization of an installation. The PEAR installer implements post-installation scripts by defining sets of questions to ask the user in the `package.xml` file, and by passing the answers a user gives to a special PHP file. Here is a simple set of questions and a post-install script to match:

First, the XML from `package.xml`:

```
<file name="rolesetup.php" role="php">
 <tasks:postinstallscript>
  <tasks:paramgroup>
   <tasks:id>setup</tasks:id>
   <tasks:param>
    <tasks:name>channel</tasks:name>
    <tasks:prompt>Choose a channel to modify configuration
    values from</tasks:prompt>
    <tasks:type>string</tasks:type>
    <tasks:default>pear.php.net</tasks:default>
   </tasks:param>
  </tasks:paramgroup>
  <tasks:paramgroup>
   <tasks:id>driver</tasks:id>
   <tasks:instructions>
In order to set up the database, please choose a database
driver.
```

```
This should be a MDB2-compatible driver name, such as mysql, mysqli,
Pgsql, oci8, etc.
   </tasks:instructions>
   <tasks:param>
    <tasks:name>driver</tasks:name>
    <tasks:prompt>Database driver?</tasks:prompt>
    <tasks:type>string</tasks:type>
   </tasks:param>
  </tasks:paramgroup>
  <tasks:paramgroup>
   <tasks:id>choosedsn</tasks:id>
   <tasks:param>
    <tasks:name>dsnchoice</tasks:name>
    <tasks:prompt>%sChoose a DSN to modify, or to add a new
dsn, type
&quot;new&quot;.  To remove a DSN prepend with
&quot;!&quot;</tasks:prompt>
    <tasks:type>string</tasks:type>
    <tasks:default>new</tasks:default>
   </tasks:param>
  </tasks:paramgroup>
  <tasks:paramgroup>
   <tasks:id>deletedsn</tasks:id>
   <tasks:param>
    <tasks:name>confirm</tasks:name>
    <tasks:prompt>Really delete &quot;%s&quot; DSN? (yes to
delete)</tasks:prompt>
    <tasks:type>string</tasks:type>
    <tasks:default>no</tasks:default>
   </tasks:param>
  </tasks:paramgroup>
  <tasks:paramgroup>
   <tasks:id>modifydsn</tasks:id>
   <tasks:name>choosedsn::dsnchoice</tasks:name>
   <tasks:conditiontype>!=</tasks:conditiontype>
   <tasks:value>new</tasks:value>
   <tasks:param>
    <tasks:name>user</tasks:name>
    <tasks:prompt>User name</tasks:prompt>
    <tasks:type>string</tasks:type>
   </tasks:param>
   <tasks:param>
    <tasks:name>password</tasks:name>
    <tasks:prompt>Database password</tasks:prompt>
```

```
  <tasks:type>password</tasks:type>
 </tasks:param>
 <tasks:param>
  <tasks:name>host</tasks:name>
  <tasks:prompt>Database host</tasks:prompt>
  <tasks:type>string</tasks:type>
  <tasks:default>localhost</tasks:default>
 </tasks:param>
 <tasks:param>
  <tasks:name>database</tasks:name>
  <tasks:prompt>Database name</tasks:prompt>
  <tasks:type>string</tasks:type>
 </tasks:param>
</tasks:paramgroup>
<tasks:paramgroup>
 <tasks:id>newpackagedsn</tasks:id>
 <tasks:param>
  <tasks:name>package</tasks:name>
  <tasks:prompt>Package name</tasks:prompt>
  <tasks:type>string</tasks:type>
 </tasks:param>
 <tasks:param>
  <tasks:name>host</tasks:name>
  <tasks:prompt>Database host</tasks:prompt>
  <tasks:type>string</tasks:type>
  <tasks:default>localhost</tasks:default>
 </tasks:param>
 <tasks:param>
  <tasks:name>user</tasks:name>
  <tasks:prompt>User name</tasks:prompt>
  <tasks:type>string</tasks:type>
  <tasks:default>root</tasks:default>
 </tasks:param>
 <tasks:param>
  <tasks:name>password</tasks:name>
  <tasks:prompt>Database password</tasks:prompt>
  <tasks:type>password</tasks:type>
 </tasks:param>
 <tasks:param>
  <tasks:name>database</tasks:name>
  <tasks:prompt>Database name</tasks:prompt>
  <tasks:type>string</tasks:type>
 </tasks:param>
</tasks:paramgroup>
```

```
  <tasks:paramgroup>
   <tasks:id>newdefaultdsn</tasks:id>
   <tasks:param>
    <tasks:name>host</tasks:name>
    <tasks:prompt>Database host</tasks:prompt>
    <tasks:type>string</tasks:type>
    <tasks:default>localhost</tasks:default>
   </tasks:param>
   <tasks:param>
    <tasks:name>user</tasks:name>
    <tasks:prompt>User name</tasks:prompt>
    <tasks:type>string</tasks:type>
    <tasks:default>root</tasks:default>
   </tasks:param>
   <tasks:param>
    <tasks:name>password</tasks:name>
    <tasks:prompt>Database password</tasks:prompt>
    <tasks:type>password</tasks:type>
   </tasks:param>
   <tasks:param>
    <tasks:name>database</tasks:name>
    <tasks:prompt>database name</tasks:prompt>
    <tasks:type>string</tasks:type>
   </tasks:param>
  </tasks:paramgroup>
 </tasks:postinstallscript>
</file>
```

Then, the post-installation script (contents of `rolesetup.php`):

```php
<?php
/**
 * Post-installation script for the Chiara_Managedb task.
 *
 * This script takes user input on DSNs and sets up DSNs, allowing
 * the addition of one custom DSN per iteration.
 * @version @package_version@
 */
class rolesetup_postinstall
{
    /**
     * object representing package.xml
     * @var PEAR_PackageFile_v2
     * @access private
     */
```

```php
var $_pkg;
/**
 * Frontend object
 * @var PEAR_Frontend
 * @access private
 */
var $_ui;
/**
 * @var PEAR_Config
 * @access private
 */
var $_config;
/**
 * The actual DSN value as will be saved to the configuration file
 * @var string
 */
var $dsnvalue;
/**
 * The actual password value as will be saved to the
 * configuration file
 * @var string
 */
var $passwordvalue;
/**
 * The channel to modify configuration values from
 *
 * @var string
 */
var $channel;
/**
 * The task object used for dsn serialization/unserialization
 * @var PEAR_Task_Chiara_Managedb
 */
var $managedb;
/**
 * An "unserialized" array of DSNs parsed from the chiaramdb2schema
 * configuration variables.
 * @var array
 */
var $dsns;
/**
 * The index of the DSN in $this->dsns we will be modifying
 * @var string
 */
```

```php
        var $choice;

        /**
         * Initialize the post-installation script
         *
         * @param PEAR_Config $config
         * @param PEAR_PackageFile_v2 $pkg
         * @param string|null $lastversion Last installed version.
         * Not used in this script
         * @return boolean success of initialization
         */
        function init(&$config, &$pkg, $lastversion)
        {
            require_once 'PEAR/Task/Chiara/Managedb.php';
            $this->_config = &$config;
            $this->_ui = &PEAR_Frontend::singleton();
            $this->managedb = new PEAR_Task_Chiara_Managedb($config,
              $this->_ui, PEAR_TASK_INSTALL);
            $this->_pkg = &$pkg;
            if (!in_array('chiaramdb2schema_dsn',
                $this->_config->getKeys())) {
                // fail: role was not installed?
                return false;
            }
            $this->channel = $this->_config->get('default_channel');
            $this->dsns = PEAR::isError(
                $e = $this->managedb->unserializeDSN($pkg)) ? array() : $e;
            return true;
        }
        /**
         * Set up the prompts properly for the script
         *
         * @param array $prompts
         * @param string $section
         * @return array
         */
        function postProcessPrompts($prompts, $section)
        {
            switch ($section) {
                case 'driver' :
                    if ($this->driver) {
                        $prompts[0]['default'] = $this->driver;
                    }
                break;
```

```
case 'deletedsn' :
    $count = 1;
    foreach ($this->dsns as $i => $dsn) {
        $text = ($i ? "(Package $i) " : '') . $dsn;
        if ($count == $this->choice) {
            break;
        }
        $count++;
    }
    $prompts[0]['prompt'] =
                sprintf($prompts[0]['prompt'], $text);
break;
case 'choosedsn' :
    $text = '';
    $count = 1;
    foreach ($this->dsns as $i => $dsn) {
        $text .= "[$count] " . ($i ? "(Package $i) " : '')
                . $dsn . "\n";
        $count++;
    }
    $prompts[0]['prompt'] =
                sprintf($prompts[0]['prompt'], $text);
break;
case 'modifydsn' :
    $count = 1;
    $found = false;
    foreach ($this->dsns as $i => $dsn) {
        if ($count == $this->choice) {
            $found = true;
            break;
        }
        $count++;
    }
    if ($found) {
        $dsn = MDB2::parseDSN($this->dsns[$i]);
        // user
        $prompts[0]['default'] = $dsn['username'];
        // password
        if (isset($dsn['password'])) {
            $prompts[1]['default'] = $dsn['password'];
        }
        // host
        $prompts[2]['default'] = $dsn['hostspec'];
        if (isset($dsn['port'])) {
```

```
                    $prompts[2]['default'] .= ':' . $dsn['port'];
                }
                // database
                $prompts[3]['default'] = $dsn['database'];
            }
        break;
    }
    return $prompts;
}

/**
 * Run the script itself
 *
 * @param array $answers
 * @param string $phase
 */
function run($answers, $phase)
{
    switch ($phase) {
        case 'setup' :
            return $this->_doSetup($answers);
        break;
        case 'driver' :
            require_once 'MDB2.php';
            PEAR::pushErrorHandling(PEAR_ERROR_RETURN);
            if (PEAR::isError($err =
                    MDB2::loadFile('Driver' . DIRECTORY_SEPARATOR .
                    $answers['driver']))) {
                PEAR::popErrorHandling();
                $this->_ui->outputData(
                'ERROR: Unknown MDB2 driver "' .
                    $answers['driver'] . '": ' .
                    $err->getUserInfo() . '. Be sure you have
                        installed ' . 'MDB2_Driver_' .
                            $answers['driver']);
                return false;
            }
            PEAR::popErrorHandling();
            $ret = $this->_config->set('chiaramdb2schema_driver',
                    $answers['driver'],
                    'user', $this->channel);
            return $ret && $this->_config->writeConfigFile();
        break;
        case 'choosedsn' :
```

```
            if ($answers['dsnchoice'] &&
                $answers['dsnchoice']{0} == '!') {
                // delete a DSN
                $answers['dsnchoice'] =
                    substr($answers['dsnchoice'], 1);
            } else {
                $this->_ui->skipParamgroup('deletedsn');
            }
            if ($answers['dsnchoice'] > count($this->dsns)) {
                $this->_ui->outputData('ERROR: No suchdsn "' .
                    $answers['dsnchoice'] . '"');
                return false;
            }
            $this->choice = $answers['dsnchoice'];
        break;
        case 'deletedsn' :
            $this->_ui->skipParamgroup('modifydsn');
            $this->_ui->skipParamgroup('newpackagedsn');
            $this->_ui->skipParamgroup('newdefaultdsn');
            if ($answers['confirm'] == 'yes') {
                $count = 1;
                foreach ($this->dsns as $i => $dsn) {
                    if ($count == $this->choice) {
                        unset($this->dsns[$i]);
                        break;
                    }
                    $count++;
                }
                $this->_ui->outputData('DSN deleted');
                $this->managedb->serializeDSN($this->dsns,
                    $this->channel);
                return true;
            } else {
                $this->_ui->outputData('No changes performed');
            }
        break;
        case 'modifydsn' :
            $count = 1;
            $found = false;
            foreach ($this->dsns as $i => $dsn) {
                if ($count == $this->choice) {
                    $found = true;
                    break;
                }
```

```
                    $count++;
                }
                if (!$found) {
                    $this->_ui->outputData('ERROR: DSN "' .
                        $this->choice . '" not found!');
                    return false;
                }
                $dsn = $answers['user'] . ':' .
                        $answers['password'] . '@' .
                        $answers['host'] . '/' . $answers['database'];
                $this->dsns[$i] = $dsn;
                $this->managedb->serializeDSN($this->dsns,
                    $this->channel);
                $this->_ui->skipParamgroup('newpackagedsn');
                $this->_ui->skipParamgroup('newdefaultdsn');
            break;
            case 'newpackagedsn' :
                $dsn = $answers['user'] . ':' .
                        $answers['password'] . '@' .
                        $answers['host'] . '/' . $answers['database'];
                $this->dsns[$answers['package']] = $dsn;
                $this->managedb->serializeDSN($this->dsns,
                    $this->channel);
                $this->_ui->skipParamgroup('newdefaultdsn');
            break;
            case 'newdefaultdsn' :
                $dsn = $answers['user'] . ':' .
                        $answers['password'] . '@' .
                        $answers['host'] . '/' . $answers['database'];
                $this->dsns[0] = $dsn;
                $this->managedb->serializeDSN($this->dsns,
                    $this->channel);
            break;
            case '_undoOnError' :
                // answers contains paramgroups that succeeded in
                // reverse order
                foreach ($answers as $group) {
                }
            break;
        }
        return true;
    }

    /**
     * Run the setup paramgroup
```

```
     *
     * @param array $answers
     * @return boolean
     * @access private
     */
    function _doSetup($answers)
    {
        $reg = &$this->_config->getRegistry();
        if (!$reg->channelExists($answers['channel'])) {
            $this->_ui->outputData('ERROR: channel "' .
                $answers['channel'] . '" is not registered,
                    use the channel-discover command');
            return false;
        }
        $this->channel = $answers['channel'];
        $this->driver = $this->_config->get('chiaramdb2schema_driver',
        null, $this->channel);
        $this->dsnvalue = $this->_config->get('chiaramdb2schema_dsn',
        null, $this->channel);
        $this->passwordvalue =
                    $this->_config->get('chiaramdb2schema_dsn', null,
                        $this->channel);
        if (!$this->dsnvalue) {
            // magically skip the "choosedsn", "deleteDSN" and
            // "modifydsn" <paramgroup>s,
            // and only create a new, default DSN
            $this->_ui->skipParamgroup('choosedsn');
            $this->_ui->skipParamgroup('deletedsn');
            $this->_ui->skipParamgroup('modifydsn');
            $this->_ui->skipParamgroup('newpackagedsn');
        }
        return true;
    }
}
?>
```

Post-installation scripts interact intimately with the different front ends that PEAR provides. There are many possibilities available to a script. In addition to using data provided by the user, a post-installation script can interactively modify prompts based on the user's previous answers, and can dynamically skip entire <tasks: paramgroup> sections. These capabilities allow significant customization of the actual script.

Components of a Post-Install Script

Every post-installation script must define two methods, `init()` and `run()`. The `init()` method should be defined somewhat like this:

```
/**
 * Initialize the post-installation script
 *
 * @param PEAR_Config $config
 * @param PEAR_PackageFile_v2 $pkg
 * @param string|null $lastversion Last installed version.
 * Not used in this script
 * @return boolean success of initialization
 */
function init(&$config, &$pkg, $lastversion)
{
    require_once 'PEAR/Task/Chiara/Managedb.php';
    $this->_config = &$config;
    $this->_ui = &PEAR_Frontend::singleton();
    $this->managedb =
        new PEAR_Task_Chiara_Managedb($config, $this->_ui,
        PEAR_TASK_INSTALL);
    $this->_pkg = &$pkg;
    if (!in_array('chiaramdb2schema_dsn',
        $this->_config->getKeys())) {
        // fail: role was not installed?
        return false;
    }
    $this->channel = $this->_config->get('default_channel');
    $this->dsns = PEAR::isError($e =
            $this->managedb->unserializeDSN($pkg)) ? array() : $e;
    return true;
}
```

Note the use of `$this->_ui = &PEAR_Frontend::singleton()`: This line of code opens up a huge array of possibilities. In addition to exposing the entire public API available to display text, such as:

- Void `outputData(string $text)`: Displays information to the user
- string `bold(string $text)`: Takes the text and returns a bold-face-transformed version of that text, which can then be passed to `outputData()`

this makes available the `skipParamGroup(string $id)` method. The `$id` parameter should be the ID of a paramgroup yet to be executed (contents of a `<tasks:id>` tag from a `<tasks:paramgroup>`).

Modifying the prompt or default value of a parameter is accomplished through the creation of a method named `postProcessPrompts()`, like so:

```php
/**
 * Set up the prompts properly for the script
 *
 * @param array $prompts
 * @param string $section
 * @return array
 */
function postProcessPrompts($prompts, $section)
{
    switch ($section) {
        case 'driver' :
            if ($this->driver) {
                $prompts[0]['default'] = $this->driver;
            }
        break;
        case 'deletedsn' :
            $count = 1;
            foreach ($this->dsns as $i => $dsn) {
                $text = ($i ? "(Package $i) " : '') . $dsn;
                if ($count == $this->choice) {
                    break;
                }
                $count++;
            }
            $prompts[0]['prompt'] =
                        sprintf($prompts[0]['prompt'], $text);
        break;
        case 'choosedsn' :
            $text = '';
            $count = 1;
            foreach ($this->dsns as $i => $dsn) {
                $text .= "[$count] " . ($i ? "(Package $i) " :
                                            '') . $dsn . "\n";
                $count++;
            }
            $prompts[0]['prompt'] =
                        sprintf($prompts[0]['prompt'], $text);
        break;
        case 'modifydsn' :
            $count = 1;
            $found = false;
```

```
            foreach ($this->dsns as $i => $dsn) {
                if ($count == $this->choice) {
                    $found = true;
                    break;
                }
                $count++;
            }
            if ($found) {
                $dsn = MDB2::parseDSN($this->dsns[$i]);
                // user
                $prompts[0]['default'] = $dsn['username'];
                // password
                if (isset($dsn['password'])) {
                    $prompts[1]['default'] = $dsn['password'];
                }
                // host
                $prompts[2]['default'] = $dsn['hostspec'];
                if (isset($dsn['port'])) {
                    $prompts[2]['default'] .= ':' . $dsn['port'];
                }
                // database
                $prompts[3]['default'] = $dsn['database'];
            }
        break;
    }
    return $prompts;
}
```

The `$prompts` parameter will be the parsed contents of a `<tasks:paramgroup>` tag.

```
<tasks:paramgroup>
 <tasks:id>databaseSetup</tasks:id>
 <tasks:param>
  <tasks:name>database</tasks:name>
  <tasks:prompt>%s database name</tasks:prompt>
  <tasks:type>string</tasks:type>
  <tasks:default>pear</tasks:default>
 </tasks:param>
 <tasks:param>
  <tasks:name>user</tasks:name>
  <tasks:prompt>%s database username</tasks:prompt>
  <tasks:type>string</tasks:type>
  <tasks:default>%s_pear</tasks:default>
 </tasks:param>
</tasks:paramgroup>
```

For this `paramgroup` the `$prompts` variable would be as follows:

```
array(
 'id' => 'databaseSetup';
 'param' =>
 array(
  array(
   'name' => 'database',
   'prompt' => '%s database name',
   'type' => 'string',
   'default' => 'pear',
  ),
  array(
   'name' => 'user',
   'prompt' => '%s database username',
   'type' => 'string',
   'default' => '%s_pear',
  ),
 ),
);
```

The `postProcessPrompts()` method should return the `$prompts` array with modifications only to the prompt and default fields. If anything else is modified, it will cause the post-install script to simply fail.

For instance, after determining that the user is using the pgSQL driver, the return value from `postProcessPrompts()` could be:

```
array(
 'id' => 'databaseSetup';
 'param' =>
 array(
  array(
   'name' => 'database',
   'prompt' => 'Postgresql database name',
   'type' => 'string',
   'default' => 'pear',
  ),
  array(
   'name' => 'user',
   'prompt' => 'Postgresql database username',
   'type' => 'string',
   'default' => 'pgsql_pear',
  ),
 ),
);
```

In addition, the entire prompt can be replaced. This could be a simple way to handle internationalization as well. For example:

```
array(
 'id' => 'databaseSetup';
 'param' =>
 array(
  array(
   'name' => 'database',
   'prompt' => 'Nom de la base de données Postgresql',
   'type' => 'string',
   'default' => 'pear',
  ),
  array(
   'name' => 'user',
   'prompt' => 'Nom d'utilisateur de la base de données Postgresql',
   'type' => 'string',
   'default' => 'pgsql_pear',
  ),
 ),
);
```

The `run()` method should accept two kinds of parameters. In normal operation, the first parameter will be an array containing the user's answers, and the second parameter will be the ID of the paramgroup. For this `<tasks:paramgroup>`, sample values might be:

```
array(
 'database' => 'huggiepear',
 'user' => 'killinator',
);
```

And the ID would be (as you might imagine) `'databaseSetup'`.

In addition to these features designed for success, sometimes, it is necessary to abort a post-installation script on error. In these cases, the `run()` method is also called with two parameters, but the second is `'_undoOnError'`, and the first is an array of completed paramgroup IDs in reverse order, to facilitate iteration for rolling back changes made by the post-install script.

_undoOnError is the Error Header and not Another Paramgroup ID?

A Paramgroup ID cannot begin with an underscore, it may only contain alphanumeric characters. Hence, _undoOnError is the error header and not another paramgroup ID.

Bundling Several Packages into a Single Archive

Often, it is a desired feature to bundle a package and its dependencies into a single installable archive. There are two ways of doing this. The simplest way is to use a `package.xml` file similar to this one:

```xml
<?xml version="1.0" encoding="UTF-8"?>
<package version="2.0" xmlns="http://pear.php.net/dtd/package-2.0"
xmlns:tasks="http://pear.php.net/dtd/tasks-1.0"
xmlns:xsi="http://www.w3.org/2001/XMLSchema-instance"
xsi:schemaLocation="http://pear.php.net/dtd/tasks-1.0
http://pear.php.net/dtd/tasks-1.0.xsd
http://pear.php.net/dtd/package-2.0
http://pear.php.net/dtd/package-2.0.xsd">
 <name>PEAR_all</name>
 <channel>pear.php.net</channel>
 <summary>PEAR Base System</summary>
 <description>
  The PEAR package and its dependencies
 </description>
 <lead>
  <name>Greg Beaver</name>
  <user>cellog</user>
  <email>cellog@php.net</email>
  <active>yes</active>
 </lead>
 <date>2005-09-25</date>
 <version>
  <release>1.4.2</release>
  <api>1.0.0</api>
 </version>
 <stability>
  <release>stable</release>
```

```
    <api>stable</api>
   </stability>
   <license uri="http://www.php.net/license">PHP License</license>
   <notes>
    This contains PEAR version 1.4.2 and its dependencies
   </notes>
   <contents>
    <bundledpackage>PEAR-1.4.2.tgz</bundledpackage>
    <bundledpackage>Archive_Tar-1.3.1.tgz</bundledpackage>
    <bundledpackage>Console_Getopt-1.2.tgz</bundledpackage>
    <bundledpackage>XML_RPC-1.4.3.tgz</bundledpackage>
   </contents>
   <dependencies>
    <required>
     <php>
      <min>4.2</min>
     </php>
     <pearinstaller>
      <min>1.4.0a12</min>
     </pearinstaller>
    </required>
   </dependencies>
   <bundle/>
  </package>
```

This simple `package.xml` can then be packaged into `PEAR_all-1.4.2.tgz`, and distributed as a single archive that users can use to upgrade all packages from a non-internet location via:

```
$ pear upgrade PEAR_all-1.4.2.tgz
```

The other way of distributing dependencies is a clever mixture of the old bundle-all-dependencies approach and the PEAR way of distributing dependencies.

Backwards Compatibility: Using package.xml 1.0 and 2.0

One of the most important new features of PEAR version 1.4.0 and newer that comes with the advent of `package.xml 2.0` is the ability to make a package installable by older PEAR versions. The package command, invoked with the following historically takes a `package.xml` and spits out a GZIP-compressed tar (`.tgz`) file.

```
$ pear package
```

If the package name is `Foo`, and the version is `1.0.0`, the `.tgz` file will be named `Foo-1.0.0.tgz`. New in version 1.4.0, if there is a second `package.xml` named `package2.xml`, the package command will attempt to include it in the archive. When PEAR downloads a package for installation, it first looks for a `package2.xml` file, which is always in version 2.0 format, and then falls back to `package.xml`. In this way, older versions of PEAR are supported, because they always look for `package.xml` first.

For this to work, PEAR does a very strict comparison of the contents of the `package.xml` files. `package.xml` version 1.0 and `package.xml` version 2.0, must satisfy the following list of constraints to be considered equivalent, otherwise validation will fail:

- Same package name
- Same package summary
- Same package description
- Same package version (release version)
- Same package stability (release stability/state)
- Same license
- Same release notes
- Same maintainers
- All files in `package.xml` 1.0 must be present in `package.xml` 2.0 `<contents>`

Note that because `package.xml` 2.0 allows files to be present but ignored during installation using the `<ignore>` tag, `package.xml` 2.0 can be used to provide an archive that is both PEAR-installable as well as unzip-and-go.

Why Support Old and Crusty package.xml 1.0?

This is a common debate in the PHP world. Why support backwards compatibility? These are old, buggy versions of PEAR, right? Yes, they are old and buggy versions and anyone using them is asking for trouble, but people may not find a compelling reason to upgrade their PEAR installer just so that they can use your package because what they have already "works for them". It is (or should be) your goal as a package distributor to make the process of upgrading as painless as possible. You should only drop `package.xml` version 1.0 support if you are in fact using new features of PEAR itself in the PHP code, or your package is a new one without an installed userbase.

PEAR development has progressed at a rapid pace, but the adoption of the new installer will not happen overnight. Large software projects like Linux distributions need time to evaluate the new features and make sure that everything works properly prior to adopting a new version. As PEAR developers, we must honor this need.

Once the installed userbase is no longer using the old and buggy versions of PEAR, upgrading the installer dependency is an option that should be taken up as soon as possible, for the sake of the users themselves. Having said this, PEAR users need to upgrade as soon as possible to avoid security holes discovered in older versions of the PEAR installer.

Security Issues in PEAR 1.4.3 and Older

A few months before writing this chapter, two major security holes were discovered in PEAR. Basically, if you're using PEAR 1.4.3 or older, you need to upgrade as soon as possible.

Details are available at:
`http://pear.php.net/advisory-20051104.txt` and
`http://pear.php.net/advisory-20060108.txt`.

Case Study: The PEAR Package

PEAR is a perfect example of a package that will always need to support `package.xml` 1.0. We will always have users who are upgrading from an earlier version to the latest one and PEAR 1.3.6 and older simply doesn't know anything about `package.xml` 2.0. If we don't make it possible to upgrade PEAR, there isn't much point in making the code available.

However, at the same time, the new dependency features and tasks of `package.xml` 2.0 are very important for the PEAR package, and so both `package.xml` 1.0 and `package.xml` 2.0 are needed. For instance, the `pear` command itself is a shell script on UNIX (with UNIX \n line endings) and a batch file on Windows (with Windows \r\n line endings). Before `package.xml` 2.0, it was necessary to add these scripts as binary files to CVS, so that the line endings are not replaced with the packager's system line endings. Now, through the use of the `<tasks:windowseol/>` and `<tasks:unixeol/>` tasks, this is no longer necessary, as the correct line endings are set at package time. In addition, because of incompatibilities between PEAR 1.4.0 and earlier versions of PEAR_Frontend_Web and the older PEAR_Frontend_Gtk (superseded by PEAR_Frontend_Gtk2), it is necessary to check for the presence of these versions, and to silently succeed if the versions are OK. `package.xml` 2.0 provides this functionality through the use of the `<conflicts/>` tag in a package dependency.

PEAR_PackageFileManager

Although the commands `convert` and `pickle` can be used in limited situations to manage both a `package.xml` version 1.0 and version 2.0, these commands can also be dangerous. A far safer way to maintain two versions of `package.xml` from a single location is through the use of the PEAR package PEAR_PackageFileManager. This package provides a simple interface from which to import an existing `package.xml` file and update with current information, or to create a new `package.xml` file from scratch. In addition, it is very simple to take an existing `package.xml 2.0`, no matter how complicated it is, and easily create an equivalent `package.xml 1.0` with absolute control over the contents of each `package.xml`.

Obtaining PEAR_PackageFileManager

PEAR_PackageFileManager can be easily obtained by using the PEAR installer. As of the writing of this book, version 1.6.0b1 is available. To install it, you must set the `preferred_state` configuration variable to `beta` via:

```
$ pear config-set preferred_state beta
```

Or you can run:

```
$ pear install PEAR_PackageFileManager-beta
```

Of course, it is always good practice to determine the latest version at `http://pear.php.net/package/PEAR_PackageFileManager` and to install that version.

PEAR_PackageFileManager Script and the package.xml Files it Generates

For our sample `PEAR_PackageFileManager` script, we will be generating a `package.xml` for the `Chiara_Managedb` task. Before writing the `package.xml` script, let's make sure we understand the components we wish to have for our `package.xml`. In our case, we will have three files to package up, the `Managedb.php` file containing the actual code for the task, the `rw.php` file containing the read/writable `PEAR_Task_Chiara_Managedb_rw` class for adding the task to `package.xml` through the `PEAR_PackageFile_v2_rw` API, and `rolesetup.php`, the post-installation script for initializing the `chiaramdb2schema` configuration variables.

There are several important details to note before diving into the source. First of all, this script generates a `package.xml` file from scratch. Most scripts will not need this kind of detail when using the `importOptions()` method. In addition, it is important to note that the `PEAR_PackageFileManager2` class extends the `PEAR_PackageFile_v2_rw` class provided with PEAR itself. This allows use of utility methods such as setPackage() and others to tweak the contents of the package.xml. Let's take a look at how to generate a somewhat complicated package.xml 2.0 with a post-installation script.

```php
<?php
/**
 * package.xml generation script for Task_Chiara_Managedb package
 * @author Gregory Beaver <cellog@php.net>
 */
require_once 'PEAR/PackageFileManager2.php';
PEAR::setErrorHandling(PEAR_ERROR_DIE);
$pfm = &PEAR_PackageFileManager2::importOptions('package.xml',
    array(
        // set a subdirectory everything is installed into
        'baseinstalldir' => 'PEAR/Task/Chiara',
        // location of files to package
        'packagedirectory' => dirname(__FILE__),
        // what method is used to glob files? cvs, svn, perforce
        // and file are options
        'filelistgenerator' => 'file',

        // don't distribute this script
        'ignore' => array('package.php', 'package2.xml', 'package.xml'),
        // put the post-installation script in a
        // different location from the task itself
        'installexceptions' =>
            array(
                'rolesetup.php' => 'Chiara/Task/Managedb',
            ),
        // make the output human-friendly
        'simpleoutput' => true,
        ));

$pfm->setPackage('PEAR_Task_Chiara_Managedb');
$pfm->setChannel('pear.chiaraquartet.net');
$pfm->setLicense('BSD license', 'http://www.opensource.org/licenses/
bsd-license.php');
$pfm->setSummary('Provides the <tasks:chiara-managedb/> file task for
    managing ' . 'databases on installation');
$pfm->setDescription('Task_Chiara_Managedb provides the code to
    implement the <tasks:chiara-managedb/> task, as well as a post-
    installation script to manage the configuration variables it needs.
```

This task works in conjunction with the chiaramdb2schema file role
(package PEAR_Installer_Role_Chiaramdb2schema) to create databases

```
used by a package on installation, and to upgrade the database
structure automatically on upgrade.  To do this,
it uses MDB2_Schema\'s
updateDatabase() functionality.
The post-install script must be run with "pear run-scripts"
to initialize configuration variables');
// initial release version should be 0.1.0
$pfm->addMaintainer('lead', 'cellog', 'Greg Beaver',
'cellog@php.net', 'yes');
$pfm->setAPIVersion('0.1.0');
$pfm->setReleaseVersion('0.1.0');
// our API is reasonably stable, but may need tweaking
$pfm->setAPIStability('beta');
// the code is very new, and may change dramatically
$pfm->setReleaseStability('alpha');
// release notes
$pfm->setNotes('initial release');
// this is a PHP script, not a PECL extension source/binary or a
// bundle package
$pfm->setPackageType('php');
$pfm->addRelease();

// set up special file properties
$pfm->addGlobalReplacement('package-info', '@package_version@',
'version');
$script = &$pfm->initPostinstallScript('rolesetup.php');

// add paramgroups to the post-install script
$script->addParamGroup(
    'setup',
    $script->getParam('channel', 'Choose a channel to modify
configuration values from',
        'string', 'pear.php.net'));
$script->addParamGroup(
    'driver',
    $script->getParam('driver', 'Database driver?'),
        'In order to set up the database, please choose a database
          driver. This should be a MDB2-compatible driver name,
          such as mysql, mysqli, Pgsql, oci8, etc.');
$script->addParamGroup(
    'choosedsn',
    $script->getParam('dsnchoice', '%sChoose a DSN to modify,
        or to add a' . ' new dsn, type "new".
            To remove a DSN prepend with "!"'));
$script->addParamGroup(
```

```
            'deletedsn',
            $script->getParam('confirm', 'Really delete "%s" DSN?
                    (yes to delete)', 'string', 'no'));
    $script->addConditionTypeGroup(
            'modifydsn',
            'choosedsn', 'dsnchoice', 'new', '!=',
            array(
                $script->getParam('user', 'User name', 'string', 'root'),
                $script->getParam('password', 'Database password',
                                    'password'),
                $script->getParam('host', 'Database host', 'string',
                                    'localhost'),
                $script->getParam('database', 'Database name'),
            ));
    $script->addParamGroup(
            'newpackagedsn',
            array(
                $script->getParam('package', 'Package name'),
                $script->getParam('user', 'User name', 'string', 'root'),
                $script->getParam('password', 'Database password',
                                    'password'),
                $script->getParam('host', 'Database host', 'string',
                                    'localhost'),
                $script->getParam('database', 'Database name'),
            ));
    $script->addParamGroup(
            'newdefaultdsn',
            array(
                $script->getParam('user', 'User name', 'string', 'root'),
                $script->getParam('password', 'Database password',
                                    'password'),
                $script->getParam('host', 'Database host', 'string',
                                    'localhost'),
                $script->getParam('database', 'Database name'),
            ));


    $pfm->addPostinstallTask($script, 'rolesetup.php');


    // start over with dependencies
    $pfm->clearDeps();
    $pfm->setPhpDep('4.2.0');
    // we use post-install script features fixed in PEAR 1.4.3
    $pfm->setPearinstallerDep('1.4.3');
    $pfm->addPackageDepWithChannel('required', 'PEAR', 'pear.php.net',
```

```
'1.4.3');
$pfm->addPackageDepWithChannel('required', 'MDB2_Schema',
    'pear.php.net', '0.3.0');
$pfm->addPackageDepWithChannel('required',
    'PEAR_Installer_Role_Chiaramdb2schmea',
        'pear.chiaraquartet.net', '0.1.0');

// create the <contents> tag
$pfm->generateContents();

// create package.xml 1.0 to gracefully tell PEAR 1.3.x users they have
// to upgrade to use this package
$pfm1 = $pfm->exportCompatiblePackageFile1(array(
        // set a subdirectory everything is installed into
        'baseinstalldir' => 'PEAR/Task/Chiara',
        // location of files to package
        'packagedirectory' => dirname(__FILE__),
        // what method is used to glob files? cvs, svn, perforce
        // and file are options
        'filelistgenerator' => 'file',

        // don't distribute this script
        'ignore' => array('package.php', 'package.xml',
                          'package2.xml', 'rolesetup.php'),
        // put the post-installation script in a
        // different location from the task itself
        // make the output human-friendly
        'simpleoutput' => true,
        ));

// display the package.xml by default to allow "debugging" by eye,
// and then create it if explicitly asked to
if (isset($_GET['make']) || (isset($_SERVER['argv']) &&
                                @$_SERVER['argv'][1] == 'make')) {
    $pfm1->writePackageFile();
    $pfm->writePackageFile();
} else {
    $pfm1->debugPackageFile();
    $pfm->debugPackageFile();
}
?>
```

And the `package.xml` it generates:

```
<?xml version="1.0" encoding="UTF-8"?>
<package packagerversion="1.4.3" version="2.0"
```

```
xmlns="http://pear.php.net/dtd/package-2.0"
xmlns:tasks="http://pear.php.net/dtd/tasks-1.0" xmlns:xsi="http://www.
w3.org/2001/XMLSchema-instance"
xsi:schemaLocation="http://pear.php.net/dtd/tasks-1.0
    http://pear.php.net/dtd/tasks-1.0.xsd
    http://pear.php.net/dtd/package-2.0
    http://pear.php.net/dtd/package-2.0.xsd">
 <name>PEAR_Task_Chiara_Managedb</name>
 <channel>pear.chiaraquartet.net</channel>
 <summary>Provides the &lt;tasks:chiara-managedb/&gt; file task for
managing databases on installation</summary>
 <description>Task_Chiara_Managedb provides the code to implement the
&lt;tasks:chiara-managedb/&gt; task, as well as a post-installation
script to manage the configuration variables it needs.

This task works in conjunction with the chiaramdb2schema file role
(package PEAR_Installer_Role_Chiaramdb2schema) to create databases
used by a package on installation, and to upgrade the database
structure automatically on upgrade.
To do this, it uses MDB2_Schema&apos;s
updateDatabase() functionality.
The post-install script must be run with &quot;pear run-scripts&quot;
to initialize configuration variables</description>
 <lead>
  <name>Greg Beaver</name>
  <user>cellog</user>
  <email>cellog@php.net</email>
  <active>yes</active>
 </lead>
 <date>2005-10-18</date>
 <time>23:55:29</time>
 <version>
  <release>0.1.0</release>
  <api>0.1.0</api>
 </version>
 <stability>
  <release>alpha</release>
  <api>beta</api>
 </stability>
 <license uri="http://www.opensource.org/licenses/bsd-
license.php">BSD license</license>
 <notes>initial release</notes>
 <contents>
  <dir baseinstalldir="PEAR/Task/Chiara" name="/">
```

```
    <dir name="Managedb">
     <file name="rw.php" role="php">
      <tasks:replace from="@package_version@" to="version"
type="package-info" />
     </file>
    </dir> <!-- //Managedb -->
    <file name="Managedb.php" role="php">
     <tasks:replace from="@package_version@" to="version"
type="package-info" />
    </file>
    <file name="rolesetup.php" role="php">
     <tasks:postinstallscript>
      <tasks:paramgroup>
       <tasks:id>setup</tasks:id>
       <tasks:param>
        <tasks:name>channel</tasks:name>
        <tasks:prompt>Choose a channel to modify configuration values
        from</tasks:prompt>
        <tasks:type>string</tasks:type>
        <tasks:default>pear.php.net</tasks:default>
       </tasks:param>
      </tasks:paramgroup>
      <tasks:paramgroup>
       <tasks:id>driver</tasks:id>
       <tasks:instructions>In order to set up the database,
       please choose a database driver.
       This should be a MDB2-compatible driver name,
       such as mysql, mysqli, Pgsql, oci8, etc.
       </tasks:instructions>
       <tasks:param>
        <tasks:name>driver</tasks:name>
        <tasks:prompt>Database driver?</tasks:prompt>
        <tasks:type>string</tasks:type>
       </tasks:param>
      </tasks:paramgroup>
      <tasks:paramgroup>
       <tasks:id>choosedsn</tasks:id>
       <tasks:param>
        <tasks:name>dsnchoice</tasks:name>
        <tasks:prompt>%sChoose a DSN to modify,
        or to add a new dsn, type &quot;new&quot;.
        To remove a DSN prepend with &quot;!&quot;
        </tasks:prompt>
        <tasks:type>string</tasks:type>
       </tasks:param>
```

```
    </tasks:paramgroup>
    <tasks:paramgroup>
     <tasks:id>deletedsn</tasks:id>
     <tasks:param>
      <tasks:name>confirm</tasks:name>
      <tasks:prompt>Really delete &quot;%s&quot;
       DSN? (yes to delete)</tasks:prompt>
      <tasks:type>string</tasks:type>
      <tasks:default>no</tasks:default>
     </tasks:param>
    </tasks:paramgroup>
    <tasks:paramgroup>
     <tasks:id>modifydsn</tasks:id>
     <tasks:name>choosedsn::dsnchoice</tasks:name>
     <tasks:conditiontype>!=</tasks:conditiontype>
     <tasks:value>new</tasks:value>
     <tasks:param>
      <tasks:name>user</tasks:name>
      <tasks:prompt>User name</tasks:prompt>
      <tasks:type>string</tasks:type>
      <tasks:default>root</tasks:default>
     </tasks:param>
     <tasks:param>
      <tasks:name>password</tasks:name>
      <tasks:prompt>Database password</tasks:prompt>
      <tasks:type>password</tasks:type>
     </tasks:param>
     <tasks:param>
      <tasks:name>host</tasks:name>
      <tasks:prompt>Database host</tasks:prompt>
      <tasks:type>string</tasks:type>
      <tasks:default>localhost</tasks:default>
     </tasks:param>
     <tasks:param>
      <tasks:name>database</tasks:name>
      <tasks:prompt>Database name</tasks:prompt>
      <tasks:type>string</tasks:type>
     </tasks:param>
    </tasks:paramgroup>
    <tasks:paramgroup>
     <tasks:id>newpackagedsn</tasks:id>
     <tasks:param>
      <tasks:name>package</tasks:name>
      <tasks:prompt>Package name</tasks:prompt>
```

```
  <tasks:type>string</tasks:type>
 </tasks:param>
 <tasks:param>
  <tasks:name>user</tasks:name>
  <tasks:prompt>User name</tasks:prompt>
  <tasks:type>string</tasks:type>
  <tasks:default>root</tasks:default>
 </tasks:param>
 <tasks:param>
  <tasks:name>password</tasks:name>
  <tasks:prompt>Database password</tasks:prompt>
  <tasks:type>password</tasks:type>
 </tasks:param>
 <tasks:param>
  <tasks:name>host</tasks:name>
  <tasks:prompt>Database host</tasks:prompt>
  <tasks:type>string</tasks:type>
  <tasks:default>localhost</tasks:default>
 </tasks:param>
 <tasks:param>
  <tasks:name>database</tasks:name>
  <tasks:prompt>Database name</tasks:prompt>
  <tasks:type>string</tasks:type>
 </tasks:param>
</tasks:paramgroup>
<tasks:paramgroup>
 <tasks:id>newdefaultdsn</tasks:id>
 <tasks:param>
  <tasks:name>user</tasks:name>
  <tasks:prompt>User name</tasks:prompt>
  <tasks:type>string</tasks:type>
  <tasks:default>root</tasks:default>
 </tasks:param>
 <tasks:param>
  <tasks:name>password</tasks:name>
  <tasks:prompt>Database password</tasks:prompt>
  <tasks:type>password</tasks:type>
 </tasks:param>
 <tasks:param>
  <tasks:name>host</tasks:name>
  <tasks:prompt>Database host</tasks:prompt>
  <tasks:type>string</tasks:type>
  <tasks:default>localhost</tasks:default>
 </tasks:param>
```

```
      <tasks:param>
       <tasks:name>database</tasks:name>
       <tasks:prompt>Database name</tasks:prompt>
       <tasks:type>string</tasks:type>
      </tasks:param>
     </tasks:paramgroup>
    </tasks:postinstallscript>
    <tasks:replace from="@package_version@" to="version"
type="package-info" />
   </file>
  </dir> <!-- / -->
 </contents>
 <dependencies>
  <required>
   <php>
    <min>4.2.0</min>
   </php>
   <pearinstaller>
    <min>1.4.3</min>
   </pearinstaller>
   <package>
    <name>PEAR</name>
    <channel>pear.php.net</channel>
    <min>1.4.3</min>
   </package>
   <package>
    <name>MDB2_Schema</name>
    <channel>pear.php.net</channel>
    <min>0.3.0</min>
   </package>
   <package>
    <name>PEAR_Installer_Role_Chiaramdb2schema</name>
    <channel>pear.chiaraquartet.net</channel>
    <min>0.1.0</min>
   </package>
  </required>
 </dependencies>
 <phprelease />
 <changelog>
  <release>
   <version>
    <release>0.1.0</release>
    <api>0.1.0</api>
   </version>
   <stability>
    <release>alpha</release>
```

```
      <api>beta</api>
    </stability>
    <date>2005-10-18</date>
    <license>BSD license</license>
    <notes>initial release</notes>
  </release>
 </changelog>
</package>
```

How PEAR_PackageFileManager Makes a Hard Life Easy

Astute readers may have noticed that the `package.xml` generation script is quite extensive and long. The good news is that in many cases, this will be unnecessary. In fact, the initial generation of `package.xml` is generally not the most important feat accomplished by PEAR_PackageFileManager. Far more significant is the management of release data. Maintaining a `package.xml` file, and in many instances `package.xml` and `package2.xml` is a serious problem. Although the PEAR installer makes it a bit easier by doing a careful equivalency comparison between package files, this process is not perfect.

PEAR_PackageFileManager takes the same data and uses explicit logic to generate the metadata that is `package.xml` guaranteeing that equivalent `package.xml` files will be created. In addition, the centralization of data means that you need to modify only the script when updating release notes. In addition, it is impossible to generate an invalid `package.xml`, as PEAR's built-in `package.xml` validation is used to validate generated `package.xml` files—the same validation used on packaging and on installation.

Globbing Files for package.xml

The single most important function that PEAR_PackageFileManager performs is the creation of the file list. Our simple package only has a few files in it, but for large, complex packages like PhpDocumentor (`http://pear.php.net/PhpDocumentor`), it becomes an increasingly difficult task to manage `package.xml`. PhpDocumentor not only has several hundred files in it, but they also tend to change dramatically from release to release because of the use of Smarty templates.

By turning off the `simpleoutput` option, it is possible to easily detect modified files and monitor this from release to release without having to rely upon external tools.

Why was PEAR_PackageFileManager Conceived?

Originally, PEAR_PackageFileManager was a single script for generating PhpDocumentor's `package.xml`. Over time, as more requests for the script came in, it improved and eventually it became clear that it should be a standalone project.

At first, PEAR_PackageFileManager simply globbed all of the files in the current file list, using an `'ignore'` option with shell wildcards to exclude files. For instance, we can ignore all files containing "test" in their name with this wildcard: `"*test*"`. In addition, entire directories and all contents including subdirectories can be ignored by appending a "/" to the pattern as in `"CVS/"`.

The previous example highlights one of the problems with this approach: In a CVS-based package, there may be files that are not part of the project inside the package and would not be exported with the `cvs export` command. As such, PEAR_PackageFileManager has several file-globbing drivers, or file list generators. The choice of which file list generator driver to use is controlled by the `'filelistgenerator'` option in the `setOptions()`/`importOptions()` family of methods. The simplest is the `file` generator.

Other drivers are `'cvs'`, `'svn'`, and `'perforce'`. Each of these drivers is identical to the `'file'` driver except that instead of simply globbing every file in a directory and all subdirectories, it limits the list of files to those in a local checkout of a remote revision source control repository. Concurrent Versioning System (CVS), Subversion, and Perforce are all revision source control repository systems. If you don't know what they are, it would be a good idea to investigate Subversion and CVS, as both are free, open-source solutions. Subversion is much more full-featured than CVS, and is newer, whereas CVS is a tried-and-true warhorse.

Managing Changelog

PEAR_PackageFileManager automatically generates a changelog for the current release, by default from oldest to newest. There are a few options for controlling this. First, the `'changelogoldtonew'` option, if set to false, will re-order the changelog so that newer entries are closer to the top of the file. In addition, if a different set of notes is to be used for the changelog than the release notes, use the `'changelognotes'` option to control this.

Synchronizing package.xml Version 1.0 and package.xml Version 2.0

In some cases, it might be necessary to generate an equivalent `package.xml` version 1.0. For instance, we may wish to allow PEAR 1.3.x users to gracefully fail with a "requires PEAR 1.4.3 or newer" error message. Doing this with PEAR_PackageFileManager is a piece of cake. Change the `importOptions` line from:

```
$pfm = &PEAR_PackageFileManager2::importOptions('package.xml',
```

To this:

```
$pfm = &PEAR_PackageFileManager2::importOptions('package2.xml',
```

Then, change the last few lines of the script to:

```
// create the <contents> tag
$pfm->generateContents();

// create package.xml 1.0 to gracefully tell PEAR 1.3.x users they
// have to upgrade to use this package
$pfm1 = $pfm->exportCompatiblePackageFile1(array(
        // set a subdirectory everything is installed into
        'baseinstalldir' => 'PEAR/Task/Chiara',
        // location of files to package
        'packagedirectory' => dirname(__FILE__),
        // what method is used to glob files? cvs, svn, perforce
        // and file are options
        'filelistgenerator' => 'file',

        // don't distribute this script
        'ignore' => array('package.php', 'package.xml',
        'package2.xml', 'rolesetup.php'),
        // put the post-installation script in a
        // different location from the task itself
        // make the output human-friendly
        'simpleoutput' => true,
        ));

// display the package.xml by default to allow "debugging" by eye,
// and then create it if explicitly asked to
if (isset($_GET['make']) || (isset($_SERVER['argv']) &&
@$_SERVER['argv'][1] == 'make')) {
    $pfm1->writePackageFile();
    $pfm->writePackageFile();
```

```
    } else {
        $pfm1->debugPackageFile();
        $pfm->debugPackageFile();
    }
    ?>
```

The script will then output both `package.xml` and `package2.xml`.

Creating a Package for Installation with the PEAR Installer

The final step in the process is creating a package. Once you have a `package.xml` file that has been generated, you can use it to create a file containing the contents of the package. To do this, you should use the `package` command:

$ pear package

This command should be executed from the directory containing the `package.xml` file. This will create a `.tgz` file like `Package-version.tgz` where `Package` is the package name, and `version` is the release version. If your package is named `Foo` and is version `1.2.3` the package command will create a file named `Foo-1.2.3.tgz`. This file can be installed with:

$ pear install Foo-1.2.3.tgz

Or can also be uploaded to a channel server for public release (discussed in Chapter 5).

The package command can also be used to create an uncompressed `.tar` file with the `--uncompress` or `-Z` option:

$ pear package -Z

In some cases, you may have renamed a package file. In this case, it is necessary to explicitly specify a `package.xml` to be used for packaging as in:

$ pear package package-PEAR.xml package2.xml

This is the actual command line used to create the PEAR package for release. Note that it does not matter which `package.xml` (version 1.0 or version 2.0) is passed in, the following command-line sequence is identical.

$ pear package package2.xml package-PEAR.xml

However, if both `package.xml` are the same version, the packaging will fail. In addition, there is a strict comparison made between the two `package.xml` files. If there is even the slightest difference between the texts of the `<description>` tag,

`<summary>` tag, or `<notes>` tag, validation will fail. In fact, every file within the `package.xml 1.0` must be contained with the `package.xml 2.0`. The number of maintainers and their roles must be identical.

However, there are a few differences that are allowed. For instance, the dependencies of `package.xml 1.0` need not match those of `package.xml 2.0` whatsoever, due to the fact that `package.xml 2.0` simply represents a far greater set of possible dependencies than `package.xml 1.0`. In addition, the introduction of the `<ignore>` tag in `package.xml 2.0` makes it possible to distribute files that are ignored by the PEAR installer. In this way, an application that will run out-of-the-box can also be easily installed with PEAR by distributing files needed for the out-of-the-box run and asking the PEAR installer to ignore them. These files will not be present in the `package.xml 1.0` because PEAR 1.3.x did not have this capability.

Summary

At this stage, we've explored the inner workings of the PEAR installer and of `package.xml` to the highest level—it is safe to say that you are now a `package.xml` expert.

4

Clever Website Coordination Using the PEAR Installer

In the last two chapters, we learned how to use the PEAR installer's features to manage libraries and applications for public distribution. In this chapter, we'll learn how the PEAR installer can be used to make managing the contents of a complex and rapidly evolving website easy. In fact, the PEAR installer can be used to provide an extra level of insurance that a website will function as expected, and even make diagnosing problems easier.

In this chapter, we'll begin by understanding the details of our problem at a high level, and seeing how PEAR installer can help us to solve it. Then we'll look at the first step of the solution, setting up the source control system, and we will finally finish off with managing the complexity of a multi-segment website using a live site as an example.

Overview of the Problem

One of the most important tasks is keeping the structure of a complex and dynamic website coherent and up to date as the information represented evolves. In many cases, re-organization may result in files that are no longer in use cluttering the directory layout. Worse, when deleting unused files, there is a risk of accidentally removing an essential file without realizing it. In addition, coordinating a multi-developer modular website presents an obvious challenge: how does one prevent conflicts in updates and additions?

In conjunction with a revision control system such as CVS (Concurrent Versions System), the PEAR installer provides a unique and battle-tested solution to manage all of these problems effectively. Revision control systems provide a combination of redundancy and flexibility that cannot be matched by simple file systems. The ability to check out a personal **sandbox** in which to do development without the fear of disrupting the primary code base is an essential part of any serious code development.

Traditionally, branches (CVS and Subversion) and tags (CVS only) are used to document "release points", where a program is ready for usage. For instance, PEAR version 1.4.5 can be retrieved directly from `cvs.php.net` via these commands:

```
$ cvs -d :pserver:anoncvs@cvs.php.net:/respository login
Password:<enter your email address>
$ cvs -d :pserver:anoncvs@cvs.php.net:/respository co -r RELEASE_1_4_5
pear-core
```

This sequence checks out the source of the PEAR installer, which is located at `cvs.php.net` in `/repository/pear-core`, and then retrieves the tag `RELEASE_1_4_5`, which was set at the release time of PEAR version 1.4.5 via the convenient `cvstag` command (covered in depth later in the chapter):

```
$ pear cvstag package2.xml package-PEAR.xml tests
```

The above example is the most complex possible command. In most cases, a developer can tag a package simply with the following command:

```
$ pear cvstag package.xml
```

Of course, the PEAR installer and a revision control system is only as effective as the coordinating plan behind them, and so devising a good strategy for developing the website in conjunction with the two tools is an essential part of the equation, and is covered in the last segment of this chapter.

Using a **roadmap** or a development timeline describing approximately when new features will be added and old ones removed is a good first step. Defining ways in which developers should coordinate and synchronize their efforts is another. Using design tools and strategies such as UML and extreme programming (test-driven development and its friends) may also be of use, but ultimately the clarity of thought present in the website architects' design goals is usually far more significant, and will lead to the best solution, regardless of the tools chosen to get there.

 The primary problem we will address is how to coordinate a complex website, specifically, how to safely and systematically update the live website from a development machine.

Understanding the Problem

To understand the solution to a problem, it makes sense that we should understand the problem at a high level. In our case, it is important to understand the main issues that surround coordinating the development of a major website. A good website will draw users back to view it as often as possible, developing a community. This will only happen if there is both exciting content and pleasing visual and logical layout. Often, content can be updated without changing any code (think of blogs or content management systems), but changing the visual layout and logical structure of a site requires more extensive internal changes to a site.

Even if you design the perfect site on the first attempt (congratulations!) and have a simple method for adjusting the content and even the logical structure of a site, this may lead to the largest challenge of transitioning from a small website to a hugely successful website with thousands of hits per minute: **scalability**. Often at this stage, a comprehensive redesign may be necessary to accommodate unexpected needs. Success inevitably leads to the need for bringing on new developers who may be unfamiliar with the website structure or design goals. The constant threat of re-factoring to improve things also threatens to bring unexpected chaos to even the best-intentioned web team.

All of this uncertainty will lead to greater potential for breakage of code, confusing and cluttered directory structure, and other problems.

We'll look at four typical problem areas, and get a better picture of how PEAR Installer will help us:

- Managing code breakage and reverting to a previous version
- Managing missing or extraneous files
- Coordinating development with a team of developers
- Backing up code: redundancy as a necessary precaution

Managing Code Breakage and Reverting to Previous Versions

Occasionally, it becomes apparent that in spite of careful design and even more careful testing, something in a recent update has broken a critical portion of a website. Even worse, a security breach may have resulted in a rogue hacker destroying a carefully worked out web structure.

In the past, this could mean hoping that a restore from backup would do the trick. In some cases, a hack was not noticed for a long time, requiring restoration from an early backup. This can result in tremendous difficulty determining the correct files to transfer and delete.

The PEAR installer manages these problems in a tremendously efficient manner. Instead of spending feverish hours going over each directory by hand, two commands are sufficient to completely remove and restore the most current website structure:

```
$ rm -rf /path/to/htdocs
$ pear upgrade --force WebSite-1.2.3.tgz
```

The difference in complexity between this and a frantic *"is-everything-all-right-oops-I-need-to-restore-that-file-and-delete-this-one"* is staggering.

PEAR Installer or rsync?

Experienced web developers should also know about the rsync command, which facilitates remote synchronization of directories on machines separated by a great distance. In many cases, this is a very efficient way of ensuring that local and remote repositories are in sync. However, if you are coordinating between several developers, or developing some portions of a site while others are stable, it may cause more difficulty than ease. In this case, you will benefit more from the strengths of the versioning and simple reversion provided by the PEAR installer.

Managing Missing or Extraneous Files

Theoretically, problems of missing or extra files should never happen if you fully test a website on a development machine prior to upload, but there are times when a mistake in a rsync transfer occurs and files are removed that should not be. In the best-case scenario, this will result in the immediate breakage of the site, and will be easily tracked down and fixed. In the worst case, however, the breakage may be subtle, and in fact not apparent until a rare but crucial task is performed by one of your website's end users or a hacker discovers a security vulnerability in an unused file. This can lead to scaring off users, lost profits for commercial websites, or even legal problems if your site was used by a hacker to commit a crime and negligence on your part can be proven.

How are these problems any different when managing a website using the PEAR installer? There are two features of the PEAR installer that set it apart from traditional solutions:

- Versioning
- File Transactions

Through the concept of versioning, it is possible to determine precisely which files are present by either examining the contents of package.xml or by running the list-files command like so:

```
$ pear list-files mychannel/PackageName
```

Missing or extraneous files are easily detectable with this system without the need to resort to a slow recursive check of actual directories. In addition, the ability to quickly revert to an earlier version, even temporarily, and then restore a newer fixed version is also incredibly simple, as evidenced by this sample command sequence:

```
$ pear upgrade --force mychannel/PackageName-1.0.2
<after fixing things>
$ pear upgrade mychannel/PackageName
```

The PEAR installer takes advantage of a concept from relational databases and implements transaction-based file installation and removal. This means that no changes to the directory structure occur until all have been successfully completed. In addition, atomic file operations are performed whenever possible. The life cycle of a file is rather simple, and consists of these steps:

- File `path/to/foo.php` is installed as `/path/to/pear/path/to/.tmpfoo.php`
- File `/path/to/pear/path/to/foo.php` if present, is renamed to `/path/to/pear/path/to/foo.php.bak`.
- File `/path/to/pear/path/to/.tmpfoo.php` is renamed to `/path/to/pear/path/to/foo.php`.

After installation, all of the `.bak` files created are removed.

However, if there is a problem at any step along the way, the installed files are removed, and the `.bak` files are renamed to the original filename. In this way, it is possible to very safely manage file upgrades. Additional checks are performed to ensure that the installer is capable of writing to the directory of the installation, and that the files are actually installed as expected. All of this extra work helps to guarantee the success of an installation.

Coordinating Development with a Team of Developers

The PEAR installer also helps coordinate a team of web developers in two ways:

- Discrete packaging
- File conflict resolution

Discrete packaging simply means that each developer or sub-team's set of files can occupy its own package and be installed/upgraded independently of the others. In addition, they can all be managed from a central package using dependencies.

File conflict resolution solves the potential for accidentally overwriting files from another team and makes it possible to share directory space safely. The PEAR installer does not allow different packages to conflict with any files from other packages. This simple technical fact will augment your team's file naming conventions with an additional layer of error-checking.

Even when the `--force` option is specified, file conflict resolution is used. Only the dangerous `--ignore-errors` option overrides file conflict checking.

Backing Up Code: Redundancy as a Necessary Precaution

Managing a website using the PEAR installer provides what is perhaps a less obvious benefit by duplicating the code. The need to back up code from a website is often thought of only in terms of keeping a duplicate of the entire site. This is important, but may not be enough. The ability to quickly restore corrupted segments of a website, if only a few files are corrupted, is again quite simple with the PEAR installer; one only needs to run:

```
$ pear upgrade --force mychannel/MyPackage
```

In addition, the storage of website code as packaged archives at the channel server provides an additional level of redundancy above and beyond the redundancy provided by source control and traditional full back-up methods.

Now that we know the problem areas and how PEAR installer can help us deal with them, let's get into the solution in detail.

The Solution, Part I: All-Important Source Control

Before taking advantage of the PEAR installer, it is important to set up a source control system. There are many fine commercial software programs that can be used to perform source control, including **Perforce** and **Visual SourceSafe**, but we will focus on the tried and true, free open-source revision control systems: **CVS** and **Subversion**.

CVS (Concurrent Versioning System) is one of the oldest source-control products, and is based on the even older **RCS (Revision Control System)** source control program. CVS implements its source control by using a client-server model. The server contains the final code, organized into directories and files. However, on the server, each file actually contains a full revision history of that file. On the client end, users check out a local **sandbox**—a copy of the server code, which can then be developed independently of other developers. When the code is ready to be committed to the server, the user sends a special command to the server. At that time, the server checks to see if there have been any changes to the repository by other users, and if so, prevents the conflict that may occur. Conflict resolution between users' commits is fully supported, as well as merging compatible changes.

Although CVS does a very good job, there are a few limitations that prompted the Subversion development team to begin work on a new model. Like CVS, Subversion provides the same collaborative tools. The difference is in how Subversion stores its information. Using a Berkeley database file to document changes and revisions (or in the latest releases, the FSFS file-based database), Subversion has the capability to track changes to groups of files and directories as well as to individual files, something that is far more difficult to do with CVS. In addition, Subversion stores a complete copy of the server code in the client sandbox, allowing for very efficient use of bandwidth when performing actions such as checking changes and making patches.

Providing Redundancy and Revision History

The primary benefit of a source control system is the combination of redundancy and revision history. Source control systems are designed around the principle of human fallibility: we just make mistakes sometimes, and it is important to be able to recover from those mistakes as easily as possible. Through the redundancy provided by separating a developer sandbox from the server repository, it becomes possible to quickly recover from a mistake on the developer's machine. The existence of revision history, and CVS/Subversion's sophisticated ability to check out code from a particular point in time, or a particular tag or branch, mean that it is also a simple matter to revert a faulty commit, or change to the server repository.

Installing CVS or Subversion

In most cases, setting up a revision control system is easy. This text is not the best resource for installation, but does cover the basics. For extended support, it is best to consult the support resources of CVS or Subversion directly.

In the next few sections, you will learn how to initialize a repository in CVS or Subversion and to create new projects within the repository, and how to create a local sandbox for development. There are a few prerequisites for setting up a revision control system. It is important that you have access to a shell on the host for which you wish to set up the revision control system. If you do not have access to the file system, it will be exceedingly difficult to fix any problems with the repository.

If you do not have shell access to your remote host, and do not have the resources to switch to an internet provider that does provide shell access, all is not lost.

On Windows-based systems, it is very easy to set up a local repository using the freeware TortoiseCVS or TortoiseSVN programs, and on unix-based systems like Mac OS X or Linux, you can compile and use the CVS and Subversion tools directly to initialize a repository. The only drawback to this approach is that you lose some of the fail-safe advantages of having a remote repository.

In either case, remote or local repository, you will need to make regular backups of the system to avoid trouble in case of catastrophic hardware failure or other unpleasant truths of Murphy's Law.

Here is Murphy's Law:

"If anything can go wrong, it will."

Always plan for problems—Hardware failure, data corruption, and security breaches just begin the list of issues plaguing our work.

Concurrent Versions System

Concurrent Versions System (CVS) is hosted at `http:\\www.nongnu.org/cvs/` and is the oldest form of revision control. CVS is very stable, and has been stable for years. As such, it is the old warhorse of revision control, having stood the test of time. CVS is based on a very simple file-based revision control. In the repository, each file contains content and metadata containing differences between revisions. The repository should never be used for direct access or work. Instead, a complete copy of a directory is checked out for development. No changes are saved to the main repository until you check in or commit the code.

CVS is designed to coordinate the work of multiple developers, and as such has the capability to refuse a commit if there may be a conflict between the work of two different developers. Let's look at an example.

The PHP repository has several modules hosted by `cvs.php.net`, which are organized like a file system. To check out a module, you must first log into the CVS server. Users with accounts will use their account name, but PHP also provides anonymous read-only CVS access. To log into the CVS server, one types:

```
$ cvs -d :pserver:cvsread@cvs.php.net:/repository login
```

At this point, the `cvs` command will prompt for a password. For anonymous CVS access, enter your email address. Once you are logged in, check out a module. For instance, to view the source of the PEAR_PackageFileManager package, you would type:

```
$ cvs -d :pserver:cvsread@cvs.php.net:/repository checkout pear/
PEAR_PackageFileManager
```

This command creates the directory `pear` and subdirectory `PEAR_PackageFileManager`, and populates them with all the files and directories contained within the project. In addition, it creates special directories named `CVS` that contain information about the state of the local copy of the repository. Each directory must contain files named `Entries`, `Root`, and `Repository`. Depending on the state of the repository, there may be other files as well. These files should *never* be hand-altered except in extreme circumstances, but it is important to know what controls your CVS checkout.

For more information and help on using CVS, it is probably good to start by reading the *manpage on unix* via `man cvs`, and to read the CVS book published by O'Reilly and distributed online under the GNU General Public Licence at `http://cvsbook.red-bean.com/`.

On Windows, it is probably easiest to use a tool like **TortoiseCVS**, which is available from `http://www.tortoisecvs.org`. This free tool adds an extension to Windows Explorer that allows direct manipulation of CVS checkouts and repository simply by right-clicking on files or directories with the mouse. It is very intuitive and powerful.

Setting Up a CVS Repository

The first step in setting up a CVS repository is to determine where you are going to put the repository. CVS has several methods of connecting to the repository remotely. In most cases, it is best to require access through secure shell (**SSH**), via the `ext` method, as in:

```
$ cvs -d :ext:cellog@cvs.phpdoc.org:/opt/cvsroot
```

Parsing this command line further, the `-d` option tells CVS where to locate the root of CVS, or `CVSROOT`. In this case, it tells CVS to connect to the remote CVSROOT at `cvs.phpdoc.org` via the `pserver` protocol, using the `cellog` username. In addition, it informs the remote CVS daemon that the CVSROOT is located at `/opt/cvsroot`. On `cvs.php.net`, the CVSROOT is located at `/repository`.

If you're on a shared host, assuming your remote username is `youruser`, it is probably best to put the `cvsroot` in `/home/youruser/cvs` or something of that nature. Otherwise, you are not likely to have write access to the directory in which you initialize your CVS repository. Obviously, write access is very important; otherwise there is no way to commit code from a development sandbox.

Once you have decided where to put the CVS repository, the next step is to initialize it. This is straightforward:

```
$ cvs -d /home/youruser/cvs init
```

This creates the `/home/youruser/cvs/CVSROOT` directory.

The next step is to create the module you will use for the website. Before importing the website, first create the module for the website.

```
$ mkdir /home/youruser/website
$ cd /home/youruser/website
$ echo "hi" >> README
$ cvs -d /home/youruser/cvs imoort website tcvs-vendor tcvs-release
```

This will create a module named `website` that can be checked out. To ensure success, check out a copy of the `website` module:

```
$ cd
$ cvs -d /home/youruser/cvs checkout website
```

If all goes well, this will result in the creation of directory /home/youruser/website and the file /home/youruser/website/README. To test that CVS is accessible remotely, check out a copy of the `website` module via something like:

```
$ cvs -d :ext:youruser@example.com:/home/youruser/cvs checkout website
```

The next step is adding the contents of the website into the CVS repository. Simply copy all of the website files with the directory hierarchy you desire into your local checkout of the `website` module. The next step is the most complicated.

Most websites contain both text files (like our PHP scripts) and binary files, like images or sound clips. CVS treats binary and text files differently. Text files are processed, and special CVS in-file tags like Id or $Revision$ are replaced with special values based on the state of the file in the repository. Tags like "Id" must be manually added to the files by the developer, CVS does not create them automatically. Binary files are treated as a single entity, and their contents are not touched.

When adding files to a CVS module, they must first be added via the `cvs add` command, and then committed via the `cvs commit` command. Text files and directories are simply added like this:

```
$ cvs add file
```

Binary files are added with the `-kb` switch:

```
$ cvs add -kb file
```

Files can be added with wildcards, but be very careful to ensure that you do not add image files as text files or text files as binary! In the worst case, you can remove files prior to committing with:

```
$ cvs remove file
```

Note that files that have been committed to the repository must be deleted prior to removal:

```
$ rm file
$ cvs remove file
```

If you are using Windows, TortoiseCVS makes adding files far easier, as it does so recursively and hides the implementation details.

Subversion

Subversion was developed a few years ago to address some of the shortcomings of CVS. Specifically, Subversion stores the repository information using a database, and so supports grouping changes together by commit rather than by file. Subversion is newer and as such has not been battle-tested as long as CVS, but both have been used in production for years.

 http://svnbook.red-bean.com contains several different formats of the same book as published by O'Reilly. The Subversion book contains everything needed to set up, configure, and administer a Subversion repository.

Subversion differs from CVS in a few important ways:

- A complete copy of the remote repository is stored locally, simplifying diffs and making it possible to do this offline.

- Tags are stored as branches, unlike CVS. In CVS, tags are read-only and it is difficult to accidentally modify a tag. Modifying a branch is quite simple, and because tags are branches in Subversion, this makes it more difficult to implement a read-only tag.

- Large files are easier to manage. Because the sandbox contains a complete copy of the current state of the repository module, this means that committing large text files only requires sending a diff. Ultimately, this saves both bandwidth and processor cycles on the server, which can be very important. (I once locked up the entire live server requiring a reboot just by committing a minor change to a 133MB database dump in a CVS repository. This was bad.)

- Keywords (Id, $Revision$, and so on) are not substituted by default; all files in subversion are treated as binary files. To set a keyword substitution for a file, you need to set a property with something like:

```
$ svn propset svn:keywords "Id" blah.php
```

More information is available at
`http://svnbook.red-bean.com/nightly/en/svn.advanced.props.html#svn.advanced.props.special.keywords`

Setting Up a Subversion Repository

Like CVS, setting up a repository is relatively painless. Simply run:

```
$ svnadmin create /path/to/subversion
```

This will create a Subversion repository as a subdirectory of the current directory. To import your website code into the repository, first set up the standard Subversion directories:

```
$ mkdir ~/tmp
$ cd ~/tmp
$ mkdir website
$ cd website
$ mkdir trunk
$ mkdir tags
$ mkdir branches
```

Next, copy the complete contents of your current website into the `website/trunk` directory. Finally execute:

```
$ cd ~/tmp
$ svn import . file:///path/to/subversion -m "initial import"
```

Once you have successfully imported, test by checking out the module:

```
$ svn checkout file:///path/to/subversion/website/trunk website
```

WARNING: check out website/trunk, not website.

If you check out the entire module, you will get all branches and tags as well. This will eventually eat up all available disk space.

Accessing the `website` module remotely requires that either the `svnserve` daemon is running or that `mod_svn` is running as an Apache web-server module. Consult the Subversion book at `http://svnbook.red-bean.com` for extended details on setting this up if one is not set up for you.

If you are running `svnserve`, either check out via:

```
$ svn checkout
svn://yourwebsite.example.com/path/to/subversion/website/trunk website
```

Or, if you support the highly recommended secure shell (SSH) tunneling:

```
$ svn checkout
svn+ssh://yourwebsite.example.com/path/to/subversion/website/
trunk website
```

Instead, if you have `mod_svn` running, checking out is far simpler:

```
$ svn checkout http://yourwebsite.example.com/subversion/website/
trunk website
```

Or, if you have a secure server:

```
$ svn checkout https://yourwebsite.example.com/subversion/website/
trunk website
```

These commands will create a directory named `website` that contains the code for your website.

Adding and removing files in a Subversion repository is very straightforward, and similar to CVS. Simply use this format to add a file or directory from within the `website` directory:

```
$ svn add file.php
```

Use this format to remove a file or directory:

```
$ svn delete file.php
```

Unlike with CVS, it is possible to move files around or copy them, retaining their revision history, with the `move` and `copy` commands:

```
$ svn copy file.php newfile.php
```
```
$ svn move oldfile.php anotherfile.php
```

If you wish to have keywords like `$Id$` or `$Revision$` replaced, you need to manually tell Subversion to perform this substitution:

```
$ svn propset svn:keywords "Id Revision" file.php
```

This should be enough information to get started with using the repository that you choose to use.

Intelligent Source Control

OK, now you have a version control repository set up and configured. Great! What next? Using a version control system intelligently is a very important step. Basic principles should be followed to ensure this is happening. Although many are common sense, it is not easy to remain vigilant and adhere to them.

- Make regular backups of your repository and store them on independent media from the machine hosting the repository. If you remember nothing else, remember this!

- Only commit working code to the repository – test before committing to avoid obvious errors like syntax errors.

- Use tags to mark point releases of working code that will be deployed to a live server.

- Use branches to support innovation and stable code bases simultaneously.

- If you have multiple developers, define some basic coding standards (like PEAR's coding standards) so that diffs between revisions do not contain spurious changes to whitespace and other noise.

- If you have multiple developers, set up a mailing list that is explicitly for commits to the repository. There are many excellent programs available for use in post-commit scripts that will mail diffs to a mailing list. Ensure that every developer is subscribed to the mailing list.

Maintaining Branches for Complex Versioning Support

Branches allow development of more than one version of the same software at the same time. For instance, when software has reached stability, and major new features will be added, branch off a copy of the software so that small bugs can be fixed in the stable version at the same time as development continues. Best practice has the stable version branched off and development continuing on HEAD.

To develop the stable version 1.2.X in a branch using CVS:

```
$ cvs tag -b VERSION_1_2
$ cvs update -b DEVEL_1_2
```

The update command is an unintuitive requirement, but is very important; without updating your sources, you will not be editing the branch code, and any changes will end up on HEAD.

It is a good idea to have two separate directories. For instance, when developing PEAR version 1.5.0 I have two directories that I use, which are created like so:

```
$ cvs -d :pserver:cellog@cvs.php.net:/repository co -r PEAR_1_4 -d
pear1.4 pear-core
```

```
$ cvs -d :pserver:cellog@cvs.php.net:/repository co pear-core
```

Because I specified the `-d pear1.4` option to the `checkout` command (abbreviated as `co`), the files will be checked out to the `pear1.4` directory. The `-r PEAR_1_4` option retrieves the PEAR_1_4 branch for fixing bugs in PEAR version 1.4.X. In the second case, files from the default HEAD branch are checked out to the `pear-core` directory.

The same task using Subversion is performed by something like:

```
$ svn checkout http://yourwebsite.example.com/subversion/website/
trunk website
```

Using Tags to Mark Point Releases

Tags are important for several reasons, not the least of which is the ability to reconstruct older releases in the event of a disastrous loss of data. There are two ways to create a tag using CVS. The recommended way is very simple:

```
$ pear cvstag package.xml
```

This command parses `package.xml`, and for each file found, that file is tagged with RELEASE_X_Y_Z where X_Y_Z is the version number. Version 1.2.3 will be tagged with RELEASE_1_2_3.

Tagging manually from within the module checkout can be accomplished with:

```
$ cvs tag -r RELEASE_1_2_3
```

Subversion does not differentiate between tags and branches, so the only difference between creating a tag and a branch is where you copy it with the `svn copy` command. By default, tags should be copied to the trunk/tags branch using `svn` copy:

```
$ svn copy trunk tags/RELEASE_1_2_3
```

```
$ svn commit -m "tag release version 1.2.3"
```

The Solution, Part II: Using the PEAR Installer to Update the Website

At this point, you should be familiar with the basic usage of both the PEAR installer and a source control system. Now we will take that knowledge to the next level and discover how to use the strengths of both tools to manage the complexity of a multi-segment website with inter-dependencies. First, it is important to think of the website code in terms of discrete packages and dependencies. To do this, it is often helpful to use a diagram. For complex systems, it makes a great deal of sense to use the **Uniform Modelling Language** (**UML**) to describe the system, as this is the universal standard of description.

Let's examine a real-world example: the Chiara String Quartet website, `http://www.chiaraquartet.net`. As of early 2006, this is a mid-size website designed by a single developer, but the principles would scale well to a multi-developer situation. The website consists of a number of sub-sites as well as the main site.

As of a few days prior to publication, the Chiara Quartet's website is now managed by an independent developer, and is no longer maintained directly by the author as described. For an example of a website that is being manged using `package.xml`, at the time of publication, `pear.php.net` was migrating to this approach. Check out the pearweb module from `cvs.php.net`, and the `package.php` script and corresponding `package.xml` and post-installation script which can be used to set up a MySQL database and configure `http.conf` file for a development copy of `pear.php.net`'s code.

The public sites are:

- `http://www.chiaraquartet.net` (main site)
- `http://music.chiaraquartet.net` (MP3s/audio samples)
- `http://calendar.chiaraquartet.net` (schedule information)

The private back-end sites include:

- `http://addressbook.chiaraquartet.net` (data entry for contact database)
- `http://database.chiaraquartet.net` (management of general back end data)

Each of these sites has an independent code base, but there are interlinked dependencies on elements such as images and templates used to unify the look of different sites. In addition, as the quartet's career grows, the needs of the website change dramatically, and the ability to add new sub-sites and remove obsolete ones is very important.

Also important is to note that very large files are needed, such as high resolution press pictures and MP3 audio clips that will not change as regularly as the PHP code.

As such, the website can be grouped into several simple packages:

- website
- website database back end
- website contact data entry back end
- website images
- website MP3s
- website photos
- website press PDFs

The primary website package itself can be broken up at a later date into separate packages such as a primary website and a website blog package without penalty through a couple of methods that we will examine later on in the chapter.

Once we have determined the logical partitioning of the website into packages, all that is needed is to create a private channel, generate proper `package.xml` files for each package, and install the website. Each component can be upgraded—and downgraded—independently, making maintenance and tracking changes far less of a magical ritual.

A wonderful technique for backing up a database is not only to save full dumps, but to commit these to a Subversion repository. This way, you are storing smaller versions and have the capability to check out the database dump on a remote machine for development and testing purposes.

Subversion is greatly preferred to CVS because it handles extremely large files far more gracefully. CVS can easily bring down an entire machine when calculating the difference between two 150 MB database dumps. I learned this the hard way. Subversion is far superior in this regard simply because it calculates differences using the local copy, and so only differences are sent back and forth, reducing net traffic exponentially.

It is important to note that if there is any private data in the database, access should be restricted to svn+ssh in order to reduce the possibility of accidentally giving the sensitive data to the wrong people.

Needless to say, if there are any crucially sensitive data such as credit-card numbers or data that identity thieves would love to get their hands on, do not allow any remote access to the data whatsoever; instead resort to a tool like rdiff-backup (http://www.nongnu.org/rdiff-backup/).

When porting an existing website, it is best to add it to CVS/Subversion in exactly the source layout of the existing website.

One difficulty in developing a remote website is the need for code that understands it will run on a different IP and possibly a different hostname. There are three ways of handling this problem:

- Add the live host name to the /etc/hosts file as an alias to localhost, so all requests go to localhost.
- Use host-neutral code, for example depending on the $_SERVER['HTTP_HOST'] variable used by the Apache web server, or $_SERVER['PHP_SELF'].
- Use PEAR's replacements facility and custom file roles to define per-machine host information.

Adding the live host name to the /etc/hosts file (usually C:\WINDOWS\system32\drivers\etc\hosts on Microsoft Windows systems) will make it impossible to actually access the live web server — or FTP server — from the development machine, and so is no solution at all.

Using host-neutral code appears to be a good idea at first, but as recent security concerns have shown, cross-site scripting (XSS) attacks thrive on vulnerabilities created through the use of these tools. Although it is not difficult to avoid the security issues, it does add considerable complexity, and makes the chance of introducing another bug or security issue higher than is comfortable.

The third option involves creating custom PEAR installer file roles that define special configuration variables, and then coupling these with PEAR's replacement task to customize files automatically per-machine.

Specifically, our example website, http://www.chiaraquartet.net, would require setting up virtual hosts www.chiaraquartet.net, database.chiaraquartet.net, music.chiaraquartet.net, and calendar.chiaraquartet.net on the development machine. What a pain! Instead, I created two custom packages that define five configuration variables:

- `root_url`: This defines the base URL of the website.
- `music_url` :This defines the base URL of the music-audio portion of the website.
- `calendar_url`: This defines the base URL of the concert and event schedule.
- `addressbook_url`: This defines the base URL of the back-end contact list.
- `database_url`: This defines the base URL of the back-end database.

On the *development* server, I set these configuration variables to their needed values with:

```
$ pear config-set root_url http://localhost
$ pear config-set music_url http://localhost/music
$ pear config-set calendar_url http://localhost/calendar
$ pear config-set addressbook_url http://localhost/addressbook
$ pear config-set database_url http://localhost/database
```

On the *live* server, I set the configuration variables to their needed values with:

```
$ pear config-set root_url http://www.chiaraquartet.net
$ pear config-set music_url http://music.chiaraquartet.net
$ pear config-set calendar_url http://calendar.chiaraquartet.net
$ pear config-set addressbook_url http://addressbook.chiaraquartet.net
$ pear config-set database_url http://database.chiaraquartet.net
```

Then, to set this information directly in the source, I use something like this:

```
$ajaxHelper->serverUrl = '@DATABASE-URL@/rest/rest_server.php';
```

The `@DATABASE-URL@` value will be replaced with the value of the `database_url` configuration variable if this tag is specified in `package.xml`:

```
<file name="blah.php" role="php">
 <tasks:replace from="@DATABASE-URL@" to="database_url"
  type="pear-config" />
</file>
```

After this work, when installed on the local *development* machine, the code will be:

```
$ajaxHelper->serverUrl =
    'http://localhost/database/rest/rest_server.php';
```

And on the *live* server, the code will be:

```
$ajaxHelper->serverUrl = 'http://database.chiaraquartet.net/rest/
rest_server.php';
```

The best thing about this is that the URL is guaranteed to be correct on both machines without any extra work. This basic principle can also be applied for any important difference between development and live servers.

Another specific difference between standard library packages and websites is that websites should be installed into publicly accessible directories, but standard library package files should be installed into non-accessible locations. For this purpose, we have default configuration variables like `php_dir`, `data_dir`, and `test_dir`. There is no default role for web files. Fortunately, a custom file role package does exist on the `pearified.com` channel. To acquire this package, follow these steps:

```
$ pear channel-discover pearified.com
$ pear install pearified/Role_Web
$ pear run-scripts pearified/Role_Web
```

Then, to use it in `package.xml`, simply write:

```
<file name="foo.html" role="web" />
```

In addition, you should specify a required dependency on `pearified.com/Role_Web` and a `<usesrole>` tag as described in Chapter 2.

After these details are worked out, it is time to generate the `package.xml` files that are needed by the PEAR installer in order to manage installation of the website.

Generating package.xml from the Source Control Checkout

To generate `package.xml`, there are a number of options available. The oldest and simplest for a complex website is to use the PEAR_PackageFileManager package to create a `package.xml` generation script. The script should generate each `package.xml` file that is needed, making it simple to update. In addition, it should correctly ignore irrelevant files and sub-packages.

The generation script for our real website, `http://www.chiaraquartet.net`, was maintained using this method:

```
<?php
require_once 'PEAR/PackageFileManager2.php';
PEAR::setErrorHAndling(PEAR_ERROR_DIE);
```

The next section simply sets release notes and versions for each sub-package's `package.xml` in a centralized location near the top of the file, making it easier to edit the file.

```
$imageversion = '0.1.0';
$imagenotes = <<<EOT
initial release
EOT;

$mp3version = '0.1.0';
$mp3notes = <<<EOT
initial release
EOT;

$photoversion = '0.1.0';
$photonotes = <<<EOT
initial release
EOT;

$pressversion = '0.1.0';
$pressnotes = <<<EOT
initial release
EOT;

$dataversion = '0.10.3';
$datanotes = <<<EOT
fix saving multiple program items
EOT;

$version = '0.10.0';
$apiversion = '0.1.0';
$notes = <<<EOT
split off database from main package
EOT;
```

Next, we create each of the package.xml files by importing from the existing package.xml for each sub-package. We'll cut out a few of the sub-packages, just for brevity. Here is a typical one (website images):

```
$package_images =
  PEAR_PackageFileManager2::importOptions(dirname(__FILE__) .
  DIRECTORY_SEPARATOR . 'images' . DIRECTORY_SEPARATOR .
  'package.xml',
    $options = array(
    'ignore' => array('package.xml'),
    'filelistgenerator' => 'cvs', // other option is 'file'
    'changelogoldtonew' => false,
    'baseinstalldir' => 'images',
    'packagedirectory' => dirname(__FILE__) . DIRECTORY_SEPARATOR .
                                                'images',
```

```php
    'simpleoutput' => true,
    'roles' => array('*' => 'web'),
  ));

$package_images->setPackageType('php');
$package_images->setReleaseVersion($imageversion);
$package_images->setAPIVersion($imageversion);
$package_images->setReleaseStability('alpha');
$package_images->setAPIStability('alpha');
$package_images->setNotes($imagenotes);
$package_images->clearDeps();
$package_images->resetUsesRole();
$package_images->addUsesRole('web_dir', 'Role_Web', 'pearified.com');
$package_images->addPackageDepWithChannel('required', 'Role_Web',
                                          'pearified.com');
$package_images->setPhpDep('5.1.0');
$package_images->setPearinstallerDep('1.4.3');

$package_images->generateContents();

$package_images->addRelease();


// snip

$package_data =
    PEAR_PackageFileManager2::importOptions(dirname(__FILE__) .
    DIRECTORY_SEPARATOR . 'database' . DIRECTORY_SEPARATOR .
                                        'package.xml',
    $options = array(
    'ignore' => array('package.xml'),
    'filelistgenerator' => 'cvs', // other option is 'file'
    'changelogoldtonew' => false,
    'baseinstalldir' => 'database',
    'packagedirectory'  => dirname(__FILE__) . DIRECTORY_SEPARATOR .
                                        'database',
    'simpleoutput' => true,
    'roles' => array('*' => 'web'),
  ));

$package_data->setPackageType('php');
$package_data->setReleaseVersion($dataversion);
$package_data->setAPIVersion($dataversion);
$package_data->setReleaseStability('alpha');
$package_data->setAPIStability('alpha');
$package_data->setNotes($datanotes);
```

```
$package_data->clearDeps();
$package_data->resetUsesRole();
$package_data->addPackageDepWithChannel('required', 'HTML_AJAX',
                                                'pear.php.net');
$package_data->addPackageDepWithChannel('required',
                          'HTML_Javascript', 'pear.php.net');
$package_data->addPackageDepWithChannel('required', 'XML_RPC2',
                                                'pear.php.net');
$package_data->addUsesRole('web_dir', 'Role_Web', 'pearified.com');
$package_data->addUsesRole('root_url', 'Role_Chiara',
                              'pear.chiaraquartet.net/private');
$package_data->addUsesRole('music_url', 'Role_Chiara',
                              'pear.chiaraquartet.net/private');
$package_data->addUsesRole('calendar_url', 'Role_Chiara',
                              'pear.chiaraquartet.net/private');
$package_data->addUsesRole('database_url', 'Role_Chiara2',
                              'pear.chiaraquartet.net/private');
$package_data->addPackageDepWithChannel('required', 'Role_Web',
                                                'pearified.com');
$package_data->setPhpDep('5.1.0');
$package_data->setPearinstallerDep('1.4.3');
```

Here, we will add replacement tasks to all files, demonstrating the customization we need for development versus production machine:

```
$package_data->addGlobalReplacement('pear-config', '@ROOT-URL@',
                                                'root_url');
$package_data->addGlobalReplacement('pear-config', '@MUSIC-URL@',
                                                'music_url');
$package_data->addGlobalReplacement('pear-config', '@CALENDAR-URL@',
                                                'calendar_url');
$package_data->addGlobalReplacement('pear-config', '@DATABASE-URL@',
                                                'database_url');
$package_data->addGlobalReplacement('pear-config', '@WEB-DIR@',
                                                'web_dir');

$package_data->generateContents();

$package_data->addRelease();


$package_website =
    PEAR_PackageFileManager2::importOptions(dirname(__FILE__) .
                        DIRECTORY_SEPARATOR . 'package.xml',
```

This next line is crucial; we need to ignore the contents of all the sub-packages, or they will be duplicated and will conflict with the parent package!

```
$options = array(
'ignore' => array('package.php', 'package.xml', '*.bak',
    'chiaraqu_Chiara', '*.tgz', 'README', 'Chiara_Role/',
    'images/', 'photos/', 'music/mp3/', 'press/', 'database/'),
'filelistgenerator' => 'cvs', // other option is 'file'
'changelogoldtonew' => false,
'baseinstalldir' => '/',
'packagedirectory' => dirname(__FILE__),
'simpleoutput' => true,
'roles' => array('*' => 'web'),
));

$package_website->setPackageType('php');
$package_website->setReleaseVersion($version);
$package_website->setAPIVersion($apiversion);
$package_website->setReleaseStability('alpha');
$package_website->setAPIStability('alpha');
$package_website->setNotes($notes);
$package_website->clearDeps();
$package_website->resetUsesRole();
$package_website->addUsesRole('web_dir', 'Role_Web',
                                    'pearified.com');
$package_website->addUsesRole('root_url', 'Role_Chiara',
                    'pear.chiaraquartet.net/private');
$package_website->addUsesRole('music_url', 'Role_Chiara',
                    'pear.chiaraquartet.net/private');
$package_website->addUsesRole('calendar_url', 'Role_Chiara',
                    'pear.chiaraquartet.net/private');
$package_website->addUsesRole('database_url', 'Role_Chiara2',
                    'pear.chiaraquartet.net/private');
$package_website->addPackageDepWithChannel('required', 'PEAR',
                                'pear.php.net', '1.4.3');
$package_website->addPackageDepWithChannel('required', 'Role_Web',
                                    'pearified.com');
$package_website->addPackageDepWithChannel('required', 'Role_Chiara',
                    'pear.chiaraquartet.net/private');
$package_website->addPackageDepWithChannel('required',
                'Role_Chiara2', 'pear.chiaraquartet.net/private');
```

Here, we add dependencies on each of the sub-packages:

```
$package_website->addPackageDepWithChannel('required',
```

```
                        'website_photos', 'pear.chiaraquartet.net/private');
$package_website->addPackageDepWithChannel('required',
                    'website_mp3s', 'pear.chiaraquartet.net/private');
$package_website->addPackageDepWithChannel('required',
                    'website_press', 'pear.chiaraquartet.net/private');
$package_website->addPackageDepWithChannel('required',
                    'website_images', 'pear.chiaraquartet.net/private');
$package_website->setPhpDep('5.1.0');
$package_website->setPearinstallerDep('1.4.3');

$package_website->addGlobalReplacement('pear-config', '@ROOT-URL@',
                                                    'root_url');
$package_website->addGlobalReplacement('pear-config', '@MUSIC-URL@',
                                                    'music_url');
$package_website->addGlobalReplacement('pear-config',
                            '@CALENDAR-URL@', 'calendar_url');
$package_website->addGlobalReplacement('pear-config',
                            '@DATABASE-URL@', 'database_url');
$package_website->addGlobalReplacement('pear-config', '@WEB-DIR@',
                                                    'web_dir');

$package_website->generateContents();
$package_website->addRelease();
```

Finally, we create each of the package.xml files or display them for error-checking:

```
if (isset($_SERVER['argv'][1]) && $_SERVER['argv'][1] == 'commit') {
    $package_press->writePackageFile();
    $package_images->writePackageFile();
    $package_mp3s->writePackageFile();
    $package_photos->writePackageFile();
    $package_website->writePackageFile();
    $package_data->writePackageFile();
} else {
    $package_press->debugPackageFile();
    $package_mp3s->debugPackageFile();
    $package_images->debugPackageFile();
    $package_photos->debugPackageFile();
    $package_website->debugPackageFile();
    $package_data->debugPackageFile();
}


?>
```

Each sub-package has its own PEAR_PackageFileManager2 object, and imports options from an existing `package.xml`, only modifying what is necessary. To create the `package.xml`, I copied an existing one from a PEAR package (in this case, PEAR's own `package2.xml`), and modified the sections `<summary>`, `<description>`, `<license>`, and the list of maintainers to suit the website package.

To use the script, I saved it as `package.php` and now run it with PHP 5.1.0 or newer, like this:

```
$ php package.php
```

This allows me to view the `package.xml` files and check them for errors. To save changes to `package.xml`, I run:

```
$ php package.php commit
```

Voilà! `package.xml` is created in `website/`, `website/database`, `website/calendar`, `website/press`, and `website/music`.

At this stage, we are ready to start making releases of the code and deploying it to a test server.

Packaging: Coordinating Release Versions with Tags and Branches

Arriving at this stage means we are ready to start packaging our website up into PEAR packages for installation. At this point, the process begins to merge with the packaging we learned to do in the previous chapter. Ultimately, this is the reason that packaging a website using the PEAR installer is a good idea. The process of installing, upgrading, and even reverting the website is no different from installing, upgrading, and reverting any PEAR package. This process makes it incredibly simple to manage.

When converting from the old way of managing a website to the PEAR way, there are several important steps that must be undertaken:

1. Test the release on a local development server.
2. Back up the live server immediately prior to deployment if possible.
3. Deploy the PEAR package on the remote server.

Once the website has been successfully deployed, then it is a simple process of upgrading the respective package on the remote server.

When a release is made, it is very important to mark that release in the source control system using a tag. If you chose to use CVS, tagging is straightforward:

```
$ pear cvstag package.xml
```

This will automatically scan `package.xml` for the files contained within the release, and using the release version will create a tag named `RELEASE_X_Y_Z` and apply it to all of the files. If the release version is 0.10.0, the tag will be `RELEASE_0_10_0`, if the release version is 1.2.3, the tag will be `RELEASE_1_2_3`, and so on.

Tagging with Subversion is not quite as automatic, but is accomplished simply via:

```
$ svn copy trunk tags/RELEASE_X_Y_Z
$ svn commit -m "tag release X.Y.Z"
```

With these steps, release version X.Y.Z is tagged.

Testing the Release before Uploading

When you are ready to deploy the website, it is important to create a test package and install it locally to ensure that all is OK. Output from packaging will be something along these lines:

```
$ pear package
Analyzing addressbook/data.php
Analyzing addressbook/form.php
Analyzing addressbook/index.php
Analyzing addressbook/list.php
Analyzing addressbook/login.php
Analyzing addressbook/nameparser.php
Analyzing addressbook/usps.php
Analyzing calendar/chiaraSchedule.php
Analyzing calendar/HTMLController.php
Analyzing calendar/HTMLView.php
Analyzing calendar/index.php
Analyzing calendar/schedulelogin.php
Analyzing css/default.css
Analyzing css/history.css
Analyzing css/jonah.css
Analyzing css/music.css
Analyzing css/newindex.css
```

```
Analyzing css/news.css
Analyzing css/schedule.css
Analyzing domLib/Changelog
Analyzing domLib/domLib.js
Analyzing domLib/LICENSE
Analyzing domTT/alphaAPI.js
Analyzing domTT/domLib.js
Analyzing domTT/domTT.js
Analyzing domTT/domTT_drag.js
Analyzing music/index.php
Analyzing rest_/list/composers.php
Analyzing rest_/list/concerts.php
Analyzing rest_/list/halls.php
Analyzing rest_/list/pieces.php
Analyzing templates/bio.tpl
Analyzing templates/genericheader.tpl
Analyzing templates/header.tpl
Analyzing templates/history.tpl
Analyzing templates/index.tpl
Analyzing templates/jonahheader.tpl
Analyzing templates/jonahindex.tpl
Analyzing templates/musicbody.tpl
Analyzing templates/news.tpl
Analyzing templates/schedulebody.tpl
Analyzing bio.php
Analyzing editconcerts.html
Analyzing history.php
Analyzing index.php
Analyzing news.php
Warning: in pieces.php: class "getPieces" not prefixed with package name
"website"
Warning: in halls.php: class "getHalls" not prefixed with package name
"website"
Warning: in concerts.php: class "getConcerts" not prefixed with package
name "website"
Warning: in composers.php: class "getComposers" not prefixed with
package name "website"
```

Warning: in index.php: function "err" not prefixed with package name "website"

Warning: in index.php: class "schedulebody" not prefixed with package name "website"

Warning: in news.php: class "test" not prefixed with package name "website"

Warning: in HTMLView.php: class "HTMLView" not prefixed with package name "website"

Warning: in HTMLController.php: class "HTMLController" not prefixed with package name "website"

Warning: in chiaraSchedule.php: class "chiaraSchedule" not prefixed with package name "website"

Warning: in usps.php: class "Services_USPS" not prefixed with package name "website"

Warning: in nameparser.php: class "Spouses" not prefixed with package name "website"

Warning: in nameparser.php: class "CareOf" not prefixed with package name "website"

Warning: in nameparser.php: class "Name" not prefixed with package name "website"

Warning: in nameparser.php: class "NameParser" not prefixed with package name "website"

Warning: in schedulelogin.php: class "Login" not prefixed with package name "website"

Warning: in index.php: class "Page3Display" not prefixed with package name "website"

Warning: in index.php: class "Page1Display" not prefixed with package name "website"

Warning: in index.php: class "MyDisplay" not prefixed with package name "website"

Warning: in index.php: class "Recycle" not prefixed with package name "website"

Warning: in index.php: class "Cancel" not prefixed with package name "website"

Warning: in index.php: class "FinalPage" not prefixed with package name "website"

Warning: in index.php: class "VerifyPage" not prefixed with package name "website"

Warning: in index.php: class "FirstPage" not prefixed with package name "website"

Warning: in form.php: class "HTML_QuickForm_Action_Next" not prefixed with package name "website"

```
Warning: in data.php: class "ContactAddress" not prefixed with package
name "website"
Warning: in data.php: class "Address" not prefixed with package name
"website"
Warning: in data.php: class "Data" not prefixed with package name
"website"
Warning: Channel validator warning: field "date" - Release Date
"2006-04-08" is not today
Package website-0.10.0.tgz done
Tag the released code with `pear cvstag package.xml'
(or set the CVS tag RELEASE_0_10_0 by hand)
$ pear upgrade website-0.10.0.tgz
upgrade ok: channel://pear.chiaraquartet.net/private/website-0.10.0
```

What about all those "Warning: in index.php..." Things?

This warning is intended for those folks who are actively developing for the official PEAR repository at http://pear.php.net to help catch cases where classes are misnamed. We could easily eliminate these warnings by creating a custom channel validator as discussed in Chapter 5, but this is unnecessary since we know that they are superfluous warnings (one of the advantages of having written the software or of having read this book!)

Next, browse to every page and click links (or run your test suite if you have one) to be sure that it is working properly. Once you are convinced it is ready and working, it is time to upgrade the live server.

Upgrading the Live Server

Although it is actually possible to upgrade the live server without taking steps to shut it down, this is generally a bad idea. It is in fact best to create a test directory with an index.html and a 404.html file; something like the following:

```
<html>
 <head>
  <title>Upgrading site - check back later</title>
 </head>
 <body>
  We are currently upgrading our server, please check back later.
 </body>
</html>
```

Then, save an .htaccess file (assuming you are using Apache) that looks something like this:

```
RewriteEngine On
RewriteRule .+ test/index.html
```

This is assuming your web host has mod_rewrite enabled in Apache (not all hosts do). Better yet, if you have access to httpd.conf, simply change the directory for DocumentRoot to the test directory, and add the ErrorDocument reference.

> Because the PEAR installer uses atomic file transactions, there is very little chance of ending up with a half-done install. The purpose of the temporary site is to avoid users having to see the site should there be any major problems. You can test the site by adding a RewriteCond rule that specifies your computer's IP will ignore the rule, which allows you to see the full site and detect any problems that need to be fixed.

Once you have the site properly hidden behind a RewriteRule, it is time to actually upgrade the site. First, check out a copy of the website from source control using cvs checkout or svn checkout as we learned at the beginning of this chapter. Next, we need to create the package and install it. Before we can do this, we need to install all of the necessary custom file roles we created:

```
$ pear channel-discover pearified.com
$ pear install pearified/Role_Web
$ pear channel-discover pear.chiaraquartet.net/private
$ pear install priv/Role_Chiara
$ pear install priv/Role_Chiara2
```

Next, we need to initialize the custom file roles:

```
$ pear run-scripts pearified/Role_Web
$ pear config-set root_url http://www.chiaraquartet.net/
$ pear config-set calendar_url http://calendar.chiaraquartet.net/
$ pear config-set database_url http://database.chiaraquartet.net/
$ pear config-set music_url http://music.chiaraquartet.net/
$ pear config-set addressbook_url http://addressbook.chiaraquartet.net/
```

Once this is complete, we are ready to begin installation:

```
$ cvs checkout...etc.
```

```
$ cd website
$ pear package
$ pear install website-0.10.0.tgz
```

That's it! Now that we have finished the initial installation, upgrading to the next version when it is time is as easy as it gets.

Using the pear upgrade Command

For this section, we will use CVS as our source-control example, but substitute what we've learned about Subversion if you are using a Subversion repository.

When you need to fix a bug or add a new feature, simply modify the release notes from the `package.php` `package.xml` generation file:

```
$version = '0.11.0';
$apiversion = '0.1.0';
$notes = <<<EOT
Add a doohickey to the main page
EOT;
```

Then, create the `package.xml` files:

```
$ php package.php commit
```

Finally, commit your work:

```
$ cvs commit -m "add a doohickey to the main page, and prepare for 0.11.0
release"
```

Again, test on the local server via:

```
$ pear upgrade package.xml
```

And when you are certain it works on the remote server, simply run these commands:

```
$ cd website
$ cvs upd -P -d
$ pear package
$ pear cvstag package.xml
$ pear upgrade website-0.11.0.tgz
```

At this stage, you have successfully upgraded to version 0.11.0.

What happens if you discover a critical error in version 0.11.0 that didn't exist in version 0.10.0? Fortunately, the sequence to fix the problem is straightforward and elegant:

```
$ cd website
$ pear upgrade -f website-0.10.0.tgz
```

Two lines of typing is all that you need. This is assuming you kept the 0.10.0 release tarball sitting around. Even if you didn't, the process is still very simple:

```
$ cd website
$ cvs upd -r RELEASE_0_10_0 -P -d
$ pear upgrade -f package.xml
$ cvs upd -r HEAD -P -d
```

Technically, the last line returning to HEAD of CVS is not really necessary for the recovery of the website, but it will save later headaches when you have forgotten that you have checked out the RELEASE_0_10_0 tag. The same process is also simple in Subversion:

```
$ cd website
$ svn switch http://yourwebsite.example.com/subversion/website/tags/
RELEASE_0_10_0
$ pear upgrade -f package.xml
$ svn switch http://yourwebsite.example.com/subversion/website/trunk
```

Now for the $10 million question: how can you perform these tasks if you have no shell access on the remote server, as many folks on shared hosts have experienced? (Hint: read the section on *PEAR_RemoteInstaller* in Chapter 1, and you'll have the answer).

The Real Beauty of Using Pear to Fix Problems

The worst moment in a web developer's life is when a serious flaw is discovered in a website. It is often difficult to quickly revert to an older version. The PEAR installer makes this process simple. If testing determines that the problem was introduced in version 1.2.3 and does not exist in version 1.2.2, reverting to version 1.2.2 is as simple as:

```
$ pear upgrade --force website-1.2.2.tgz
```

Or if you have set up a channel (we'll assume you have aliased it as private):

```
$ pear upgrade --force private/website-1.2.2
```

Abbreviated:

```
$ pear up -f private/website-1.2.2
```

In addition, any required dependencies will also be downgraded if you pass in the -o command-line option.

Summary

In this chapter we have seen how to use PEAR installer to manage a complicated and rapidly evolving website. We saw a number of issues involved in the development of a website, such as code breakage, missing or extra files, and how the PEAR Installer can help us with them.

We also saw how to set up a revision control system, either CVS or Subversion. Finally, we saw how to use PEAR installer and source control systems to update a website.

In the next chapter you will learn about ways of publicly distributing your libraries and applications over the Internet.

5
Releasing to the World: PEAR Channels

One of the premier features of PEAR version 1.4.0 and newer versions is the ability to publicly distribute your own applications for installation with the PEAR installer. Although this was feasible with PEAR 1.3.6 and earlier versions, it was far more difficult, and so was rarely attempted. PEAR version 1.4.0+ adds ease to distributing packages by the use of a new distribution medium called **channels**. Each PEAR channel provides a unique set of packages that can be installed quite easily using the PEAR installer. For instance, to install a package from the `pear.chiaraquartet.net` channel, one need only type:

```
$ pear channel-discover pear.chiaraquartet.net
$ pear install chiara/Chiara_PEAR_Server
```

In the past, this was simply not possible. A non-intuitive set of keystrokes would be needed to install a package from `pear.chiaraquartet.net`:

```
$ pear config-set master_server pear.chiaraquartet.net
$ pear install Chiara_PEAR_Server
$ pear config-set master_server pear.php.net
```

The complexity is confounded by cross-channel dependencies. The `pear.chiaraquartet.net/Chiara_PEAR_Server` package depends on `pear.php.net/HTML_QuickForm`, and so the sequence would in fact need to be:

```
$ pear install HTML_QuickForm
$ pear config-set master_server pear.chiaraquartet.net
$ pear install Chiara_PEAR_Server
$ pear config-set master_server pear.php.net
```

The same process would need to be repeated upon upgrading, introducing both painful memory requirements ("Where did I get this Chiara_PEAR_Server from again?") and the chance for error. What if `pear.chiaraquartet.net` happened to provide a package named `LogXML` and `pear.php.net` introduced one? If you were to accidentally type:

```
$ pear upgrade LogXML
```

Without the necessary:

```
$ pear config-set master_server pear.chiaraquartet.net
$ pear upgrade LogXML
$ pear config-set master_server pear.php.net
```

You could unknowingly upgrade to the wrong package! Channels remove all of these troubles, and do so with rigorous security.

So how do you set up your own channel? This chapter will investigate the steps needed to install Chiara_PEAR_Server, and the structure of a channel definition file used to document your channel's unique features.

In addition, we will learn how to distribute customized PEAR applications per-user, even for pay-for-use applications. We'll discover the **Crtx_PEAR_Channel_Frontend** package used to provide a public front door for users browsing the web, and finally, we will talk about security issues.

Distributing a package.xml-Based Package

There are two ways of distributing packages (either of which can be used):

- Channel server
- Static tarball

You will learn about both approaches in this section.

Before the release of PEAR 1.4.0, the user typed:

```
$ pear remote-list
```

The PEAR installer would then use XML-RPC to send a request for the `package.listAll` method to `http://pear.php.net/xmlrpc.php`. Meanwhile, at `pear.php.net`, the database of all packages, releases, and dependencies would be queried for data (or a server-side cache accessed), and then it would be dynamically encoded into an XML-RPC response, decoded at the user end, and converted into a PHP array containing a list of all packages and their releases. This would then be formatted into a pretty list of package names and spewed out on to the screen.

XML-RPC stands for **XML Remote Procedure Call**, and is a protocol that allows a program to call a function on a remote server as if it were implemented on the local machine.

SOAP (until recently it was **Simple Object Access Protocol**, but now just "SOAP", because the developers realized there was nothing simple about it and it was a confusing name as well) is a more complex implementation of the same idea.

From the end user's perspective, there are two ways of installing a remote package using the PEAR installer. The first way is to install an abstraction, as in:

```
$ pear install PEAR
$ pear install PEAR-stable
$ pear install PEAR-1.4.3
$ pear install channel://pear/PEAR
$ pear install channel://pear.php.net/PEAR-1.4.3
```

Each of these examples takes the information passed in by the user and converts it into an actual, existing URL for retrieving a file from the channel server (pear.php. net in this case), and then downloads that package for installation. In fact, at the time of writing this chapter, each of these examples essentially converts into this:

```
$ pear install http://pear.php.net/get/PEAR-1.4.3.tgz
```

The second way of installing a package is to directly specify a URL to install, as above.

These two approaches appear to be the same to the end user. However, behind the scenes they differ significantly. When downloading and installing a package via an abstract package like PEAR or PEAR-stable, it is possible to validate all dependencies prior to downloading a single file, saving considerable time in the slowest part of installation — downloading. When installing a static URL (http://pear.php.net/ get/PEAR-1.4.3.tgz), it is necessary to download the entire package before any dependency validation can occur, possibly resulting in wasted bandwidth.

In order to convert abstract-package requests into actual physical URLs, a small amount of information is retrieved from the remote channel server. This information is used to validate dependencies prior to downloading a full package, and also to determine the correct version of a package to be downloaded based on the user's requirements.

For example, the following call first retrieves a list of all releases of PEAR organized by version number and stability:

```
$ pear upgrade PEAR-stable
```

Assume the server returns a list like this:

Version	Stability
1.5.0a1	alpha
1.4.3	stable
1.4.2	stable
1.4.1	stable
1.4.0	stable
1.4.0RC1	beta
1.4.0a14	alpha

The PEAR installer will examine version 1.5.0a1, the newest version available, and will determine it is not stable enough to install. Next, it will examine version 1.4.3 and (assuming the installed version is 1.4.2 or older) determine that this is the version that should be downloaded. Next, it will query the server and retrieve the list of dependencies for version 1.4.3, which is something like this:

Dependency type	Dependency name (if any)	Dependency version requirements
PHP		4.2.0 or newer
PEAR installer		1.3.3–1.3.6, 1.4.0a12 or newer
Package	Archive_Tar	1.3.1 or newer (1.3.1 recommended)
Package	Console_Getopt	1.2 or newer (1.2 recommended)
Package	XML_RPC	1.4.3 or newer (1.4.3 recommended)
Conflicting package	PEAR_Frontend_Web	0.4 or older
Conflicting package	PEAR_Frontend_Gtk	0.3 or older
Remote installer group	PEAR_RemoteInstaller	0.1.0 or newer
Web installer group	PEAR_Frontend_Web	0.5.0 or newer
Gtk installer group	PEAR_Frontend_Gtk	0.4.0 or newer

Before downloading PEAR 1.4.3 to install it, the PEAR installer will use this information to determine whether the package is compatible with existing installed packages, and the running version of PHP and the PEAR installer. Only if all checks pass, will the PEAR installer continue with the downloading/installation.

In addition, because PEAR 1.4.3 has a `package.xml` version 2.0, when upgrading from PEAR 1.4.0 or newer, the list of required dependencies will also be automatically downloaded and installed.

How, you might be asking yourself, can I distribute my applications and libraries to take advantage of the power and elegance built into the PEAR installer? The answer turns out to be quite simple, as evidenced by the small explosion of channel servers since the release of PEAR version 1.4.0, like eZ components (`http://www.ez.no`), and the popular pearified channel (`http://www.pearified.com`). The **Chiara_PEAR_Server** package is a fully functional PEAR channel server available for installation from the `pear.chiaraquartet.net` channel server.

Originally, Chiara_PEAR_Server was named PEAR_Server. The intention was to propose a package named "PEAR_Server" or "PEAR_Channel_Server" to the `pear.php.net` repository when the code is stable enough. Until that point, however, there are potential naming conflicts (PEAR is generally reserved for packages that originate from `pear.php.net`), and the package will be named Chiara_PEAR_Server as long as it is distributed from `pear.chiaraquartet.net`

Once you have Chiara_PEAR_Server up and running (prerequisites include a working PEAR installation and a MySQL server, plus PHP 5.0.0 or newer with the mysql or mysqli extensions), you might also consider installing Davey Shafik's public front end, **Crtx_Channel_PEAR_Server_Frontend**, available from the `crtx.org` channel. This is discussed later on in this chapter, in the section entitled *Configuring the Server; Obtaining a Front End for End Users*.

Distributing Packages through a Channel Server

When distributing packages through a channel server, there are a few things that the PEAR installer needs in order to determine which packages to install. Most important is how to communicate with the channel server. Does the server expect an incoming XML-RPC request, or is REST supported? Which XML-RPC functions are implemented, and which REST information is provided? Are there any mirrors available? What, if any, are the custom-package validation requirements?

All of these questions are answered by the simple `channel.xml` structure. Before installing Chiara_PEAR_Server, it is important to understand the underpinnings of the package, as it will make it possible to get up and run very quickly.

The channel.xml File

The first thing a channel needs in order to exist is a `channel.xml` file. The official definition of `channel.xml` in XSchema format is found at `http://pear.php.net/dtd/channel-1.0.xsd`. The `channel.xml` file *must* be named `channel.xml` and must be located in the root directory of your channel; otherwise the PEAR installer's auto-discovery mechanism will not work. For instance, the channel definition file for `pear.php.net` is located at `http://pear.php.net/channel.xml`, and the channel definition file for `pear.chiaraquartet.net` is located at `http://pear.chiaraquartet.net/channel.xml`.

This file allows the PEAR installer to quickly and efficiently determine the capabilities offered by a channel server without wasting any bandwidth. A `channel.xml` file must define the channel name (its server hostname and path), a brief summary of the channel's purpose, and then metadata used to retrieve package information for installation purposes. In addition, the `channel.xml` file allows explicit definition of channel mirrors, for the first time making it possible to mirror a channel repository.

Here is an example `channel.xml` file containing every possible tag:

```
<?xml version="1.0" encoding="ISO-8859-1"?>
<channel version="1.0" xmlns="http://pear.php.net/channel-1.0"
xmlns:xsi="http://www.w3.org/2001/XMLSchema-instance"
xsi:schemaLocation="http://pear.php.net/channel-1.0
http://pear.php.net/dtd/channel-1.0.xsd">
 <name>pear.example.com</name>
 <summary>Example channel</summary>
 <suggestedalias>example</suggestedalias>
 <validatepackage version="1.0">
    Example_Validate_Package</validatepackage>
 <servers>
  <primary ssl="yes" port="81">
   <xmlrpc path="myxmlrpc.php">
    <function version="1.0">logintest</function>
    <function version="1.0">package.listLatestReleases</function>
    <function version="1.0">package.listAll</function>
    <function version="1.0">package.info</function>
    <function version="1.0">package.getDownloadURL</function>
    <function version="1.1">package.getDownloadURL</function>
    <function version="1.0">package.getDepDownloadURL</function>
```

```
      <function version="1.1">package.getDepDownloadURL</function>
      <function version="1.0">package.search</function>
      <function version="1.0">channel.listAll</function>
     </xmlrpc>
     <soap path="soap.pl">
      <function version="1.0">customSoapFunction</function>
     </soap>
     <rest>
      <baseurl type="REST1.0">http://pear.example.com/rest/</baseurl>
      <baseurl type="REST1.1">http://pear.example.com/rest/</baseurl>
     </rest>
    </primary>
    <mirror host="poor.example.com" port="80" ssl="no">
     <xmlrpc>
      <function version="1.0">logintest</function>
      <function version="1.0">package.listLatestReleases</function>
      <function version="1.0">package.listAll</function>
      <function version="1.0">package.info</function>
      <function version="1.0">package.getDownloadURL</function>
      <function version="1.1">package.getDownloadURL</function>
      <function version="1.0">package.getDepDownloadURL</function>
      <function version="1.1">package.getDepDownloadURL</function>
      <function version="1.0">package.search</function>
      <function version="1.0">channel.listAll</function>
     </xmlrpc>
     <soap path="soap.php">
      <function version="1.0">customSoapFunction</function>
     </soap>
     <rest>
      <baseurl type="REST1.0">http://poor.example.com/rest/</baseurl>
      <baseurl type="REST1.1">http://poor.example.com/rest/</baseurl>
     </rest>
    </mirror>
   </servers>
  </channel>
```

A quick glance over the `channel.xml` file reveals a large amount of information contained in a very simple format. With this file, we tell the PEAR installer whether to use a secure connection or not, how to access the package metadata (with XML-RPC, SOAP, or REST), and how the user can access/use the channel (suggested alias, validation package).

Does PEAR Installer Support SOAP?

No. Sorry to burst your bubble, but SOAP is not necessary for the relatively simple remote communication needed by the PEAR installer; so no, SOAP is not implemented. However, should the need arise in the future, or should a channel wish to advertise custom SOAP methods implemented, the channel.xml spec supports SOAP.

However, this should only be used to inform the client that a **WSDL (Web Services Description Language)** file is present, as this format is much richer than channel.xml.

A channel may be located at a hostname's root directory (pear.example.com), or at a subdirectory (pear.example.com/subdirectory). Note that pear.example.com is a different channel from pear.example.com/subdirectory. Users would install packages from the pear.example.com/subdirectory channel as follows:

```
$ pear install pear.example.com/subdirectory/Packagename
```

Other packages would depend on packages from the pear.example.com/subdirectory channel with a package.xml tag like this:

```
<dependencies>
 <required>
  ...
   <package>
    <name>Packagename</name>
    <channel>pear.example.com/subdirectory</channel>
   </package>
  </required>
</dependencies>
```

channel.xml Tag Summary

A channel's <summary> should be a one-line description of the channel, such as "The PHP Extension and Application Repository".

The <suggestedalias> of a channel is the short name that a user can use on the command line.

For instance, the pear.php.net channel's suggested alias is pear, the pecl.php.net channel's suggested alias is pecl, and the pear.chiaraquartet.net channel's suggested alias is chiara. These aliases can be used to install packages quickly, such as:

```
$ pear install pear/DB
$ pear install chiara/Chiara_PEAR_Server
```

The alias is a suggested alias because the end user has the option to redefine the alias via the `channel-alias` command:

`$ pear channel-alias pear.chiaraquartet.net c`

This would allow the quick installation of packages with:

`$ pear install c/Chiara_PEAR_Server`

 You cannot use a channel's suggested alias in the dependencies section of a `package.xml` file. You must use the full name of channel.

A channel's validation package (controlled by the `<validatepackage>` tag) is used by the installer to perform customized validation specific to the channel. The default validation (found in the `PEAR/Validate.php` file of the PEAR package) is quite strict in terms of versioning and package naming, and attempts to implement coding standards that are specific to `pear.php.net`-based packages. These rules are stricter than the rules implemented by the `pecl.php.net` channel, and so `pecl.php.net` packages are validated using the custom channel validator found in the `PEAR/Validate/PECL.php` file of the PEAR package.

Most channels external to `pear.php.net` will want to copy the `channel.xml` file for the `pecl.php.net` channel, and use the `PEAR_Validate_PECL` validation package.

A custom channel validator must provide a class that matches the path (`PEAR/Validate/PECL.php` provides the `PEAR_Validate_PECL` class), and the package name must be identical to the class name. In addition, the class must extend `PEAR_Validate`, and implement validation with the `validate*()` methods (such as `validateVersion()`, `validatePackage()`, `validateSummary()`, and so on). In addition, the class *must* be a package distributed from the channel itself, unless the class is already loaded in memory.

 The default validation class `PEAR_Validate` and the PECL validation class `PEAR_Validate_PECL` will always be available for use by channels as custom validation packages.

To use the `PEAR_Validate_PECL` class, simply add this line to `channel.xml`:

```
<validatepackage version="1.0">
   PEAR_Validate_PECL</validatepackage>
```

The most important part of the `channel.xml` channel definition file is the `<servers>` tag. This is where the PEAR installer determines how to connect to a channel (via REST or XML-RPC) and whether any mirrors are available.

The protocols supported by the primary channel server (which must be the same as the channel name) are defined in the `<primary>` tag. Mirrors are (logically) defined by the `<mirror>` tag, which is described at the end of this section. The `<primary>` tag has a few optional attributes:

- **ssl** — legal values are *yes* and *no*. By default, `ssl` is set to *no*. If set to *yes*, then the channel server will be contacted through a secure socket.
- **port** — legal values are any positive integer. By default, `port` is set to *80*, the default HTTP port for contacting a remote web server. All data from channels are transported via HTTP, and so this is a natural choice.

REST, although very new, has several significant advantages over XML-RPC. First of all, REST content (as implemented in the PEAR channel standard) is all static files. This means that a lightweight server like thttpd can be used for high-volume sites to serve the content. In addition, channel aggregators like `http://www.pearified.com` and `http://www.pearadise.com` can crawl through your channel and provide a searchable index of the packages.

Mirroring of REST-based channels is straightforward because of the same design principles, and can be done with a simple web crawler script.

In addition, as of PEAR 1.4.3, XML-RPC support is optional in the PEAR installer, so not all users will support XML-RPC on the client-side.

There are only a few protocols recognized by the PEAR Installer. For XML-RPC, the functions recognized are:

- `logintest` (`1.0`): This simply returns true
- `package.listLatestReleases` (`1.0`): This returns an array indexed by package name containing the file size, version, state, and dependencies of its latest release, if any.
- `package.listAll` (`1.0`): This returns an array of packages with extreme details about their releases.

- `package.info` (`1.0`): This returns an array of detailed information about a single package.

- `package.getDownloadURL` (`1.0`): This returns an array with simple information about a release and a precise URL from which to download a specific release.

- `package.getDownloadURL` (`1.1`): Like version 1.0, this returns an array with simple information about a release and a precise URL. In addition, this accepts as a parameter the currently installed version of a package to narrow down the search.

- `package.getDepDownloadURL` (`1.0`): Like `package.getDownloadURL`, this returns information about a release and a precise URL to download the release from. However, as input, it accepts a dependency as parsed from `package.xml`.

- `package.getDepDownloadURL` (`1.1`): Like `package.getDepDownloadURL`, this returns information about a release and a precise URL to download the release from. It also accepts the currently installed version of the dependency as a parameter.

- `package.search` (`1.0`): Like `package.listAll`, this returns a list of packages with detailed information. However, this function limits the search of information based on input parameters.

- `channel.listAll` (`1.0`): This function returns a simple list of channels known by the current channel.

This detail is provided for informational purposes only, as XML-RPC support is deprecated for all channels.

Instead, your channel should support REST-based static files conveying information about the categories, maintainers, packages, and releases available through the channel. There are two protocols supported by the PEAR installer at the time of writing this chapter. The first is collectively known as **REST1.0**, and is defined by a set of path-related assumptions the installer makes and several XSchema files.

Inside `channel.xml`, REST is declared using a `<baseurl>` tag much like this one:

```
<baseurl type="REST1.0">http://pear.php.net/rest/</baseurl>
```

This is in fact all that the installer needs in order to fully implement REST. From this information, the installer is able to build any necessary query to determine remote information. Astute readers may have noticed a familiar word from their work with databases — query — querying is exactly what the PEAR installer does; accessing data directly rather than through an API wrapper like SOAP or XML-RPC. Unlike the procedural protocol used by XML-RPC and by RPC-based SOAP, REST is based on the principle of providing hyperlinked data, or resources, with a unique URL for each resource.

PEAR is an unusual REST interface in that it is strictly read-only, but this is an even better reason to use REST. Not only can the installer grab any data it wants without relying upon an intrinsically limited API, we can also take advantage of some of the more powerful features of the HTTP protocol itself, and implement a client-side HTTP cache, saving a tremendous amount of bandwidth and time that would otherwise be spent downloading redundant information.

This also provides an inherent security benefit to both the client and the server. The client is simply working with static XML files, and the server is not required to accept any input from the client whatsoever. In short, REST is simply the best choice from all ends.

The path structure expected by the PEAR installer when accessing REST1.0 is the following one:

```
c/ [Categories]
   CategoryName1/
       info.xml [information on the "CategoryName1" category]
       packages.xml [list of packages in the CategoryName1 category]
   CategoryName2/
       info.xml [information on the "CategoryName2" category]
       packages.xml [list of packages in the CategoryName2 category]
m/ [Maintainers]
   joe/
       info.xml [information about maintainer "joe"]
   frank/
       info.xml [information about maintainer "frank"]
   amy/
       info.xml [information about maintainer "amy"]
p/ [Packages]
   packages.xml [A list of all packages in this channel]
   PackageName1/
       info.xml [information on "PackageName1" package]
       maintainers.xml [list of maintainers of this package]
   PackageName2/
       info.xml [information on "PackageName2" package]
       maintainers.xml [list of maintainers of this package]
   PackageName3/
       info.xml [information on "PackageName3" package]
       maintainers.xml [list of maintainers of this package]
r/ [Releases]
```

```
PackageName1/ [Releases of package PackageName1]
    allreleases.xml [A brief list of all releases available]
    1.0.0.xml [summary information about version 1.0.0]
    package.1.0.0.xml [the complete package.xml of this release]
    deps.1.0.0.txt [PHP-serialized dependencies of version 1.0.0]
    0.9.0.xml [summary information about version 0.9.0]
    deps.0.9.0.txt [PHP-serialized dependencies of version 0.9.0]
    package.0.9.0.xml [the complete package.xml of this release]
    ...
    ...
    latest.txt [the latest version number, in text format]
    stable.txt [the latest stable version number, in text format]
    beta.txt  [the latest beta version number, in text format]
PackageName2/ [Releases of package PackageName2]
    allreleases.xml [A brief list of all releases available]
    1.1.0.xml [summary information about version 1.1.0]
    deps.1.1.0.txt[PHP-serialized dependencies of version 1.1.0]
    package.1.1.0.xml [the complete package.xml of this release]
    1.0.4.xml [summary information about version 1.0.4]
    deps.1.0.4.txt[PHP-serialized dependencies of version 1.0.4]
    package.1.0.4.xml [the complete package.xml of this release]
    ...
    ...
    latest.txt [the latest version number, in text format]
    stable.txt [the latest stable version number, in text format]
    beta.txt [the latest beta version number, in text format]
    alpha.txt [the latest alpha version number, in text format]
    devel.txt [the latest devel version number, in text format]
```

Note that PackageName3 has no releases, and so has no REST entry.

REST1.1 adds these files to the structure:

```
c/
    categories.xml [list of all categories]
    CategoryName1/
        packagesinfo.xml [consolidated package/release info for the entire
                                                        category]
    CategoryName2/
        packagesinfo.xml [consolidated package/release info for the entire
                                                        category]
m/
    allmaintainers.xml [list of all maintainers]
p/
r/
```

The primary purpose of REST1.1 is to enable spidering of a channel without requiring that old-fashioned directory crawling to be allowed, eliminating the potential security vulnerability intrinsic to all web servers.

A channel server mirror is defined by the `<mirror>` tag. This tag is identical to the `<primary>` tag except that it requires an additional attribute, `host`. The `host` attribute defines the URL that should be used to contact the mirror.

Obtaining Chiara_PEAR_Server

The Chiara_PEAR_Server package is easily obtained. First, you need to meet a few prerequisites. The Chiara_PEAR_Server package requires:

- PHP 5.0.0 or newer; PHP 5.1.0 or newer is recommended
- A MySQL database server
- The mysql or mysqli PHP extension
- A working web server such as Apache
- PEAR version 1.4.3 or newer

To obtain PEAR version 1.4.3 or newer, if you have PHP version 5.1.0, all you need to do on UNIX is:

```
$ cd php-5.1.0
$ ./buildconf
$ ./configure
$ make cli
$ make install-pear
```

This will install and configure PEAR automatically. Note that the `configure` command accepts a large number of options, and it is easy to learn about them through `./configure --help`.

Note that installing PHP in a web server is more complicated, and is necessary to install the Chiara_PEAR_Server package. If you are using Apache, all you need to do is pass in the `--with-apache` or `--with-apache2` directives to `configure`, and you will be up and running.

On Windows, for all PHP versions prior to version 5.2.0, you need to download the `.zip` version of PHP, *not* the `.msi` version. Then change to the directory you uncompressed PHP into and type:

```
go-pear
```

Answer the prompts and choose installation locations. In both cases, after installing, be sure to upgrade:

```
pear upgrade PEAR
```

This will ensure that you have the latest stable version of PEAR.

Installing the mysql or mysqli PHP extensions is documented at `http://www.php.net/mysql`.

After everything is ready, you can obtain the Chiara_PEAR_Server package via these simple steps:

```
$ pear channel-discover pear.chiaraquartet.net
$ pear up Chiara_PEAR_Server-alpha
```

That's it! Note that Chiara_PEAR_Server currently requires `pear.php.net` packages DB_DataObject and HTML_QuickForm, so be sure that you either have a working internet connection or have installed these packages prior to attempting to install Chiara_PEAR_Server.

Configuring the server requires running a post-installation script, which we cover in the following section.

Configuring the Server; Obtaining a Front End for End Users

Before we run the post-installation script, it is important to understand what it will need in order to function properly.

First, we need to create a MySQL user that will be used by the post-installation script to initialize the database and create tables. As such, this user needs to have `create` and `alter` permissions (use the GRANT command from within MySQL to do this). As this will be the database user used by public web scripts, for security reasons, it is best to remove `create/alter` permissions once the database has been properly initialized. The only permissions needed for everyday operations by the Chiara_PEAR_Server administrative back end are `insert/delete/update`. Note that, when upgrading Chiara_PEAR_Server, `create/alter` permissions should be re-granted again temporarily, just in case there are modifications or additions to the database.

Running the Chiara_PEAR_Server post-installation script is a simple task in PEAR, all you need to do is type:

```
$ pear run-scripts chiara/Chiara_PEAR_Server
```

The PEAR installer will walk you through several questions. After you are finished with them, and if there are no errors, the channel server will be ready for operation.

The first set of questions will ask for database-connection information, and for the `Handle` of the primary-channel administrator (you) and the name of the channel. Your `Handle` is the same as your handle or username in a `package.xml` file, and should be a single lower-cased word. For examples of choices of handles, you might browse the list of maintainers at `http://pear.php.net/accounts.php`. Your channel name must be the same as the server. So, for instance, if you are setting up a test server at localhost, your channel must be named `localhost`.

The next set of questions you will need to answer relates to the basics of your channel. It is at this time that you should have a server name in mind. Generally speaking, it is easier for users to remember a channel name if there is a direct connection to the content it serves. For instance, if your channel serves financial software, perhaps a channel name like *software.companyname.com* would be good, with an alias like *companysoftware*.

After this, information will be requested about the primary-channel administrator. Finally, information will be asked about the document root of your web server.

This section is the most important, as it will be used to create both the administrative front end used to maintain packages and upload releases, and the REST files used to support the REST protocols needed by the PEAR installer in order to function. In general, the default values provided in parentheses should be acceptable. However, it is helpful to understand the purpose of the different prompts.

- **PEAR Configuration File Location**: This specifies the location of the file that should be used to retrieve channel information. The Chiara_PEAR_Server channel simply will not function at all unless it can retrieve information about its own channel, so this value needs to be right.

- **Path to document root of web server for localhost**: This should be the full path on your local file system to the base of your web server. If your web server reads `/var/lib/web/htdocs/servername/index.php` when a user requests `http://servername/index.php`, then your document root is `/var/lib/web/htdocs/servername`.

- **name of frontend.php HTML admin frontend file**: This is the filename of your administrative front-end file. Choosing a unique file name will help prevent annoying or prevent malicious people from unwanted attempts to access the channel administrative interface.

- **temporary path to save release uploads in**: This should be a web server-writeable location in which you initially save uploaded releases.

- **port clients should connect to (443 is SSI, 80 is regular HTTP)**: Follow the instructions. If you have a typical configuration, 80 is normal for `http://` and 443 is typical for `https://`.

- **protocol clients should use to connect (http or https)**: Again, choose one of the two options.

Adding a Package and Releasing Packages

Once you have completed the post-installation script, navigate to the administrative front-end file, whose name you specified in the **name of frontend.php HTML admin frontend file** section. For instance, if your front-end file is named `foo.php`, and your channel is `localhost`, navigate to `http://localhost/foo.php`. You should see something like this:

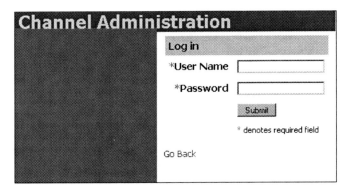

To log in as the administrator, enter the handle and password that you specified for the administrator in the post-installation script. After logging in, prior to uploading a release, you first need to create the package on the server, and then add maintainers.

When you log in, you will see a screen similar to this one:

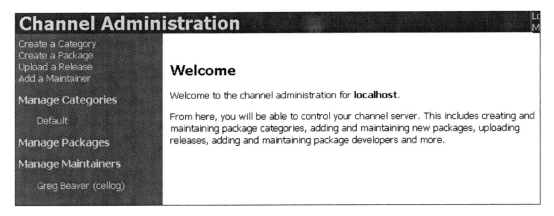

Links for configuring the channel are on the left side of the screen. To get started, you may also want to create some categories for the software you are releasing, such as "Database" or "XML Processing." For examples of categories, see `http://pear.php.net/packages.php`.

After you have created categories, you will want to add maintainers and create packages. Creating a package is straightforward. First, click **Create a Package**, and you will see a screen like the following:

Channel Administration

Create a Category
Create a Package
Upload a Release
Add a Maintainer

Manage Categories

   Default

Manage Packages

Manage Maintainers

   Greg Beaver (cellog)

Add a New Package

Channel	localhost
***Name**	Test
Category	Default ▾
***License**	BSD License
License URL	licenses/bsd-license.php
***Summary**	Test the Channel
***Description**	This tests the channel Enjoy
Parent Package	▾
Web CVS URL	
Bug Tracker URL	
Documentation URL	
	Save Changes

Fill in the required fields (marked by a red asterisk), and then click **Save Changes**. The next step is very important: before you can upload a release, you will need to create maintainers and add them as maintainers to the package. To do this, click on the **(Maintainers)** link next to your newly created package seen at the left side of the screen:

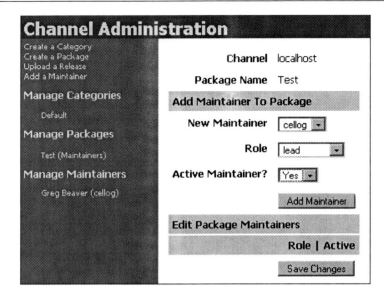

Once you have chosen the maintainer, and the role, and whether the maintainer is active, click **Add Maintainer**, and the maintainer will show up on the list of package maintainers.

Who can Upload Releases?

The channel administrator can upload a release for any package on the channel, and also package maintainers who are listed as a lead at the channel can upload packages. Note that a maintainer listed as lead in the package.xml file but not at the channel's administrative front end will *not* be able to upload a release for security reasons.

Installing a Public Channel Front End

After Chiara_PEAR_Server is configured and running, you may wish to install Davey Shafik's **Crtx_PEAR_Channel_Frontend** package from channel pear.crtx.org. The Crtx_PEAR_Channel_Frontend package provides a browsable website that allows developers to look at the packages your channel offers and how to acquire them. In addition, it has a support for linking to a bug tracker, online revision control browser, and other features. Crtx_PEAR_Channel_Frontend is to Chiara_PEAR_Server as http://pear.php.net is to the installer data provided at http://pear.php.net/rest.

Acquiring Crtx_PEAR_Channel_Frontend can be done via these steps:

```
$ pear channel-discover pear.crtx.org
$ pear upgrade crtx/Crtx_PEAR_Channel_Frontend
```

Once you have installed the package, there are some minor configurations to be performed (this may be automated by a post-installation script in future releases). First, you need to locate the pear_frontend.css file, which is installed into data_dir/Crtx_PEAR_Channel_Frontend/data/pear_frontend.css.

data_dir is the path to data (normally /usr/local/lib/php/data on UNIX, and C:\php5\PEAR\data or C:\php4\PEAR\data on Windows) as defined by the PEAR data_dir configuration variable. Once the file is located, copy this to the document root of your channel.

After copying the pear_frontend.css file, you need to create the public front-end PHP file. A sample front end follows:

```php
<?php
/**
 * An example of Crtx_PEAR_Channel_Frontend Usage
 *
 * @copyright Copyright © David Shafik and Synaptic Media 2004.
 *All rights reserved.
 * @author Davey Shafik <davey@synapticmedia.net>
 * @link http://www.synapticmedia.net Synaptic Media
 * @version $Id: $
 * @package
 * @category Crtx
 */

/**
 * Crtx_PEAR_Channel_Frontend Class
 */
require_once 'Crtx/PEAR/Channel/Frontend.php';

$frontend = new Crtx_PEAR_Channel_Frontend('localhost',
array('database' => 'mysqli://user:pass@localhost/pearserver',
      'index' => 'index.php', 'admin' => 'admin_myfront.php'));
?>
<html>
    <head>
        <title>localhost Channel Server</title>
        <link rel="stylesheet" type="text/css"
         href="pear_frontend.css" />
        <?php
```

```
            $frontend->showLinks();
        ?>
    </head>
    <body>
        <div id="top">
            <h1><a href="index.php">localhost Channel Server</a></h1>
        </div>
        <div id="menu">
            <?php
                $frontend->showMenu();
            ?>
            <div id="releases">
                <?php
                    $frontend->showLatestReleases();
                ?>
            </div>
        </div>
        <div id="content">
            <?php
            if (!$frontend->run()) {
                $frontend->welcome();
            }
            ?>
        </div>
    </body>
</html>
```

This file, if saved as index.php in the document root of the localhost web server, will provide an attractive screen similar to the following:

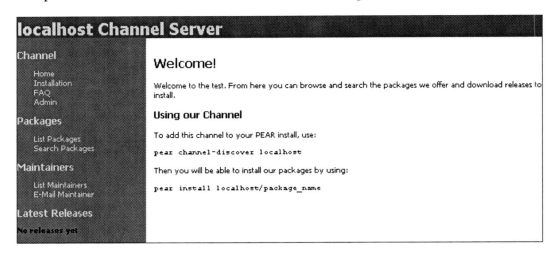

There are several nice features built into this package, including RSS feeds and the ability to email maintainers. In addition, customization of the look and feel is straightforward, accomplished through elementary modification of the `pear_frontend.css` file and the `index.php` front end. With very little work, a very attractive front end can be created. Examples of the diversity of possibilities include `http://pear.crtx.org` and `http://pear.php-tools.net`.

Distributing Pay-For-Use PHP Applications through a Channel

One of the more common questions posed about channels is: "Can my business distribute pay-for-use PHP applications through a channel, and restrict access?" The answer is a resounding yes.

The PEAR installer implements HTTP authentication through the use of the `pear login` command. To distribute your non-free applications, it is best to rely upon the strengths of web servers like Apache. For instance, by making "get" a file and using the `ForceType` directive in `httpd.conf` like the following:

```
<Location /get>
  ForceType application/x-httpd-php
</Location>
```

You can use a file named `get` that contains PHP code to process the login/password supplied by a user and direct them to a restricted package customized for their login. In fact, normal users could be directed to a trial version of the software, without any change to their installation process.

Note that the PEAR Installer only supports HTTP Basic authentication, and for a truly secure connection, SSL (HTTPS) should be used, otherwise anyone can glean the restricted passwords. Here is a sample script for the `get` file:

```
<?php
/**
 * Example restricted access file
 *
 *
 * This example requires Apache, PHP 4.3+, the mysqli extension, and
 * this code to be added to httpd.conf/.htaccess:
 * <pre>
 *  <Location "/get">
 *    ForceType application/x-httpd-php
 *  </Location>
```

```
 * </pre>
 *
 * In addition, it assumes that a mysql database is set up with users
 * who have purchased the packages, and that database connection
 * info is set in php.ini
 * @package download
 */

// shut up or we risk getting corrupted tgz files
error_reporting(0);

function error($message)
{
    header('HTTP/1.0 404 Not Found');
    echo $message;
    exit;
}

/**
 * Downloader class, handles authentication and actual downloading
 * @package download
 */
class Download
{
    var $user = false;
    var $passwd = false;
    /**
     * A list of purchased versions that the current user may
     *download
     *
     * @var array
     */
    var $purchased = array();
    /**
     * MySQL database connection
     *
     * @var resource mysqli resource
     */
    var $db;
    /**
     * Full path to offline location of package releases
     *
     * @var string
     */
```

```
var $path = '/path/to/releases/';
/**
 * Hash of package names to demo versions
 *
 * This probably should be constructed from a database,
 * but for our simple example it will be hard-coded
 *
 * @var array
 */
var $demo_versions = array(
        'Foo' => array('1.0demo'),
        'Bar' => array('1.1demo', '2.0demo'),
    );
/**
 * Hash of package names to full versions
 *
 * This probably should be constructed from a database,
 * but for our simple example it will be hard-coded
 *
 * @var array
 */
var $full_versions = array(
        'Foo' => array('1.0'),
        'Bar' => array('1.1', '2.0'),
    );


/**
 * Connect to the database, authenticate the user,
 * and grab the list
 * of purchased packages for this user
 */
function Download()
{
    // assume we have specified connection details in php.ini
    $this->db = mysqli_connect();

    if ($this->db) {
        // on database connect failure,
        // we can still download demos,
        // so fail silently
        if (isset($_SERVER['PHP_AUTH_USER']) &&
            isset($_SERVER['PHP_AUTH_PASSWD'])) {
            $this->user = $_SERVER['PHP_AUTH_USER'];
            $this->passwd = $_SERVER['PHP_AUTH_PASSWD'];
```

```php
                // construct a list of purchased packages
                // for this user/pass combination
                if ($res = mysqli_query($this->db, '
                    SELECT purchased_package FROM regusers
                    WHERE user = "' .
                     mysqli_real_escape_string($this->db,
                     $this->user) . '", AND pass = "' .
                     mysqli_real_escape_string($this->db,
                     $this->passwd) . '"')) {
                    while ($row = mysqli_fetch_row($res)) {
                        $this->purchased[$row[0]] = true;
                    }
                }
            }
        }
    }

/**
 * Feed the file to the user, or display an error
 *
 * @param string $path
 */
function downloadPackage($path)
{
    // note that we assume the case is correct
    // (the PEAR Installer always gets
    // this correct, only manual downloads will fail)
    if (!preg_match('/^([a-zA-Z0-9_]+)-(.+)\.(tar|tgz)$/',
      $path, $matches)) {
        error('invalid package/version: "' . $path . '"');
    }
    list(, $package, $version, $ext) = $matches;
    // sanity check #1: does the release exist on the disk?
    if (!file_exists($this->path . $package . '-' . $version .
        '.' . $ext)) {
        error('unknown package/release: "' . $path . '"');
    }
    // sanity check #2: do we know anything about this version?
    if (!isset($this->demo_versions[$package]) &&
         !isset($this->full_versions[$package])) {
        error('unknown package: "' . $package . '"');
    }
    // check to see if it is a demo version, and return right
    // away if so
```

```
        // if you have more purchaser downloads than demos,
        // put this after
        // purchased check for slight speed increase
        if (isset($this->demo_versions[$package]) &&
                in_array($version, $this->demo_versions[$package],
                true)) {
            $this->_doDownload($package, $version, $ext);
        }
        if (isset($this->full_versions[$package]) &&
                in_array($version, $this->full_versions[$package],
                true)) {
            if (isset($this->purchased[$package])) {
                $this->_doDownload($package, $version, $ext);
            }
            // if we get here, the user has not purchased this
            // version
            error('version "' . $version . '" is restricted and
                    must be purchased.  ' .
                'Use "pear login" to set purchase key first');
        }
        // fall-through: this line of code should be unreachable
        error('internal error, please report attempt to download "
                ' . $path . '" failed');
    }


    /**
     * Do the actual downloading.
     *
     * @param string $package
     * @param string $version
     * @param string $ext this is either "tar" or "tgz"
     * @access private
     */
    function _doDownload($package, $version, $ext)
    {
        // construct local path to the downloadable object
        $path = $this->path . $package . '-' . $version . '.' . $ext;
        header('Last-modified: ' .
            gmdate('D, d M Y H:i:s \G\M\T', filemtime($path)));
        header('Content-type: application/octet-stream');
        header('Content-disposition: attachment; filename="' .
            $path . '"');
        header('Content-length: ' . filesize($path));
        readfile($path);
```

```
        exit;
    }
}


if (!isset($_SERVER['PATH_INFO']) || $_SERVER['PATH_INFO'] == '/') {
    error('no package selected');
}
$info = explode('/', $_SERVER['PATH_INFO']);
switch (count($info)) {
    case 2:
        $dl = new Download;
        $dl->downloadPackage($info[1]);
        break;
    default:
        error('no package selected');
}

?>
```

The above example shows how easily even complex version validation can be accomplished. However, this approach does not scale very efficiently — every download is funneled through the PHP interpreter, which is considerably slower than fetching a static file. Another option, which will only work with PEAR versions 1.4.9 or newer, is to send a redirect header (402), and allow Apache to handle the actual file download. However, the savings are minimal enough over using readfile() that it may not be worth requiring users to upgrade.

Another option is to simply restrict access to files using HTTP Basic authentication in .htaccess files for individual tarballs. This is most likely to be scalable.

Then, instruct users to take these steps when first setting their login/password:

```
$ pear -d "default_channel=your.channel.com" login
Logging into your.channel.com
Username: myuser
Password: mypassword
```

The user/password will only be sent when the user requests a package from your. channel.com, taking advantage of per-channel configuration.

It is highly recommended to use SSL for your channel, so that username/password pairs are never sent in plaintext.

That's all that is necessary!

Distributing Packages through Static tarballs for Single-Client Installations

In addition to distributing packages via a channel, it is also possible to distribute a single release and post it to the Web.

PEAR 1.4.10 is needed to Install Static Releases with Dependencies

A bug in the PEAR installer prevents installing static tarballs; use version 1.4.10 or newer to get the fix for this problem.

This basically involves packaging up a release via `pear package` and then uploading it to a website, where it can then be downloaded, or installed directly via:

```
$ pear install http://www.example.com/Package-1.0.0.tgz
```

This is nothing new: the earliest versions of the PEAR installer supported this syntax. What is new is the ability to depend on these **static tarballs** in other package releases.

Who Needs this Feature?

In some cases, it is not necessary to set up a channel server. In general, it is better to set up a channel server and distribute packages in that manner. However, a common real-world situation is a PHP consultant who is providing services to multiple clients, and also maintaining their websites for them. Although every site is unique, it is very helpful to have a set of utility packages that can be used by each specific site. To provide a channel for these packages only introduces unneeded complexity.

By installing your client's website as a PEAR package, it becomes possible for you as the software consultant to easily maintain the site and regulate its content in a much stricter manner than channels allow.

Differences in package.xml and Dependencies

In order to prevent name collisions between channels and static tarballs, a static tarball's `package.xml` file cannot use the `<channel>` tag, and must instead use the `<uri>` tag. In addition, the `<uri>` tag must contain the actual location of the tarball on the Internet. If the static tarball is located at `http://www.example.com/tarballs/Package-1.0.0.tgz`, the `package.xml` file should begin with something like this:

```
<?xml version="1.0" encoding="UTF-8"?>
<package packagerversion="1.4.3" version="2.0"
xmlns="http://pear.php.net/dtd/package-2.0"
xmlns:tasks="http://pear.php.net/dtd/tasks-1.0"
xmlns:xsi="http://www.w3.org/2001/XMLSchema-instance"
xsi:schemaLocation="http://pear.php.net/dtd/tasks-1.0
http://pear.php.net/dtd/tasks-1.0.xsd
http://pear.php.net/dtd/package-2.0
http://pear.php.net/dtd/package-2.0.xsd">
 <name>Package</name>
 <uri>http://www.example.com/tarballs/Package-1.0.0</uri>
```

It is very important to notice that the uri has the file extension, .tgz, removed. This is because when providing a static tarball, it is expected that you will also provide an uncompressed .tar for users who do not have the zlib extension enabled.

To depend on this static tarball, a dependency tag like the following should be used:

```
<package>
 <name>Package</name>
 <uri>http://www.example.com/tarballs/Package-1.0.0</uri>
</package>
```

Versioning has no meaning when working with static tarballs as dependencies, and so none of the normal versioning tags (<min>, <max>, <recommended>) are allowed. However, it is possible to upgrade static tarballs.

Each static tarball package has an implied <channel>__uri</channel> tag — all static tarballs are installed/upgraded/uninstalled as if in the pseudo-channel __uri. This channel is treated just like other channels except that it cannot be modified via the channel-update command, deleted via the channel-delete command, and it does not contain a server, and so will never attempt to contact the Internet to query a remote channel server. Running pear channel-info __uri results in:

```
CHANNEL __URI INFORMATION:
==========================
Name and Server          __uri
Summary                  Pseudo-channel for static packages
Validation Package Name  PEAR_Validate
Validation Package       default
Version
SERVER CAPABILITIES
===================
TYPE                     VERSION/REST TYPE FUNCTION NAME/REST BASE
No supported protocols
```

In addition to demonstrating the qualities of the __uri pseudo-channel, it tells us that static tarball packages are validated with the same strictness that `pear.php.net` channel packages are validated (using `PEAR_Validate`). If you need flexibility of validation, it is necessary to use a channel instead of distributing your software as a static tarball.

However, this also means that after installing our static package via:

```
$ pear install http://www.example.com/tarballs/Package-1.0.0.tgz
```

It is possible to upgrade this package, should a new version be released, via:

```
$ pear upgrade http://www.example.com/tarballs/Package-1.0.1.tgz
```

In addition, it is possible to uninstall the package via the simple:

```
$ pear uninstall __uri/Package
```

If you wish to see a list of all static tarball packages installed, simply run the `list` command with the -c option:

```
$ pear list -c __uri
```

Beware the simplicity of static tarballs! If there is any chance your end user will install static tarballs from any other source, you must distribute your packages from a channel. Otherwise, the user could run into a name collision between two different packages, as illustrated by these two hypothetical install commands:

```
$ pear install http://www.example.com/tarballs/Foo-1.0.0.tgz
```

```
$ pear upgrade http://www.notexample.com/Foo-1.2.3.tgz
```

In this case, the package named `Foo` distributed from `www.example.com/tarballs` is not the same code-base as the package named `Foo` distributed from `www.notexample.com`, but the PEAR installer treats them both as if you had typed:

```
$ pear install __uri/Foo
```

```
$ pear upgrade __uri/Foo
```

In this situation, the chance of subtle to severe breakage is immediate and difficult to debug. Don't push your luck; use a channel if there is any chance that this situation could occur.

Releasing Equals Uploading

As stated earlier, the biggest advantage to using a static tarball instead of a channel is that releasing a new package simply involves uploading both a `.tgz` and a `.tar` of the release as created by the commands:

```
$ pear package
$ pear package -Z
```

It doesn't get any easier than this!

Security Issues Inherent in Remote Installation

As evidenced by the advent of internet worms taking advantage of vulnerabilities in phpBB, MySpace.com, and XML_RPC, security holes are no laughing matter, and it is critical that you are aware of the potential risks involved in installing software you have not written yourself.

Fortunately, the PEAR-installer model provides both ease of upgrading to obtain needed security fixes and intrinsic security to ensure you won't become a victim of malicious hackers just by using the PEAR installer.

Although the PEAR developers have taken every step to ensure the safety of your code without restricting its usefulness, it is still very important that you understand some basics of security, as PEAR will not be able to protect you from yourself, should you choose to use or write insecure code. There are several excellent references written recently on PHP security and on internet security in general. Both Ilia Alshanetsky's *php|architect's Guide to PHP Security* and Chris Shiflett's *Essential PHP Security* guide are a good place to start if you are unfamiliar with concepts such as escaping output, filtering input, or terms like XSS, arbitrary code execution, security through obscurity, and so on.

Many developers mistakenly develop and operate under the old golden rule: "Do unto others as you would have them do unto you." This approach is fatally flawed when you are developing code that has a component of internet connectivity. If it is possible for anyone other than you to access the PHP application you have written, then you need to assume that they have only the worst intentions.

As you design a feature, think to yourself: "How could I use this feature to modify the environment of the machine it is running on? Can I use it to perform unexpected actions?"

If the answer is "yes" or even "maybe" then the feature is intrinsically insecure and must be restricted until the answer is "no" or "only in extreme circumstances that would render it useless by other safeguards that are in place".

How do PEAR Installer and Chiara_PEAR_Server Provide Security?

The PEAR installer has taken a number of important steps to provide security. However, at its essence, the PEAR installer is ultimately designed to install arbitrary PHP code — this is its raison d'être, so the first rule of security with PEAR must be:

 Never install a package on a live, production site without first looking at the code it provides on a development server.

Extra Security beyond what PEAR Provides

Although most basic actions taken by the PEAR installer have a reasonable expectation of security, there are a few that should be avoided.

This means, for instance, that `upgrade-all` should be avoided at all costs on production servers. This command upgrades all existing packages to the latest version, which intrinsically removes your ability to control upgrades. This command is best used on a development server when testing newer versions of packages prior to upgrading them individually on the production server.

In addition, if you are installing a package distributed by a channel other than those hosted at `php.net` (`pear.php.net` and `pecl.php.net` at the time of writing this chapter), first download the package and run two commands on the package to learn more about it:

```
$ pear info Packagename-1.0.0.tgz
$ pear list-files Packagename-1.0.0.tgz
```

The first will tell you dependencies that the package has. If you don't recognize those dependencies, then you will need to perform the same steps on them.

The `list-files` command lists all files in the archive. Look for files installed into the PEAR/ subdirectory. Unless the package is providing a custom file role, custom file task, or a custom command, a package generally has no business installing files into this location, as this is the directory used by the PEAR Installer. Any files installed into this directory could be attempting to maliciously affect the way the installer works.

The most obvious exceptions to this rule are packages whose names contain PEAR such as PEAR_PackageFileManager. If a package is installing files into locations that don't appear to have much to do with the stated purpose, you should immediately be suspicious. Contact the package maintainer, and ask why the package needs to install files there.

If you do not receive a satisfactory response, notify the PEAR developer's mailing list immediately at pear-dev@lists.php.net. Any channel that attempts to provide malicious packages will be blacklisted by the PEAR installer.

Even more importantly, if there is only one thing that you remember from this book, let it be this one:

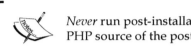 *Never* run post-installation scripts without looking over the PHP source of the post-installation script.

Post-installation scripts are by definition arbitrary PHP code. Anything that can be done in PHP can be done by a post-installation script. This includes actions like installing spyware, erasing your hard disk, and other things you probably don't intend when running the pear run-scripts command. It is never worth risking your entire system for the minor convenience of not looking at a script.

Ultimately, the chance of a malicious package being distributed by a channel is extremely low, due to the extreme ease of tracing a malicious package to the source, as well as requiring explicit user installation of the package. Both of these factors will not be enough to discourage evildoers out there unless you also are vigilant about installing packages from unknown sources, so that they are caught before any significant damage is done.

In addition, it is crucial that you upgrade the PEAR installer to version 1.4.3 or newer, and continually upgrade as new versions of the installer are released. Bugs, security issues, and minor fixes are sure to be addressed in newer versions.

Specific Security Principles Applied in Designing the PEAR Installer and Chiara_PEAR_Server

When designing and implementing the latest versions of the PEAR installer, one of the primary concerns was preventing unanticipated modifications of the user environment. By opening up the installer to take advantage of sources other than pear.php.net/pecl.php.net for packages, and adding features like post-installation scripts, custom file roles, and custom file tasks, there is an element of risk. Every new feature balances openness to legitimate activity with restriction of dangerous activity.

For instance, channels are defined by their server name. This means that you cannot automatically and secretly change the source of packages distributed by `pear.php.net`. In addition, when a user runs:

```
$ pear channel-update mychannel.example.com
```

The PEAR installer attempts to retrieve `http://mychannel.example.com/channel.xml`. A clever and evil channel administrator could in fact serve a `channel.xml` file that did not define `mychannel.example.com`. This kind of mischief is immediately detected by the installer, and is disallowed.

The addition of channel mirrors also introduces an element of risk. By defining these mirrors in `channel.xml`, it is not possible to subvert the installer into believing another channel is a legitimate mirror of a channel.

When downloading a package from a channel, strict verification of the `package.xml` is performed. If a package is downloaded from channel `foo.example.com` and its `package.xml` claims to be from `pear.php.net`, the PEAR installer refuses to install or upgrade the package, as this would be a blatant security exploit.

In addition, if the requested package name is not the same as the package name in `package.xml`, the PEAR installer will refuse to install or upgrade the package. Otherwise, it would be possible to distribute a package claiming to be `foo.example.com/Foo` and actually distributing `pear.php.net/PEAR`. The same mechanism prevents dependencies on malicious packages. A package downloaded from a channel/package must be that channel/package, period. The same is true for static tarballs. A package depended on using a static-tarball package dependency cannot distribute a channel-based package.

The most potentially dangerous features implemented in the PEAR installer are post-installation scripts and custom file tasks. Both of these features automatically execute arbitrary code when invoked. PEAR provides a layer of security by making it extremely difficult to accidentally execute malicious code. A user must:

- Explicitly install a malicious file task
- Explicitly install a package that uses the malicious file task

For post-installation scripts, the end user must:

- Explicitly install a package containing malicious post-installation scripts
- Explicitly type pear `run-scripts maliciouschannel/maliciouspackage` for the malicious package

These extra steps allow the PEAR installer to make it very difficult to accidentally compromise a system, and also to provide extreme visibility to the fact that an unusual circumstance is being executed.

It is important to note that until PEAR version 1.4.3, the PEAR installer had two security vulnerabilities. Both require a user to install a publicly distributed malicious package. Both were caused by improper implementation of the command pattern.

The command pattern is a method of providing extensibility based on loading files in a special subdirectory. The PEAR installer has been using this pattern since version 1.0 to load the actual commands shown when you type:

```
$ pear help
```

The files implementing this pattern are located in `PEAR/Command/*.php` (`PEAR/Command/Auth.php`, `PEAR/Command/Install.php`, etc.), and in PEAR versions 1.4.2 and older, these files were loaded up every time the user used the `pear` command.

This ultimately provides a vector for a malicious package to execute arbitrary PHP code in an uncontrolled situation. PEAR 1.4.3 and newer versions fix this through the implementation of an XML format describing commands. No actual PHP code is loaded unless the user explicitly requests a command other than `help`.

The command pattern is also used for custom file roles, first introduced in PEAR 1.4.x. All files `PEAR/Installer/Role/*.php` were loaded up every time the `pear` command was executed in order to construct the list of custom configuration variables. The same solution that fixed the arbitrary code execution vulnerability in commands is implemented to fix this vulnerability.

Summary

This chapter showed us that channels are designed to make it easy to install packages from any location, but difficult to compromise your system in the process, following a basic security principle: always make the easiest way to do things the most secure way.

Channels open up `pear.php.net`'s monopoly over the PEAR installer to the entire Internet. Custom-built packages distributed through your channel can even be sold and made available to specific users while co-existing peacefully with publicly available open source-packages.

6

Embedding the PEAR Installer: Designing a Custom Plug-In System

At this point, practically everything that can be done with the `pear` and `pecl` commands and existing PEAR software has been revealed. In the previous chapter, we learned how to set up a custom PEAR channel, completing our quest to master the usage of the PEAR installer. Now that we can conquer the universe of PEAR, let's look even further, and see how we can solve some of the most common problems of a web-based framework with the PEAR installer.

In this chapter, we will design a custom plug-in system for a fake blog application, called **MyBlog**. For MyBlog, we will design a plug-in system to manage templates, and use the PEAR installer to manage the details of querying the remote server for templates, handling dependencies between versioning, and doing the actual installation process as well. In addition, it will use an extension of REST on the remote server to store thumbnail images of the templates to aid in choosing a template. Of course, since this is a fake blog, the thumbnail images are pictures of cats, but they would be screenshots of the templates for a real blog.

For those who do not wish to type in every character, the code for MyBlog is always available for download directly from Packt website, or by direct installation using the PEAR installer (the fun way) via:

```
pear channel-discover pear.chiaraquartet.net
pear install MyBlog
pear run-scripts chiara/MyBlog
```

Although a bit ugly (I never claimed to be a designer), here is the administration page of our fake MyBlog application, demonstrating the image pulled from a remote server and pagination:

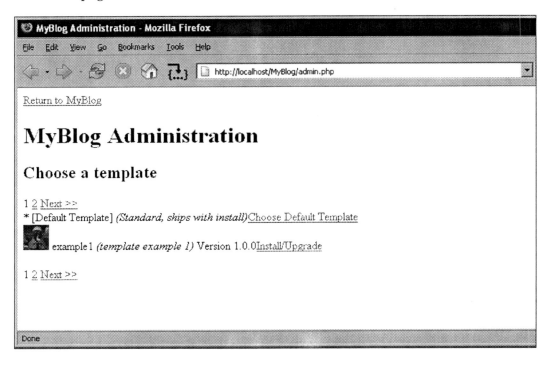

Here is a screenshot of the post-install process after clicking on the second template to install it:

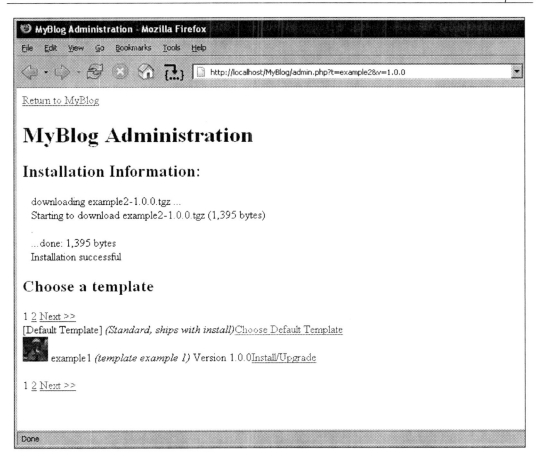

Why Embed PEAR?

In many cases, PHP applications are web applications like Content Management Systems (CMS) or some other customizable framework that can be extended. Inevitably, at some point, end users will think: "Wouldn't it be nice to just click and get the functionality that I want downloaded and installed automatically?"

At this point, it would be simpler for you to require users to install the extra functionality using the PEAR installer, but what if we don't want our application's users to have to learn how to use PEAR at all? Users who download your CMS or framework (let's call it the XYZ framework) already have a lot to learn about how the framework is designed, how to customize and use it to author content. The last thing they want to learn is some external tool just in order to install a special voting plug-in or a new template.

What we really need is a simple page on the administration portion of the XYZ framework that allows the user to browse plug-ins, and click on one for installation, without worrying about details. Even better would be to allow the possibility for advanced users to customize the remote server used for download, whether to install experimental plug-ins, and so on.

In other words, we need to embed the PEAR installer directly inside the XYZ framework, and use it to handle the dirty work of querying remote servers, retrieving plug-ins, and doing the actual installing/upgrading process.

Simplify User Choices for Installation

Embedding the PEAR installer makes it possible to focus on the important part of your application: ease of use and features for your users. The last thing you need is for confused users to simply give up on your application because you wasted too much time on re-inventing the internals, and not enough time on the visual and logical layout.

Relying on the PEAR installer will give both, more time for streamlining the look and flow of the plug-ins page, and also allow creation of simple "click here to install" links that will properly download the right plug-in for the current combination of PHP version, framework version, and requested stability level.

Eliminate Chances for Error

As always, by avoiding the urge to re-invent the wheel, this cuts down on the complexity of your application, making it much less likely that a bug will be introduced, and saving both time and future effort. PEAR's robust test suite and large community of users can be relied upon to ensure the stability of the PEAR installer, freeing you to work on the robustness of your own code.

Other Plug-In Systems

Before diving in, let's take a look at other possibilities for bundling plug-ins. There are three models currently employed by major PHP applications:

- Bundling plug-ins directly in the source code
- Using PEAR dependencies for subpackages
- Customized remote plug-in servers

Bundling Plug-Ins Directly in the Source Code

By far, the most common solution employed in the PHP world is bundling plug-ins directly in the source code. This method, as explored in previous chapters results in code that can be simpler to create, but is far more difficult to maintain, and particularly to upgrade, often resulting in out-of-date code. As recent security vulnerabilities in popular programs demonstrate, keeping code up-to-date and bug-free is not just important for minor annoyances; it can make the difference between a secure and an insecure application.

Although it is the most common choice, bundling plug-ins directly in the source code is just not a very flexible idea, and so we won't explore this idea in depth.

Subpackages – PEAR Dependencies

Using the PEAR installer's facility to manage dependencies is another approach to bundling plug-ins, which is starting to gain momentum at `pear.php.net`. This approach was first suggested by the work I did on maintaining phpDocumentor. I noticed that when implementing a new template or a new converter for phpDocumentor, this often meant that point releases of the entire phpDocumentor package was necessary even when a small change was made to a template or to a converter. Although it is not necessarily bad to be releasing often, it is important to provide a good reason for users to upgrade. In this case, it meant choosing between a release with a small change and postponing the release.

In addition, when a new experimental converter, such as the PDF converter, was introduced, the stability level of the converter could only be documented as being less stable. Users often became confused about why an unstable converter was released with a stable phpDocumentor.

All of the problems pointed to the need for a better way to handle sub-sections of an application. The answer came in the form of subpackages. Subpackages are discrete PEAR packages that define a parent-child relationship between the larger application and a smaller section of the application.

 A subpackage is a self-contained portion of an application that can not work without a parent application; for example, the **MDB2_mysqli** subpackage to the **MDB2** package. MDB2 can handle connections to the mysqli driver for MySQL versions 4.1 and newer if the MDB2_mysqli package is installed. MDB2_mysqli cannot work on its own, and requires MDB2 in order to be useful. Hence, MDB2_mysqli is a subpackage of MDB2.

Case Study: MDB2

The first package to take advantage of this idea was the MDB2 package (`http://pear.php.net/MDB2`) designed by Lukas Smith and Lorenzo Alberton to supersede the MDB package designed by Smith, Alberton, and inspired by Metabase created by Manuel Lemos.

MDB2 is a database abstraction layer that has a core set of functionality contained in the basic MDB2 package. Each specific database is accessed using a driver package. For instance, the mysqli driver is accessed using the MDB2_Driver_mysqli package. Unlike older database abstraction packages like the popular DB package, MDB2 has split off these drivers, so that each driver is maintained separately.

Each driver encapsulates the functionality of a single database, and as such, the subpackages are:

- MDB2_Driver_mssql (`http://pear.php.net/MDB2_Driver_mssql`)
- MDB2_Driver_sqlite (`http://pear.php.net/MDB2_Driver_sqlite`)
- MDB2_Driver_querysim (`http://pear.php.net/MDB2_Driver_querysim`)
- MDB2_Driver_pgsql (`http://pear.php.net/MDB2_Driver_pgsql`)
- MDB2_Driver_oci8 (`http://pear.php.net/MDB2_Driver_oci8`)
- MDB2_Driver_mysqli (`http://pear.php.net/MDB2_Driver_mysqli`)
- MDB2_Driver_mysql (`http://pear.php.net/MDB2_Driver_mysql`)
- MDB2_Driver_ibase (`http://pear.php.net/MDB2_Driver_ibase`)
- MDB2_Driver_fbsql (`http://pear.php.net/MDB2_Driver_fbsql`)

Each driver has its own versioning, stability, and more importantly, a dependency on the database driver needed.

The old model used by the DB package makes it impossible to specify dependencies on database extensions. In other words, to require the needed extensions for each driver would mean a dependency on the mssql, sqlite, pgsql, oci8, mysqli, mysql, ibase, and fbsql PHP extensions. Not only would this force unnecessary database extensions to be loaded in `php.ini`, it would cause potential conflicts between database extensions.

In addition, if a new driver was introduced, the stability of the DB package (stable) would automatically filter down to the extension. To get around this problem, DB uses a text file in the documentation describing the stability of each driver using a table. This information does not show up at installation time. If a new driver is introduced for MDB2, it could have a stability of `devel` or `alpha` even though MDB2 is `stable`. Also beneficial is the ability to release a new version of a driver independent from the parent MDB2 package. Any time a change is made to a DB driver, the entire DB package with all of its other drivers must be released.

There are some drawbacks to the MDB2 approach. First, in order to install MDB2, there are two steps needed:

```
$ pear install MDB2
$ pear install MDB2_Driver_pgsql
```

This requires knowing how to use the pear command-line as well as the name of the drivers. A common mistake (one I, myself, have made) is to instead type:

```
$ pear install MDB2
$ pear install MDB2_pgsql
```

This, of course, results in a very unhelpful error message:

```
$ pear install MDB2_pgsql
No releases available for package "pear.php.net/MDB2_pgsql"
Cannot initialize 'MDB2_pgsql', invalid or missing package file
Package "Mdb2_pgsql" is not valid
Install failed
```

In addition, uninstalling requires the same two steps, or passing both packages on the command-line:

```
$ pear uninstall MDB2 MDB2_Driver_pgsql
```

There is, however, a better way to implement the subpackages model when using package.xml version 2.0 (MDB2 still uses the original version 1.0 implementation of package.xml as of the writing of this chapter). If MDB2 were to define install groups for each driver, this would allow users to install MDB2 and the proper database. For instance, consider this approach in package.xml:

```
<dependencies>
  ...
  ...
 <group name="mssql" hint="Microsoft SQL Server driver">
  <package>
   <name>MDB2_Driver_mssql</name>
   <channel>pear.php.net</channel>
  </package>
 </group>
 <group name="sqlite" hint="SQLite driver">
  <package>
   <name>MDB2_Driver_sqlite</name>
```

```
   <channel>pear.php.net</channel>
  </package>
 </group>
 <group name="querysim" hint="Query Simulator driver">
  <package>
   <name>MDB2_Driver_querysim</name>
   <channel>pear.php.net</channel>
  </package>
 </group>
 <group name="pgsql" hint="Postgresql driver">
  <package>
   <name>MDB2_Driver_pgsql</name>
   <channel>pear.php.net</channel>
  </package>
 </group>
 <group name="oci8" hint="Oracle 8 driver">
  <package>
   <name>MDB2_Driver_oci8</name>
   <channel>pear.php.net</channel>
  </package>
 </group>
 <group name="mysqli" hint="MySQL 4.1+ driver">
  <package>
   <name>MDB2_Driver_mysqli</name>
   <channel>pear.php.net</channel>
  </package>
 </group>
 <group name="mysql" hint="MySQL 4.0- driver">
  <package>
   <name>MDB2_Driver_mysql</name>
   <channel>pear.php.net</channel>
  </package>
 </group>
 <group name="ibase" hint="Interbase driver">
  <package>
   <name>MDB2_Driver_ibase</name>
   <channel>pear.php.net</channel>
  </package>
 </group>
 <group name="fbsql" hint="Firebird driver">
  <package>
   <name>MDB2_Driver_fbsql</name>
   <channel>pear.php.net</channel>
  </package>
```

```
  </group>
  <group name="all" hint="all drivers [for uninstall]">
   <package>
    <name>MDB2_Driver_fbsql</name>
    <channel>pear.php.net</channel>
   </package>
   <package>
    <name>MDB2_Driver_ibase</name>
    <channel>pear.php.net</channel>
   </package>
   <package>
    <name>MDB2_Driver_mysql</name>
    <channel>pear.php.net</channel>
   </package>
   <package>
    <name>MDB2_Driver_mysqli</name>
    <channel>pear.php.net</channel>
   </package>
   <package>
    <name>MDB2_Driver_oci8</name>
    <channel>pear.php.net</channel>
   </package>
   <package>
    <name>MDB2_Driver_pgsql</name>
    <channel>pear.php.net</channel>
   </package>
   <package>
    <name>MDB2_Driver_querysim</name>
    <channel>pear.php.net</channel>
   </package>
   <package>
    <name>MDB2_Driver_sqlite</name>
    <channel>pear.php.net</channel>
   </package>
   <package>
    <name>MDB2_Driver_mssql</name>
    <channel>pear.php.net</channel>
   </package>
  </group>
 </dependencies>
```

This `package.xml` would allow users much more flexibility. When installing, users would see:

```
$ pear install MDB2
Install ok: channel://pear.php.net/MDB2-2.2.0
MDB2: Optional feature mssql available (Microsoft SQL Server driver)
MDB2: Optional feature sqlite available (SQLite driver)
MDB2: Optional feature querysim available (Query Simulator driver)
MDB2: Optional feature pgsql available (Postgresql driver)
MDB2: Optional feature oci8 available (Oracle 8 driver)
MDB2: Optional feature mysqli available (MySQL 4.1+ driver)
MDB2: Optional feature mysql available (MySQL 4.0- driver)
MDB2: Optional feature ibase available (Interbase driver)
MDB2: Optional feature fbsql available (Firebird driver)
MDB2: Optional feature all available (all drivers [for uninstall])
```

In order to install MDB2 with mysqli support, the user would simply type:

```
$ pear install MDB2#mysqli
```

Then, the MDB2_Driver_mysqli package would be downloaded and installed. Better yet, if at some point in time, MDB2 needs to be uninstalled, MDB2 and all of its drivers could be installed with a single command:

```
$ pear uninstall MDB2#all
```

The disadvantage to this approach is that the output when installing or upgrading MDB2 is quite wordy, and could make it difficult to notice a stray error or warning. In addition, should a new driver be released, it must be added to `package.xml` in order to make the handy feature available. On the other hand, this could be an easy way to differentiate between recommended and experimental drivers.

In short, this approach is ripe for exploration.

Custom Plug-In Systems: Remote Server

The primary drawback of the subpackage approach used by MDB2 is that the end-user of MDB2 must have a working understanding of the PEAR installer in order to properly install the drivers. This can be a significant stumbling block for graphically-oriented users who are expecting to go to one location in order to manage and use your application. For instance, bloggers expect to be able to concentrate on authoring and the tasks associated with blogging. Very few bloggers want to spend time studying the intricacies of a subtle and powerful installation system like the PEAR installer.

Instead, they want to be able to customize the look and feel of their blog, add or remove functional components of the blog at will, and do all of this from the same visual interface that is used for blogging.

If your application fits into a similar one-stop-for-everything model (and most web-based applications do fit this model), you will want to consider a way to remotely manage plug-ins and/or templates. In order to do this, your application needs to have three abstract components:

- The application plug-in manager
- The remote plug-in server
- A plug-in downloader/installer

If you've been paying attention in the last four chapters, you might note the striking similarity this bears to the goals of the PEAR Installer. Pairing up a PEAR Channel Server (refer Chapter 5) with a customized embedded PEAR installer will enable construction of a highly sophisticated plug-in manager with minimal coding.

However, before we dive into the PEAR-based solution, let's look at another example from the current state of affairs, the fantastic **Serendipity** blog (http://www.s9y.org). The Serendipity blog is an easy-to-install, highly configurable PHP-based blogging program that is very stable and feature-rich. In addition, it has had full support for PHP 5 and the latest database extensions for longer than most PHP-based blogging software, and has just recently reached the landmark of version 1.0. Serendipity is licensed under the BSD license.

Case Study: Serendipity Blog's Spartacus Plug-In Manager

The Serendipity blog manages plug-ins through the use of a specialized plug-in called **Spartacus**. Spartacus is designed to work in the same way as any other Serendipity plug-in, but has the ability to query a list of trusted servers for both plug-ins and templates for the Serendipity blog, and then to easily allow users to download and/or upgrade the plug-ins.

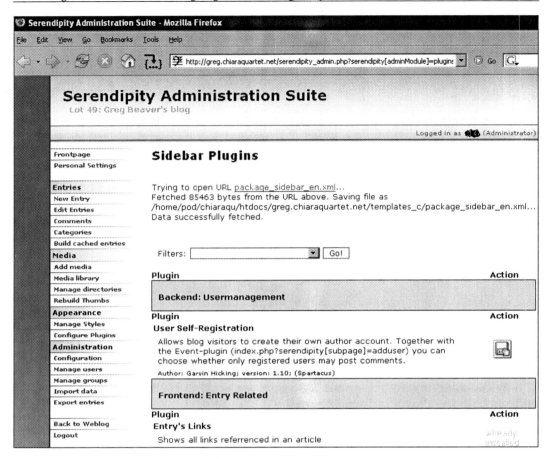

The structure of a Serendipity plug-in consists of a single PHP file located at a special location. Each plug-in resides within a separate directory, and the directory may contain a number of additional files. As such, the Spartacus plug-in consists of the `serendipity_event_spartacus.php` file and a number of different language translations for text prompts used in the plug-in.

Within the `serendipity_event_spartacus.php` file, there is a single class containing a number of different methods. The methods can be roughly grouped into a few simple categories:

- Utility methods such as `microtime_float()`, which works around deficiencies in PHP's internal `microtime()` function in PHP versions prior to 5.0.0.
- Universal plug-in methods, common to every plug-in needed for introspection of plug-in name/author, Serendipity events hooked into, configuration variables, and so on.

- XML-manipulation methods for processing remote meta-data about plug-ins and templates.

- File-management methods for installing and uninstalling plug-ins and templates.

- Remote HTTP download methods based on PEAR's **HTTP_Request** package.

- Data-caching methods for storing downloaded plug-in information.

- Methods for building plug-in list.

- Methods for building the template list and downloading the preview thumbnail.

Even with all of this functionality, the entire plug-in file weighs in at 805 lines with comments.

The basic design behind Spartacus is to fetch a descriptive XML file (basically a REST service) from a trusted server, parse information about plug-ins or templates from the file, format this into the style needed by Serendipity to display plug-ins, and then to process user requests from Serendipity's event hooks and download/install plug-ins and templates.

In order to download the plug-ins, Serendipity uses a simple but inflexible system based on static URLs. Constructing the URL for a plug-in's meta-data takes place in this manner:

```
switch($type) {
    // Sanitize to not fetch other URLs
    default:
    case 'event':
        $url_type = 'event';
        $i18n     = true;
        break;

    case 'sidebar':
        $url_type = 'sidebar';
        $i18n     = true;
        break;

    case 'template':
        $url_type = 'template';
        $i18n     = false;
        break;
}

if (!$i18n) {
    $lang = '';
```

```
        } elseif
(isset($serendipity['languages'][$serendipity['lang']])) {
        $lang = '_' . $serendipity['lang'];
    } else {
        $lang = '_en';
    }

    $mirrors = $this->getMirrors('xml', true);
    $mirror  = $mirrors[$this->get_config('mirror_xml', 0)];

    $url = $mirror . '/package_' . $url_type . $lang . '.xml';
```

The $url is then used to download the actual meta-data.

Displaying the meta-data requires a check to see if the plug-in is already installed:

```
    if (in_array($data['class_name'], $plugins)) {
        $infoplugin =&
    serendipity_plugin_api::load_plugin($data['class_name']);
        if (is_object($infoplugin)) {
            $bag     = new serendipity_property_bag;
            $infoplugin->introspect($bag);
            if ($bag->get('version') == $data['version']) {
                $installable = false;
            } elseif (version_compare($bag->get('version'),
              $data['version'], '<')) {
                $data['upgradable'] = true;
                $data['upgrade_version'] = $data['version'];
                $data['version'] = $bag->get('version');
                $upgradeLink =
                '&amp;serendipity[spartacus_upgrade]=true';
            }
        }
    }
```

Note the highlighted entries showing the essential test of whether the plug-in can be upgraded. This is used to decide whether a plug-in is clickable (installable/upgradable).

Once a user decides to download a plug-in, Spartacus cycles through the list of files from the plug-in's metadata, and downloads them one-by-one using a static URL and a ViewCVS trick (highlighted in the following example) to retrieve them. Here is the code:

```
    foreach($files AS $file) {
        $url     = $mirror . '/' . $sfloc . '/' .
        $file . '?rev=1.9999';
```

```
        $target = $pdir . $file;
        @mkdir($pdir . $plugin_to_install);
        $this->fetchfile($url, $target);
        if (!isset($baseDir)) {
            $baseDirs = explode('/', $file);
            $baseDir  = $baseDirs[0];
        }
    }
}
```

This ViewCVS trick (retrieving revision 1.9999) is a very simple way of retrieving the correct version of files to install, but it does not allow for much flexibility, and requires strict control over revisions on the server—a single mistake will bring down the installation of an entire plug-in, and potentially the entire local install of our personal Serendipity blog.

As such, the Serendipity developers have placed a to-do note at the top of the page with some ideas for the next implementation of Spartacus to address these issues:

```
/************
   TODO:

   - Perform Serendipity version checks to only install plugins
     available for version
   - Allow fetching files from mirrors / different locations -
     don't use ViewCVS hack (revision 1.999 dumbness)

***********/
```

Both of these are hard problems to solve. To solve the first, we need to be able to do some relatively complex dependency validation, and have the ability to cycle through available versions of the plug-in until we find one that can work with the current Serendipity version. The second also requires some sophisticated server/ client communication, and could add significant bloat to Serendipity as they move forward in development of Spartacus.

Fortunately, there is a solution to this issue. The PEAR installer is specifically designed to handle situations even more complex than what Serendipity's Spartacus plug-in is attempting to grapple with, and can be embedded within an application with surprisingly minimal effort.

Case Study: Seagull Framework's Embedded PEAR Installer

Seagull Framework (http://www.seagullproject.org/) is an example of a web-based application that takes an extremely minimal approach to embedding the

PEAR installer. Unlike Serendipity, Seagull is more of a general-purpose framework, designed to make it easy to build other things. Seagull provides glue and more than a few handy buzzword-friendly ideas for your development pleasure, like software patterns implemented in PHP (Front Controller, Observer, Service Locator, Task Runner, Wizard, etc.), and utility classes such as HtmlRenderer, UrlParser, and Emailer.php. A quick browse of `http://trac.seagullproject.org/browser/ trunk/lib/SGL` shows the full range of power available.

Like phpDocumentor, Seagull is available as a one-stop unzip-and-go zip file, or can be installed using the PEAR installer. Also like phpDocumentor, lesser configuration is needed on installation or upgrade, when installing via the PEAR Installer.

In addition, Seagull bases much of its work on the pre-existing foundation of PEAR packages available from `http://pear.php.net`. Seagull uses a full range of PEAR packages. Here's a sampling of some of the dependencies:

- Archive_Tar
- Cache_Lite
- Config
- Date
- DB
- DB_DataObject
- DB_NestedSet
- File
- HTML_Common
- HTML_TreeMenu
- HTML_QuickForm
- HTML_Template_Flexy
- HTTP_Header
- HTTP_Download
- Log
- Mail_Mime
- Net_Socket
- Net_Useragent_Detect
- Pager
- Text_Password
- Translation2
- Validate
- XML_Parser
- XML_Util

Whew!

In addition, Seagull makes use of the **Role_Web** package available from the
`pearified.com` channel so that installation and upgrading is a one-stop shop.

Managing all of these PEAR dependencies can be a real pain in the rear end,
especially when users are installing Seagull expecting to only use Seagull. When they
discover that they need to use the PEAR installer to manage Seagull's dependencies,
this confuses the issue.

As such, Seagull creator Demian Turner has developed the first-ever experimental
embedding of the PEAR installer into Seagull. The embedding is only available in
the latest versions of Seagull, and is considered to be of alpha-code quality, but is
well worth examining for the principles the code employs. Here is a screenshot of the
actual Seagull PEAR Manager:

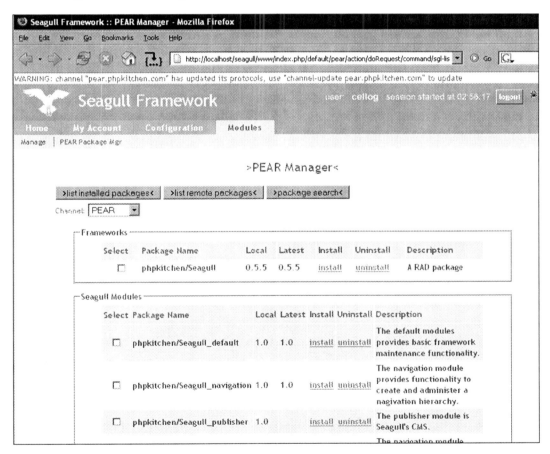

Found in the `modules/default/classes/PearMgr.php` file, the PEAR Manager for Seagull provides a customized web-based front end to any PEAR channel for listing of packages, installation, and upgrading.

Location of PearMgr.php

Seagull takes advantage of the subpackage feature of `package.xml` version 2.0, and has split its large code base into a base package and three subpackages. The `PearMgr.php` file is found in the `pear.phpkitchen.com/Seagull_Default` package, which is required and automatically installed by default when installing Seagull. Users installing from SourceForge unzip-and-go will get all the files in one zip file.

Seagull uses a customized version (one line is changed, and the templates are different) of the **PEAR_Frontend_Web** package available from `pear.php.net` along with `PearMgr.php` to manage PEAR installation/upgrading. Seagull also adds seven commands to the PEAR installer: `sgl-clear-cache`, `sgl-download`, `sgl-list-all`, `sgl-list-upgrades`, `sgl-remote-info`, and `sgl-search`. These commands are again implemented in a near carbon-copy of the PEAR equivalents, except they remove all calls to the `outputData()` method, something we will address later on in the text.

The code in `PearMgr.php` is approximately 200 lines. So, in a quarter of the length of Serendipity's Spartacus, Seagull has implemented a fully functional remote plug-in installer that can also be used to upgrade Seagull itself!

Let's take a look at the code that is used to determine which channels can be used:

```
$this->aChannels = array(
    'pear.phpkitchen.com'   => 'Seagull',
    'pear.php.net'          => 'PEAR',
    'pearified.com'         => 'Pearified',
);
```

As with Spartacus, the servers are hard-coded. However, unlike Spartacus, should any of these channels add a mirror at any point in the future, PEAR will take care of updating this information, and the mirror will automatically be available to the user.

The actual package download/install/upgrade management all uses PEAR's abstract command interface:

```
switch ($input->command) {

case 'sgl-list-all':
```

```
        if ($serialized = $cache->get($cacheId, 'pear')) {
            $data = unserialize($serialized);
            SGL::logMessage('pear data from cache',
            PEAR_LOG_DEBUG);
        } else {
            $cmd = PEAR_Command::factory($input->command,
                                                $config);
            $data = $cmd->run($input->command, $opts, $params);
            $serialized = serialize($data);
            $cache->save($serialized, $cacheId, 'pear');
            SGL::logMessage('pear data from REST call',
                                        PEAR_LOG_DEBUG);

        }
        break;

    case 'sgl-install':
    case 'sgl-uninstall':
    case 'sgl-upgrade':
        $params = array($input->pkg);
        ob_start();
        $cmd = PEAR_Command::factory($input->command, $config);
        $ok = $cmd->run($input->command, $opts, $params);
        $pearOutput = ob_get_contents();
        ob_end_clean();
        if ($ok) {
            $this->_redirectToDefault($input, $output);
        } else {
            print '<pre>';print_r($ok);
        }
        break;
}
```

The PEAR-specific code has been highlighted in the example. The entire complexity of listing packages is taken care of in just two lines of code. The same is true of installation, uninstallation, and upgrading.

There is a rather curious usage of output buffering to capture the informational output of the PEAR command. This appears to be necessary because PEAR will output information to the screen if given a choice, but in fact it is possible to capture this output without resorting to hacks. In defense of the Seagull developers, I can't imagine much more cutting edge code than what they are trying to do, and they did it without the benefit of this book!

The key to capturing the output of the PEAR-installation process is in fact to register a front-end object. The code below shows an example of the right way to do this kind of thing:

```
require_once 'PEAR/Frontend.php';
class CaptureStuff extends PEAR_Frontend
{
    public $data = array();
    function log($msg)
    {
        $this->data[] = array('log' => $msg);
    }

    function outputData($data, $command = '_default')
    {
        $this->data[] = array('outputData' => array($data,
                                            $command));
    }

    function userConfirm()
    {
        // needed to satisfy interface contract PHP4-style
    }
}
$capture = new CaptureStuff;
PEAR_Frontend::setFrontendObject($capture);
// $config is a PEAR_Config object
$cmd = PEAR_Command::factory($command, $config);
$cmd->run($command, array(), $params);
```

At this point, the `$capture->data` array contains all of the information that would normally be displayed by the PEAR installer in the order in which it occurred, and it can be ignored or displayed in appropriate fashion.

Now that we have seen an example of embedding the PEAR installer, it is time for our feature attraction: designing a customized PEAR channel-based plug-in system that takes full advantage of the customizability of the PEAR installer.

Designing a Custom PEAR Channel-Based Plug-In System

For this system, we will design a template installer that is for the fictional blogging program "MyBlog." Before we look at the code, it is important to understand the problem. Here are the requirements of the MyBlog template system:

- Templates need to have thumbnail images associated with them that the user can use to visually preview the template.

- Templates must be listed without requiring scrolling (paginated results).

- It must be possible to label new templates as experimental.

- Templates must be matched to the MyBlog version they are intended for.

- Any template that does not fit the needs of the blog user should not be displayed in the list of templates, like the templates that are too experimental or do not work with the current version of MyBlog.

- Templates must be remotely installable only from a discrete list of trusted servers.

- Template should also be installable from a locally downloaded template.

- The plug-in manager should work in PHP 5.0.0 and later. PEAR is of course compatible with PHP versions 4.2.0 and newer, but let's assume that MyBlog is designed to take advantage of some of the fantastic new features in PHP version 5. Porting this code to work with PHP 4 is a simple task, it would involve replacing a few keywords and using PEAR_Error instead of exceptions; an exercise left to the reader.

With all of these requirements, we will need to take advantage of `channel.xml`'s ability to specify customized web services, in this case an additional REST protocol for the template thumbnail images. In addition, we will need to implement a customized remote listing of templates that is able to filter out templates that will not work with the current version of MyBlog, and also filter by stability. The rest of the requirements can be handled easily by existing PEAR functionality.

In this section, we will implement the PEAR-specific code. As such, we will not make the next cool CMS out of our MyBlog program nor will we implement the server-side template thumbnail uploader, as this is a common task that is easily implemented using PHP.

In order to implement the tasks required, we will create a class responsible for downloading and processing REST from the remote server, a class for organizing and paginating the templates, and a class for downloading and installing the templates. In this case, once a template is installed, there is no need to uninstall directly, but implementing this is quite simple once the basic principles are understood. Our template switcher simply installs or upgrades if necessary.

Reusing Existing Functionality

In this example, we will make full use of the PEAR_REST class, PEAR_Downloader and PEAR_Installer classes, and also the PEAR_Config/PEAR_Registry internal classes. Re-using components is the primary strength of this approach, and is of course the primary purpose of the PEAR repository. It cannot be overstressed how important this is for both cutting down on initial development time and on the pain of debugging later on.

When re-using code, it is important to verify the stability and the robustness of the user community surrounding the code. The PEAR installer of course has an extensive test suite and both a large user base and a core of experienced and dedicated developers from all over the planet, who work to maintain and enhance the package.

Let's take a look at the classes from the PEAR package that we will be using.

PEAR Installer Infrastructure: REST and PEAR Installer Classes

The PEAR installer primarily consists of several classes. The classes that we will need to understand for our template plug-in system are:

- `PEAR_Config`
- `PEAR_Dependency2`
- `PEAR_REST`
- `PEAR_REST_11`
- `PEAR_REST_10`
- `PEAR_Downloader`
- `PEAR_Downloader_Package`
- `PEAR_Installer`

The complexity of these multi-purpose classes can be quite daunting; so let's take a step back and examine what we will actually need from each class.

PEAR_Config

The `PEAR_Config` class is used to manage basic configuration issues for the PEAR installer. As such, it is designed to easily retrieve the related internal-package registry, a REST object, and all kinds of other features that we don't really need to care about.

For our purposes, we only really need to understand three things about the `PEAR_Config` object as it is used by the PEAR installer:

- A `PEAR_Config` object is generally used as a singleton by the installer.
- The `get()` method is used to retrieve configuration values.
- The `set()` method is used to set configuration values in-memory only, and will not affect on-disk configuration files unless `writeConfigFile()` is used to save the values.

When the PEAR installer is initialized, the `PEAR_Config::singleton()` method is called with default values. If these values are not set to the proper location, then our template plug-in system will save templates in the global PEAR location. In some cases, this is great, as the application is designed to work within the system context.

If your application instead uses a local install for plug-ins internal to the application, you'll need to set all of the configuration values before performing installation tasks. Seagull Framework is a good example of a program that needs to set the configuration values, and the method with which they are set, is the best practice. Here it is:

```
$conf = &PEAR_Config::singleton();

$conf->set('default_channel', 'pear.php.net');
$conf->set('doc_dir', SGL_TMP_DIR);
$conf->set('php_dir', SGL_LIB_PEAR_DIR);
$conf->set('web_dir', SGL_WEB_ROOT);
$conf->set('cache_dir', SGL_TMP_DIR);
$conf->set('data_dir', SGL_TMP_DIR);
$conf->set('test_dir', SGL_TMP_DIR);
$conf->set('preferred_state', 'devel');
```

At a minimum, you will need to set all of the `_dir` configuration values (`bin_dir`, `doc_dir`, `ext_dir`, `php_dir`, `cache_dir`, `data_dir`, `download_dir`, `temp_dir`, and `test_dir` as of PEAR 1.4.10) to valid values. The `preferred_state` variable should be set to `stable` unless the user expects to be able to install experimental templates, then one of `beta`, `alpha`, or `devel` should be used.

We will also be using the low-level registry in order to determine whether a template package is already installed, in a similar fashion to the method used by Serendipity's Spartacus plug-in:

```
$reg = $this->_config->getRegistry();
// default channel is set to the template channel
$existing = $reg->packageInfo($template, 'version',
    $this->_config->get('default_channel'));
if (version_compare($existing, $version) === 0) {
    // installed already
    $this->log('Template set as active template');
    return true;
}
```

In our example, we retrieve the currently installed version of the template, and as a sanity check, ensure that we are not attempting to install the currently installed version.

It should be noted that it may be desirable to allow the user to force re-installation. If this is the case, the code should be modified such that if the versions are the same, the `force` option is passed to installation. The topic of installation options will be discussed in the later section on `PEAR_Installer`.

PEAR_Dependency2

The `PEAR_Dependency2` class is a simple utility class that is used by the PEAR installer to validate `package.xml` dependencies against all of the variables on a system. This is a low-level class that in fact expects as its input the unserialized XML dependency straight from `package.xml`.

In other words, consider the following to be the dependency you are trying to validate:

```
<required>
 <package>
  <name>Blah</name>
  <channel>foo.example.com</channel>
  <min>1.2.3</min>
 </package>
```

`PEAR_Dependency2` then expects the variable representing the dependency to contain this array:

```
array(
    'name' => 'Blah',
    'channel' => 'foo.example.com',
    'min' => '1.2.3');
```

For our application, the only use we have for the `PEAR_Dependency2` class is to validate the dependency against the parent MyBlog application. We need to make sure that the template actually works with the current MyBlog version. As such, the only dependency we will need to validate is the required package dependency on the MyBlog package.

This greatly simplifies the usage of `PEAR_Dependency2`, and all we need to understand is how to use it to validate a package dependency. The method that will be used for this task is called `validatePackageDependency()`, as one might expect. The method signature expects the dependency array as our example above, a boolean representing whether the dependency is required or optional, and an array containing the list of all packages that will attempt to be installed in this iteration.

The third parameter is irrelevant to our task, as only one template will ever be installed at a time, and so we will always pass an empty array for this parameter.

In PHP code, the signature as we use it will look something like:

```
$e = $d2->validatePackageDependency($pdep, true, array());
```

As with all of PEAR_Dependency2's validation methods, validatePackageDependency() returns either true, an array, or a PEAR_Error object. true is returned upon success, an array containing an error message is returned if there is a warning that does not invalidate the dependency, and a PEAR_Error object is returned if the dependency validation fails.

As PEAR's error handling allows registering a callback, it is very important to disable any callbacks while calling the dependency validation, and so our total code looks like:

```
PEAR::staticPushErrorHandling(PEAR_ERROR_RETURN);
$e = $d2->validatePackageDependency($pdep, true, array());
PEAR::staticPopErrorHandling();
if (PEAR::isError($e)) {
    // skip any template releases that cannot work
    // with the current version of MyBlog
    continue 2;
}
```

The above code tells PEAR to simply return PEAR_Error objects, temporarily ignoring any special handling the user has specified, attempt to validate the dependency, and then if the validation fails, to skip this release of the template.

How do we extract the $pdep variable from dependency information? The answer is semi-intuitive, actually. Just as the example dependency from above is extracted to an array matching the XML tag name to the tag contents, the same is true of its parent tag. The full array for the dependency above is:

```
array(
    'dependencies' => array(
        'required' => array(
            'package' => array(
                'name' => 'Blah',
                'channel' => 'foo.example.com',
                'min' => '1.2.3'
            )
        )
    )
);
```

Note that if we have more than one required package dependency, the array will look like:

```
array(
    'dependencies' => array(
        'required' => array(
            'package' => array(
                0 => array(
                    'name' => 'Blah',
                    'channel' => 'foo.example.com',
                    'min' => '1.2.3'),
                1 => array(
                    'name' => 'Dep2',
                    'channel' => 'foo.example.com',
                    'min' => '1.2.3'),
            )
        )
    )
);
```

In this case, the package tags are in fact an array of arrays. I've found that the easiest way to handle this fact is to always convert the package element into an array of itself if it does not contain numeric indices.

Here is the full code that accesses the required package dependencies of a template:

```
if (isset($dep['required']) && isset($dep['required']['package'])) {
    if (!isset($dep['required']['package'][0])) {
        $dep['required']['package'] =
            array($dep['required']['package']);
    }
    foreach ($dep['required']['package'] as $pdep) {
        if (!isset($pdep['channel'])) {
            // skip uri-based dependencies
            continue;
        }
        if ($pdep['name'] == 'MyBlog' &&
            $pdep['channel'] == 'pear.chiaraquartet.net') {
            PEAR::staticPushErrorHandling(PEAR_ERROR_RETURN);
            $e = $d2->validatePackageDependency($pdep, true,
            array());
            PEAR::staticPopErrorHandling();
            if (PEAR::isError($e)) {
                // skip any template releases that cannot work
                // with the current version of MyBlog
                continue 2;
            }
        }
    }
}
```

Note that we can also easily skip static uri-based dependencies by checking for the existence of a <channel> tag inside the dependency, and skip them accordingly.

PEAR_REST and PEAR_REST_10/PEAR_REST_11

The PEAR_REST class is a general utility class for downloading, parsing, and caching remote REST files. It is the REST equivalent of the XML-RPC class that PEAR used to use for the older XMLRPC-based channels. We will be using this low-level class to retrieve the PNG thumbnail image of templates, and so need to know about the retrieveCacheFirst() method. This method first checks the local cache, and if it exists, never attempts to query the remote server. If the file has never been downloaded, it then queries the server to retrieve it. As its argument, it simply takes a full URL to the file that one wishes to download, and returns its contents in a string.

The retrieveData() method takes a different approach. If the cache is young enough (3600 seconds by default), it is used without querying the remote server. After this time, the server is queried using HTTP 1.1 and HTTP caching is used to determine whether downloading is necessary. This can dramatically cut down on bandwidth, as the file is only downloaded if there are any changes.

It should be noted that XML files (as identified by the Content-Type HTTP header) will be parsed into an array automatically by both retrieveData() and retrieveCacheFirst().

PEAR_REST_10 and PEAR_REST_11 implement the REST1.0 and REST1.1 PEAR REST standards, as described in Chapter 5. As such, the methods implement ways of retrieving useful information from the raw REST data, such as the download information for a particular package, or a list of all packages with current releases. For our purposes, we will need to implement a modified version of the REST1.1 listAll() method, one that filters out incompatible templates and experimental templates. In order to implement this, we will cut-and-paste the code from PEAR_REST_11 and use that to implement our listTemplates() method by tweaking the loop that examines each package.

Cutting and pasting from PEAR_REST_11 may seem to be an unclean approach, as cut and paste is generally frowned upon by the purist element, but in our case it demonstrates an important principle of the REST design. If PEAR still used XML-RPC, it would in fact be impossible to implement the customized template listing that we desire, because some of the necessary information would have been stripped on the server side.

The REST model makes the data available and expects the client to do any filtering of that data. This is in fact both more efficient and more flexible, which cuts down on programming time and completely eliminates the hacks that used to be necessary when designing around the system.

Yes, we are cutting and pasting, but the code is drawing upon a well-defined, simple system of remote REST resources, and so we can be certain it will continue to work as the standards evolve.

In our simple implementation, the only method of the REST1.0-based PEAR_REST_10 class that we will need is the getDownloadURL() method, in order to implement our customized template download with restrictions. The API signature of getDownloadURL() is somewhat complex, and as such it is helpful to examine the actual code with comment from the PEAR_REST_10 class:

```
/**
 * Retrieve information about a remote package to be downloaded
 * from a REST server
 *
 * @param string $base The uri to prepend to all REST calls
 * @param array $packageinfo an array of format:
 * <pre>
 *   array(
 *     'package' => 'packagename',
 *     'channel' => 'channelname',
 *   ['state' => 'alpha' (or valid state),]
 *    -or-
 *   ['version' => '1.whatever']
 * </pre>
 * @param string $prefstate Current preferred_state config
 * variable value
 * @param bool $installed the installed version of this package
```

```
 * to compare against
 * @return array|false|PEAR_Error see {@link _returnDownloadURL()}
 */
function getDownloadURL($base, $packageinfo, $prefstate, $installed)
```

getDownloadURL() either returns a PEAR_Error or an array. The array will contain
an associative index url if the package can be successfully downloaded. If none of
the releases meet the conditions specified, then the url index will not be present. As
such, we can use the getDownloadURL() method very simply:

```
$info = $this->getDownloadURL($this->_restBase,
    array('channel' => $this->_channel,
          'package' => $templateName,
          'version' => $version),
    $this->_config->get('preferred_state', null, $this->_channel),
    $installed
);
if (PEAR::isError($info)) {
    throw new MyBlog_Template_Exception($info->getMessage());
}
if (!isset($info['url'])) {
    throw new MyBlog_Template_Exception('Template "' .
    $templateName . '" cannot be installed');
}
if (!extension_loaded("zlib")) {
    $ext = '.tar';
} else {
    $ext = '.tgz';
}
return $info['url'] . $ext;
```

Note that the url does not contain a file extension, as this is determined by the
presence of the zlib extension. If we have zlib, then we can download the compressed
release, and save some time and bandwidth. Otherwise, the uncompressed .tar is
downloaded and installed instead.

This is essentially all of the code needed to successfully leverage our remote server
querying! The only task left is the actual downloading and installation.

PEAR_Downloader and PEAR_Downloader_Package

Downloading, as seen by the PEAR installer, is not just a simple task of grabbing a
url via HTTP and saving its contents locally as a file. The PEAR installer intelligently
downloads the right version of a package based on its dependencies and the local
system, and also automatically downloads package dependencies in certain situations.

The `PEAR Downloader` mechanism understands three different kinds of installable packages:

- Abstract package names, i.e. `pear install PEAR` or `pear install PEAR-beta`
- Absolute URLs, i.e. `pear install http://pear.example.com/Blah-1.2.3.tgz`
- Local files, i.e. `pear install /path/to/Blah-1.2.3.tgz`

Each instance is handled very differently. Local packages are handled in a simple manner, as one might expect. Absolute URLs are first downloaded, and then treated in the same way as local packages. Abstract packages are treated very differently. No downloading is performed until the installer is sure that all dependencies have been satisfied. This ensures that if a complex application's dependencies are not satisfied, no time or bandwidth will be wasted downloading large package files.

However, in each of the three kinds of downloadable packages, the way their dependencies and package information are handled is the same. Because of this, to avoid unnecessary code duplication, the three kinds of downloadable packages are abstracted into the `PEAR_Downloader_Package` class. Many of the API functions in `PEAR_Downloader` and `PEAR_Installer` expect or return a `PEAR_Downloader_Package` object.

However, the first and most important method to investigate is `PEAR_Downloader`'s `download()` method. This method expects as input a simple array of strings, each string representing one of the three forms of downloadable packages. Here is an example demonstrating all three:

```
$downloader->download(array('PEAR-beta',
    'http://pear.example.com/Blah-1.2.3.tgz',
    '/path/to/Blah-1.2.3.tgz'));
```

Options can be passed to the `download()` method, but they must be specified when creating the `PEAR_Downloader` object:

```
$ui = PEAR_Frontend::singleton();
$config = PEAR_Config::singleton();
$downloader = new PEAR_Downloader($ui, $config,
    array('force' => true));
```

Options available for the `PEAR_Downloader` include `force`, `downloadonly`, `soft`, `offline`, `packagingroot`, `nodeps`, `pretend`, `ignore-errors`, `nocompress`, `alldeps`, `onlyreqdeps`, and `installroot`. In other words, the options that are displayed when executing `pear help install` are all available, plus the internal option `downloadonly`, which is used by the `pear download` command.

The main options that may be of interest when designing an embedded PEAR installer are the following:

- `force`: This option forcibly installs even if dependencies are invalid, or the package is already installed. The best usage of the `force` option is to repair a corrupted installation.

- `offline`: This option prevents any attempts to contact remote servers, and can be useful in installation settings.

- `nocompress`: This option instructs the installer to download uncompressed `.tar` files rather than `.tgz` files, and is useful when the zlib extension is not present.

- `nodeps`: This option prevents the downloader from attempting to validate dependencies, or from downloading required package dependencies.

- `pretend`: This option instructs the downloader to simply grab a listing of all packages that would be downloaded, and to return that, but not to do any actual downloading. This is useful for displaying to the user what packages would need to be installed or upgraded.

- `alldeps`/`onlyreqdeps`: These options instruct the downloader to automatically download package dependencies. The `onlyreqdeps` option instructs the installer to only download required dependencies, whereas `alldeps` downloads all dependencies. `onlyreqdeps` is obsolete by `package.xml` version 2.0, but is still useful for the many PEAR packages that still use `package.xml 1.0` at `pear.php.net`

The `download()` method can return either a `PEAR_Error` object, or an `array()`. Now this is where things get a bit tricky. A `PEAR_Error` object is only returned in the case of an egregious error, such as the inability to access the local package registry, or some other exceptional circumstance. An array is returned in other situations.

In other words, if downloading fails because every package passed in failed dependency validation, an empty array will be returned instead of a `PEAR_Error` object. Another way of thinking about this is that `PEAR_Downloader` is smart enough to skip downloads that fail and continue with ones that work, rather than halting the entire download experience just because a single package depended on the Gronk_Wzilnk package and it was unavailable.

To handle the condition of multiple errors, `PEAR_Downloader` provides a `getErrorMsgs()` method that should always be checked after downloading. This method implements a simplistic array of multiple error messages that predated the advanced `PEAR_ErrorStack` class (and incidentally helped to inspire its creation). As such, the code that is used to download should look something like this:

```
$ui = PEAR_Frontend::singleton();
$config = PEAR_Config::singleton();
$dl = new PEAR_Downloader($this, array('upgrade' => true),
                                        $this->_config);
// download the actual URL to the template
$downloaded = $dl->download(array($info));
if (PEAR::isError($downloaded)) {
    throw new MyBlog_Template_Exception($downloaded->getMessage());
}
$errors = $dl->getErrorMsgs();
if (count($errors)) {
    $err = array();
    foreach ($errors as $error) {
        $err[] = $error;
    }
    if (!count($downloaded)) {
        throw new MyBlog_Template_Exception('template "' .
        $template . '" installation failed:<br />' .
        implode('<br />', $err));
    }
}
```

Note that the `$info` variable should contain the name of a template to download in this example.

PEAR_Installer

Finally, we arrive at the `PEAR_Installer` class. This class is monstrous, containing code for handling file transactions, basic installation, uninstallation, and is very significantly huge in general. `PEAR_Installer` is also one of the oldest classes in the PEAR package and although it has undergone a serious liposuction in PEAR 1.4.0 and newer, it will undergo further trimming in future versions.

File transactions are the PEAR installer's equivalent to database transactions. When installing a package, the PEAR installer either fully installs a package, or rolls back the installation completely. When upgrading, the PEAR installer makes a backup copy of the previous version. If there are any problems in upgrading, the previous version is completely restored. This ensures that it is *impossible* for the package to be in a half-installed state of limbo if there are any errors.

The method we need to know about in our quest to install templates is not too surprisingly named `install()`. The `install()` method is rather flexible in its input, because of backwards compatibility. It is possible to pass in the array that we would pass to `PEAR_Downloader->download()`, but this results in significant guesswork by the installer to do what you should be telling it to do, and is deprecated. It is better is to pass in the array returned from `PEAR_Downloader->downloader()`, and to prepare for installation with a few helper methods:

```
// $templatePackage is the PEAR_Downloader_Package object
// we received from PEAR_Downloader->download()
// $template is the name of the template
$ui = PEAR_Frontend::singleton();
$installer = new PEAR_Installer($ui);
$packages = array($templatePackage);
// always upgrade
$installer->setOptions(array('upgrade' => true));
$installer->sortPackagesForInstall($packages);
PEAR::staticPushErrorHandling(PEAR_ERROR_RETURN);
$err = $installer->setDownloadedPackages($packages);
if (PEAR::isError($err)) {
    PEAR::staticPopErrorHandling();
    throw new MyBlog_Template_Exception($err->getMessage());
}
// always upgrade
$info = $installer->install($templatePackage,
                            array('upgrade' => true));
PEAR::staticPopErrorHandling();
if (PEAR::isError($info)) {
    throw new MyBlog_Template_Exception($info->getMessage());
}
if (is_array($info)) {
    $this->log('Installation successful');
    return true;
} else {
    throw new MyBlog_Template_Exception('install of "' . $template .
                                            '" failed');
}
```

Code specifically relating to installation has been highlighted above. Again, because the `PEAR_Installer` class is an older relic within the larger PEAR installer package, some of the things we can do with `PEAR_Downloader` must be done manually. For instance, options should be set with the `setOptions()` method. In addition, packages should be sorted for proper installation order using `sortPackagesForInstall()`. This ensures that dependencies are installed before any packages that depend upon them, as packages are installed by the `install()`

method one at a time, without knowledge of the other packages that are being installed. This system also helps to ensure that the packages are rarely left in a dangerously corrupted state, should installation of any package fail.

Immediately preceding the `install()` method, packages that have already been downloaded should be registered as such so that pre-installation validation is only performed once. This must be done with the `setDownloadedPackages()` method.

Now that we have a working understanding of the internals of the PEAR installer, let's look at the server side.

Extending REST with Custom Information

In order to implement thumbnails on the server, first we need to implement customized REST for the server. Let's look at a typical `channel.xml`:

```
<?xml version="1.0" encoding="ISO-8859-1" ?>
<channel version="1.0" xmlns="http://pear.php.net/channel-1.0"
  xmlns:xsi="http://www.w3.org/2001/XMLSchema-instance"
  xsi:schemaLocation="http://pear.php.net/dtd/channel-1.0
  http://pear.php.net/dtd/channel-1.0.xsd">
 <name>pear.chiaraquartet.net/template</name>
 <summary>Template example for book</summary>
 <suggestedalias>te</suggestedalias>
 <servers>
  <primary>
   <rest>
    <baseurl type="REST1.0">
     http://pear.chiaraquartet.net/Chiara_PEAR_Server_REST/</baseurl>
    <baseurl type="REST1.1">
     http://pear.chiaraquartet.net/Chiara_PEAR_Server_REST/</baseurl>
   </rest>
  </primary>
 </servers>
</channel>
```

If we want to add support for our custom-thumbnail REST, all we need to do is add another `<baseurl>` tag:

```
<?xml version="1.0" encoding="ISO-8859-1" ?>
<channel version="1.0" xmlns="http://pear.php.net/channel-1.0"
  xmlns:xsi="http://www.w3.org/2001/XMLSchema-instance"
  xsi:schemaLocation="http://pear.php.net/dtd/channel-1.0
  http://pear.php.net/dtd/channel-1.0.xsd">
 <name>pear.chiaraquartet.net/template</name>
```

```
<summary>Template example for book</summary>
<suggestedalias>te</suggestedalias>
<servers>
 <primary>
  <rest>
   <baseurl type="REST1.0">
    http://pear.chiaraquartet.net/template/Chiara_PEAR_Server_REST/
   </baseurl>
   <baseurl type="REST1.1">
    http://pear.chiaraquartet.net/template/Chiara_PEAR_Server_REST/
   </baseurl>
   <baseurl type="MyBlogThumbnail1.0">
    http://pear.chiaraquartet.net/template/thumbnails/
   </baseurl>
  </rest>
 </primary>
</servers>
</channel>
```

The new `baseurl` is highlighted in the previous example. This allows us to retrieve a template-thumbnail image with one line of code:

```
$thumbnail = $this->_rest->retrieveCacheFirst($this->_thumbnailBase .
$template . '/' . $version . 'thumbnail.png');
```

Now, we finally have enough information to actually implement our template manager!

Designing a Lightweight Installer Plug-In: The Code At Last

For our fake MyBlog, we will use this directory tree:

```
MyBlog/
    Template/
        Exceptions.php
        Fetcher.php
        Interfaces.php
        Lister.php
        REST.php
        Config.php
        Main.php
        admin.php
        index.php
        image.php
        blogsetup.php
```

The PEAR-embedding occurs in the files located in the `Template/` subdirectory. The blog is implemented in the abstract by the `Config.php` and `Main.php` files, and the actual web files are `index.php`, `image.php`, and `admin.php`. We won't concern ourselves yet with the design of the fake MyBlog blog. If you would like to play around with the fake MyBlog, you can install it via these steps:

```
$ pear channel-discover pearified.com
$ pear install pearified/Role_Web
$ pear run-scripts pearified/Role_Web
$ pear channel-discover pear.chiaraquartet.net
$ pear up chiara/MyBlog
$ pear run-scripts chiara/MyBlog
```

> The MyBlog package from `pear.chiaraquartet.net` makes use of a post-installation script that has no prompting of the user at all. We'll go into the details of the post-install script in greater detail later on, as it shows another side of PEAR's versatility.

MyBlog_Template_IConfig and MyBlog_Template_Config

Let's dive in; first, `Interfaces.php`:

```php
<?php
interface MyBlog_Template_IConfig
{
    function getTemplateChannel();
    function getCurrentTemplate();
}
```

It doesn't get much simpler than that! This allows flexibility, loosely coupling the embedded PEAR with the template's configuration, and is always a good idea.

Next, let's see the exception class, yet another example of complexity:

```php
<?php
class MyBlog_Template_Exception extends Exception {}
?>
```

OK, I know what you're thinking: that doesn't look very complex. Actually, you're right. I was just kidding. Now for the real deal; let's start off with the configuration class from the MyBlog package. The `getTemplateChannel()` and getCurrentTemplate() methods are simply hard-coded strings for our sample application, but let's look at the getPearConfig() method:

```
/**
 * Get a customized PEAR_Config object for our blog template system
 * @return PEAR_Config
 */
function getPearConfig(){
    static $done = false;
    $config = PEAR_Config::singleton();
    if ($done) {
        return $config;
    }
    $config->set('php_dir', '@php-dir@' . DIRECTORY_SEPARATOR .
                 'MyBlog' . DIRECTORY_SEPARATOR . 'templates');
    $config->set('data_dir', '@php-dir@' . DIRECTORY_SEPARATOR .
                 'MyBlog' . DIRECTORY_SEPARATOR . 'templates');
    // restrict to the template channel
    $config->set('default_channel', $this->getTemplateChannel());
    return $config;
}
```

Much like Seagull's package, we grab the PEAR_Config singleton object and customize it. However, our blog's templates will only ever use the php or the data role, and we are installing into an internal PEAR repository, so we can take advantage of PEAR's replacement tasks (see Chapter 3 for a refresher on replacement tasks) to replace @php-dir@ with the value of the php_dir configuration variable on the local computer.

In essence, this instructs PEAR to install templates into @php-dir@/MyBlog/templates/, which is exactly where we want them to go.

MyBlog_Template_REST

Next, let's jump into the REST class. This class simply requires a PEAR_Config object to get started, and is instantiated in admin.php like so:

```
$conf = new MyBlog_Config;
$config = $conf->getPearConfig();
$rest = new MyBlog_Template_REST($config, array());
```

Again, simplicity of use is the emphasis. Let's see the complete code:

```
<?php
/**
 * MyBlog_Template_REST
```

```
 *
 * PHP version 5
 *
 * @package    MyBlog
 * @author     Greg Beaver <cellog@php.net>
 * @copyright  2006 Gregory Beaver
 * @license    http://www.opensource.org/licenses/bsd-license.php BSD
License
 * @version    CVS: $Id$
 * @link       http://pear.chiaraquartet.net/index.php?package=MyBlog
 * @since      File available since Release 0.1.0
 */
/**
 * Helper files from PEAR and our template system
 */
require_once 'PEAR/REST/11.php';
require_once 'PEAR/REST/10.php';
require_once 'PEAR/Dependency2.php';
require_once 'MyBlog/Template/Exceptions.php';
/**
 * Perform needed remote server REST actions.
 *
 * This class implements multiple inheritance through the
 * use of magic functions, and extends both PEAR_REST_11 and
 * PEAR_REST_10, giving preference to PEAR_REST_11 methods.
 *
 * The class provides modified listAll in the listTemplates() method,
 * and a way to retrieve a template thumbnail image with
 * getThumbnail().
 */
class MyBlog_Template_REST extends PEAR_REST_11
{
    private $_config;
    private $_rest10;
    private $_restBase;
    private $_thumbnailBase;
    private $_channel;
    function __construct(PEAR_Config $config, $options = array())
    {
        parent::PEAR_REST_11($config, $options);
        $this->_config = $config;
        $this->_rest10 = new PEAR_REST_10($config, $options);
    }
```

```php
/**
 * Implement multiple inheritance of REST_10 and REST_11
 *
 * @param string $func
 * @param array $params
 * @return mixed
 */
function __call($func, $params)
{
    if (method_exists($this->_rest10, $func)) {
        return call_user_func_array(array($this->_rest10, $func),
        $params);
    }
}


/**
 * Retrieve the web location of a template's thumbnail image
 *
 * @param string $base URL to template REST as defined in
 * channel.xml
 * @param string $template Template name (package name on the
 * template server)
 * @param string $version Template version
 */
function getThumbnail($template, $version)
{
    return $this->_rest->retrieveCacheFirst($this->_thumbnailBase
  . $template . '/' . $version . 'thumbnail.png');
}


/**
 * Retrieve the Base URL for a channel's template REST
 *
 * @param string $channel
 * @return string
 * @throws MyBlog_Template_Exception
 */
function getRESTBase($channel)
{
    $reg = $this->_config->getRegistry();
    if (PEAR::isError($reg)) {
        throw new MyBlog_Template_Exception('Cannot initialize
        registry: ' . $reg->getMessage());
    }
```

```php
        $chan = $reg->getChannel($channel);
        if (PEAR::isError($chan)) {
            throw new MyBlog_Template_Exception('Cannot retrieve
            channel: ' . $chan->getMessage());
        }
        if
         ($chan->supportsREST($this->_config->get('preferred_mirror',
                                              null, $channel)) &&
            $base = $chan->getBaseURL('MyBlogThumbnail1.0',
            $this->_config->get('preferred_mirror', null,
                                              $channel))) {
            $this->_thumbnailBase = $base;
            return $chan->getBaseURL('REST1.1',
                $this->_config->get('preferred_mirror', null,
                                              $channel));
        }
        throw new MyBlog_Template_Exception('Unable to retrieve
            MyBlogThumbnail1.0 base URL for channel ' . $channel);
}


/**
 * Set the channel that will be used for the template locating
 *
 * @param string $channel
 */
function setTemplateChannel($channel)
{
    $this->_channel = $channel;
    $this->_restBase = $this->getRESTBase($channel);
}


/**
 * Retrieve information about all templates
 *
 * This code demonstrates the power of REST. The
 * REST information retrieved is in fact the same
 * information used by the list-all and remote-list
 * commands. However, the list-all/remote-list commands
 * do not return dependency and release information.
 *
 * This function uses dependency/release information to strip
 * away templates that are not compatible with the current
 * MyBlog version, or are not stable enough.
 * @param string $base
```

```
 * @return array
 */
function listTemplates()
{
    $d2 = new PEAR_Dependency2($this->_config, array(),
          array('package' => '', 'channel' => ''));
    $packagesinfo = $this->_rest->retrieveData($this->_restBase .
        'c/Templates/packagesinfo.xml');
    if (PEAR::isError($packagesinfo)) {
        return;
    }

    if (!is_array($packagesinfo) || !isset($packagesinfo['pi']))
    {
        return;
    }
    if (!is_array($packagesinfo['pi']) ||
                            !isset($packagesinfo['pi'][0])) {
        $packagesinfo['pi'] = array($packagesinfo['pi']);
    }

    $ret = array();
    $preferred_state = $this->_config->get('preferred_state',
                                    null, $this->_channel);
    // calculate the set of possible states sorted
    // from most stable -> least stable
    $allowed_states =
      array_flip($this->betterStates($preferred_state, true));
    foreach ($packagesinfo['pi'] as $packageinfo) {
        $info = $packageinfo['p'];
        $package = $info['n'];
        $releases = isset($packageinfo['a']) ?
                              $packageinfo['a'] : false;
        $deps = isset($packageinfo['deps']) ?
                    $packageinfo['deps'] : array('b:0;');
        $version_numbers = array(
            'latest' => false,
            'stable' => false,
            'beta' => false,
            'alpha' => false,
            'devel' => false,
        );

        if ($releases) {
```

```php
        if (!isset($releases['r'][0])) {
            $releases['r'] = array($releases['r']);
        }
        if (!isset($deps[0])) {
            $deps = array($deps);
        }
        foreach ($releases['r'] as $i => $release) {
            $dep = unserialize($deps[$i]['d']);
            if (isset($dep['required']) &&
                    isset($dep['required']['package'])) {
                if (!isset($dep['required']['package'][0])) {
                    $dep['required']['package'] =
                     array($dep['required']['package']);
                }
                foreach ($dep['required']['package'] as
                                                    $pdep) {
                    if (!isset($pdep['channel'])) {
                      // skip uri-based dependencies
                      continue;
                    }
                    if ($pdep['name'] == 'MyBlog' &&
                      $pdep['channel'] ==
                                'pear.chiaraquartet.net') {
        PEAR::staticPushErrorHandling(PEAR_ERROR_RETURN);
        $e = $d2->validatePackageDependency($pdep, true,
                                                    array());
        PEAR::staticPopErrorHandling();
                    if (PEAR::isError($e)) {
          // skip any template releases that cannot work
          // with the current version of MyBlog
          continue 2;
                    }
                  }
                }
            }
            // skip releases that are not stable enough
            if (!isset($allowed_states[$release['s']])) {
               continue;
            }
            if (!$version_numbers['latest']) {
                $version_numbers['latest'] = $release['v'];
            }
            if (!$version_numbers[$release['s']]) {
                $version_numbers[$release['s']] =
```

```
                                                    $release['v'];
                    }
                }
            }
            if (!$version_numbers['latest']) {
                // no valid releases found, so don't list this
                // template
                continue;
            }
            $ret[$package] = array('versions' => $version_numbers,
                                         'info' => $info);
        }
        return $ret;
    }


    /**
     * Retrieve the download URL for a template
     *
     * @param string $templateName template package name to download
     * @param string $version template version to download
     * @throws MyBlog_Template_Exception
     * @return string
     */
    function getTemplateDownloadURL($templateName, $version)
    {
        $reg = $this->_config->getRegistry();
        if (PEAR::isError($reg)) {
            throw new MyBlog_Template_Exception($reg->getMessage());
        }
        $installed = $reg->packageInfo($templateName, 'version',
$this->_channel);
        if ($version === $installed) {
            throw new MyBlog_Template_Exception('template version "'
            . $version . '" is already installed');
        }
        $info = $this->getDownloadURL($this->_restBase,
            array('channel' => $this->_channel,
                  'package' => $templateName,
                  'version' => $version),
            $this->_config->get('preferred_state', null,
                                     $this->_channel),
            $installed);
        if (PEAR::isError($info)) {
            throw new MyBlog_Template_Exception($info->getMessage());
```

```
        }
        if (!isset($info['url'])) {
            throw new MyBlog_Template_Exception('Template "' .
            $templateName . '" cannot be installed');
        }
        if (!extension_loaded("zlib")) {
            $ext = '.tar';
        } else {
            $ext = '.tgz';
          }
        return $info['url'] . $ext;
    }
}
?>
```

MyBlog_Template_Lister

Next, let's look at the template lister. The template lister class, aptly named `MyBlog_Template_Lister`, is instantiated via this simple code:

```
require_once 'MyBlog/Template/Lister.php';
require_once 'MyBlog/Config.php';
$blog_config = new MyBlog_Config;
$lister = new MyBlog_Template_Lister($blog_config->getPearConfig());
$lister->setConfigObject($blog_config);
```

The primary method is `listRemoteTemplates()` and is called like so:

```
list($info, $pager) = $lister->listRemoteTemplates(1);
```

The only argument passed is the number of templates to include per page. We pass in 1 because there are two sample templates for the fake MyBlog that are available for installation. The return value is a simple array, the first element being an array of data for paging, and the second a Pager object.

This is a good example of code re-use. When I first began designing the code, I thought it would make the most sense to write my own pager, as it seemed to be a 10-line deal. However, as I began to get further involved in the implementation, the complexity spiraled out of control, and I quickly switched to using the Pager package from `pear.php.net` (http://pear.php.net/Pager). This well-designed package is also well documented, and became a 10-minute job to implement the paging.

From our example usage above, the `$info` variable is an array in our application, and its format is simply a numerically indexed array of arrays:

```
array(
    array(
        'name' => 'example1',
        'version' => '1.0.0',
        'summary' => 'sample template 1'
    ),
    array(
        'name' => 'example2',
        'version' => '1.0.0',
        'summary' => 'sample template 2'
    )
);
```

This can be iterated over quite easily to create the template listings. At this point, we should be ready to see the entire `MyBlog_Template_Lister` class file `Lister.php`:

```php
<?php
/**
 * MyBlog_Template_Lister
 *
 * PHP version 5
 *
 * @package    MyBlog
 * @author     Greg Beaver <cellog@php.net>
 * @copyright  2006 Gregory Beaver
 * @license    http://www.opensource.org/licenses/bsd-license.php BSD
 * License
 * @version    CVS: $Id$
 * @link       http://pear.chiaraquartet.net/index.php?package=MyBlog
 * @since      File available since Release 0.1.0
 */
/**
 * Helper files from PEAR and our template system
 */
require_once 'PEAR/Config.php';
require_once 'Pager/Pager.php';
require_once 'MyBlog/Template/Interfaces.php';
require_once 'MyBlog/Template/REST.php';
/**
 * List local and remote templates, also the currently active
 * template.
 * @package    MyBlog
 * @author     Greg Beaver <cellog@php.net>
 * @copyright  2006 Gregory Beaver
 * @license    http://www.opensource.org/licenses/bsd-license.php BSD
```

```
 * License
 * @version      @package_version@
 * @link         http://pear.chiaraquartet.net/index.php?package=MyBlog
 */
class MyBlog_Template_Lister
{

    /**
     * Template Configuration object
     *
     * This is used to grab configuration information for
     * the current setup
     * @var Template_IConfig
     */
    private $_templateConfig;
    /**
     * PEAR configuration object
     *
     * @var PEAR_Config
     */
    private $_pearConfig;
    /**
     * Current template channel
     *
     * @var string
     */
    private $_templateChannel;
    /**
     * Current template name
     *
     * @var string
     */
    private $_currentTemplate;
    /**
     * Template REST object
     *
     * @var MyBlog_Template_REST
     */
    private $_rest;

    /**
     * @param PEAR_Config $config
     */
    function __construct(PEAR_Config $config = null)
```

```
{
    if ($config === null) {
        $config = PEAR_Config::singleton();
    }
    $this->_pearConfig = $config;
    $this->_rest = new MyBlog_Template_REST($config, array());
}

/**
 * Set our channel for retrieving templates
 * @param string $channel
 * @throws MyBlog_Template_Exception
 */
function setTemplateChannel($channel)
{
    $reg = $this->_pearConfig->getRegistry();
    if (PEAR::isError($reg)) {
        throw new MyBlog_Template_Exception('Unable to initialize
                            Registry: ' . $reg->getMessage());
    }
    if (!$reg->channelExists($channel)) {
        throw new MyBlog_Template_Exception('Channel "' .
        $channel . '" is unknown');
    }
    // translate alias into actual channel name
    $channel = $reg->channelName($channel);
    $this->_templateChannel = $channel;
    $this->_rest->setTemplateChannel($channel);
}

/**
 * set the name of the current template package
 * @param string $template
 */
function setCurrentTemplate($template)
{
    $this->_currentTemplate = $template;
}

/**
 * Set up the current template configuration, and
 * extract the channel and current template name.
 *
 * @param Template_IConfig $config
```

```
     */
    function setConfigObject(MyBlog_Template_IConfig $config)
    {
        $this->_templateConfig = $config;
        $this->setTemplateChannel($config->getTemplateChannel());
        $this->setCurrentTemplate($config->getCurrentTemplate());
    }

    /**
     * Retrieve a listing of templates
     *
     * This method paginates the data, and prepares it for display by
     * the view portion of our template lister.
     * @param int $pageNumber Page number to retrieve
     * @param int $templatesPerPage number of templates to display
     * per-page
     * @return array
     * @throws MyBlog_Template_Exception indirectly, from internal
     * REST calls
     */
    function listRemoteTemplates($templatesPerPage = 15)
    {
        $info = $this->_rest->listTemplates();
        if ($info === null || PEAR::isError($info)) {
            return array();
        }
        $params = array(
            'mode'        => 'Jumping',
            'perPage'     => $templatesPerPage,
            'delta'       => 2,
            'itemData'    => $info);
        $pager = Pager::factory($params);

        $ret = array();
        $data = $pager->getPageData();
        foreach ($data as $template => $info) {
            $ret[] = array(
                        'name' => $template,
                        'version' => $info['versions']['latest'],
                        'summary' => $info['info']['s']);
        }
        return array($ret, $pager);
    }
}
?>
```

MyBlog_Template_Fetcher

Finally, let's look at the installation manager class, which we'll call `MyBlog_Template_Fetcher`. This class is also instantiated simply, but is a bit more involved than the other classes:

```
require_once 'MyBlog/Template/Fetcher.php';
require_once 'MyBlog/Template/REST.php';
$conf = new MyBlog_Config;
$config = $conf->getPearConfig();
$rest = new MyBlog_Template_REST($config, array());
$rest->setTemplateChannel($conf->getTemplateChannel());
$fetch = MyBlog_Template_Fetcher::factory($rest, $config);
```

A `MyBlog_Template_Fetcher` is instantiated by a factory method because it must be registered as a `PEAR_Frontend` object in order for the PEAR installer to use it to display output (as was mentioned in the section on the Seagull Framework earlier).

The primary method we'll be using is `installTemplate()` and its usage is like so:

```
try {
    $fetch->installTemplate($_GET['t'], $_GET['v']);
    $out = '';
    foreach ($fetch->log as $info) {
        if ($info[0] == 'log') {
            $out .= '    ' . htmlspecialchars($info[1]) .
            '<br />';
        } else {
            $out .= htmlspecialchars($info[1]) . '<br />';
        }
    }
    // this is safe because installTemplate throws an exception
    // if the template or version are not valid PEAR package/version
    // so input is validated by this point
    $_SESSION['template'] = $_GET['t'];
    define('MYBLOG_OUTPUT_INFO', $out);
} catch (MyBlog_Template_Exception $e) {
    define('MYBLOG_OUTPUT_INFO', '<strong>ERROR:</strong> ' .
    $e->getMessage());
}
```

As the `MyBlog_Template_Fetcher` class mimics a `PEAR Frontend`, we need to define three methods, `log()`, `outputData()`, and `userConfirm()`. The first two simply store their input in an internal array for display later, and the last is a dummy method that will not be used in our sample application.

Finally, here is the class listing:

```php
<?php
/**
 * MyBlog_Template_Fetcher
 *
 * PHP version 5
 *
 * @package    MyBlog
 * @author     Greg Beaver <cellog@php.net>
 * @copyright  2006 Gregory Beaver
 * @license    http://www.opensource.org/licenses/bsd-license.php BSD
 * License
 * @version    CVS: $Id$
 * @link       http://pear.chiaraquartet.net/index.php?package=MyBlog
 * @since      File available since Release 0.1.0
 */

/**
 * Helper files from PEAR and our template system
 */
require_once 'MyBlog/Template/REST.php';
require_once 'MyBlog/Template/Exceptions.php';
require_once 'PEAR/Frontend.php';
require_once 'PEAR/Downloader.php';
require_once 'PEAR/Installer.php';
require_once 'PEAR/Config.php';
require_once 'PEAR/Downloader/Package.php';
/**
 * Control installation/upgrade of MyBlog templates
 *
 * This class makes full use of internal PEAR classes to
 * download and install/upgrade templates. To simplify
 * things, the class extends PEAR_Frontend and stores output
 * from installation directly in the class, which can then
 * be retrieved for proper formatting and display to the user
 * by the MyBlog application.
 *
 * This class should be instantiated using the factory method as in:
 * <code>
 * $fetch = MyBlog_Template_Fetcher::factory($rest, $config);
 * </code>
 * @package    MyBlog
 * @author     Greg Beaver <cellog@php.net>
```

```
 * @copyright   2006 Gregory Beaver
 * @license     http://www.opensource.org/licenses/bsd-license.php BSD
 * License
 * @version     @package_version@
 * @link        http://pear.chiaraquartet.net/index.php?package=MyBlog
 */
class MyBlog_Template_Fetcher extends PEAR_Frontend
{
    /**
     * @var Template_Fetcher_REST
     */
    private $_rest;
    /**
     * @var PEAR_Config
     */
    private $_config;

    /**
     * log messages from installation are stored here
     *
     * @var array
     */
    public $log = array();

    private function __construct(MyBlog_Template_REST $rest,
    PEAR_Config $config)
    {
        $this->_config = $config;
        $this->_rest = $rest;
    }

    /**
     * Create a new MyBlog_Template_Fetcher object, and register it
     * as the global frontend for PEAR as well
     *
     * @param MyBlog_Template_REST $rest
     * @param PEAR_Config $config
     * @return MyBlog_Template_Fetcher
     */
    static function factory(MyBlog_Template_REST $rest,
                            PEAR_Config $config){
        $a = new MyBlog_Template_Fetcher($rest, $config);
        // configure this as the frontend for all installation
        // processes
```

```
        PEAR_Frontend::setFrontendObject($a);
        return $a;
}

/**
 * Record a message logged while installing
 *
 * This can be used later to display information on the
 * template install/download
 * process
 * @param string $msg
 */
function log($msg){
    $this->log[] = array('log', $msg);
}

/**
 * Dummy function required to be a valid UI
 *
 * @return boolean
 */
function userConfirm(){
    return true;
}

/**
 * Record a message logged while installing
 *
 * This can be used later to display information on the
 * template install/download
 * process
 * @param string $msg
 */
function outputData($msg, $command){
    $this->log[] = array('out', $msg);
}

/**
 * Given a template package name, download and install a template
 *
 * @param string $templatePath template package name
 * @param string $version template package version to install
 * @throws MyBlog_Template_Exception
 */
```

```
function installTemplate($template, $version){
    // first, validate input
    if (!preg_match(PEAR_COMMON_PACKAGE_NAME_PREG, $template)) {
        throw new MyBlog_Template_Exception('SECURITY ALERT:
        template is not ' . 'a valid package name, aborting');
    }
    if (!preg_match(PEAR_COMMON_PACKAGE_VERSION_PREG, $version))
      {
        throw new MyBlog_Template_Exception('SECURITY ALERT:
        template version ' . 'is not a valid version, aborting');
    }
    $reg = $this->_config->getRegistry();
    // default channel is set to the template channel
    $existing = $reg->packageInfo($template, 'version',
        $this->_config->get('default_channel'));
    if (version_compare($existing, $version) === 0) {
        // installed already
        $this->log('Template set as active template');
        return true;
    }
    // convert the template package into a discrete download URL
    $info = $this->_rest->getTemplateDownloadURL($template,
    $version);
    if (PEAR::isError($info)) {
        throw new MyBlog_Template_Exception($info->getMessage());
    }
    // download the template and install
    // (use PEAR_Downloader/Installer)
    $dl = new PEAR_Downloader($this, array('upgrade' => true),
                              $this->_config);
    // download the actual URL to the template
    $downloaded = $dl->download(array($info));
    if (PEAR::isError($downloaded)) {
        throw new MyBlog_Template_Exception
                                    ($downloaded->getMessage());
    }
    $errors = $dl->getErrorMsgs();
    if (count($errors)) {
        $err = array();
        foreach ($errors as $error) {
            $err[] = $error;
        }
        if (!count($downloaded)) {
            throw new MyBlog_Template_Exception('template "' .
```

```
                        $template . '" installation failed:<br />' .
                        implode('<br />', $err));
                }
            }
            $templatePackage = $downloaded[0];
            $installer = new PEAR_Installer($this);
            // always upgrade
            $installer->setOptions(array('upgrade' => true));
            $packages = array($templatePackage);
            $installer->sortPackagesForInstall($packages);
            PEAR::staticPushErrorHandling(PEAR_ERROR_RETURN);
            $err = $installer->setDownloadedPackages($packages);
            if (PEAR::isError($err)) {
                PEAR::staticPopErrorHandling();
                throw new MyBlog_Template_Exception($err->getMessage());
            }
            // always upgrade
            $info = $installer->install($templatePackage,
                    array('upgrade' => true));
            PEAR::staticPopErrorHandling();
            if (PEAR::isError($info)) {
                throw new MyBlog_Template_Exception($info->getMessage());
            }
            if (is_array($info)) {
                $this->log('Installation successful');
                return true;
            } else {
                throw new MyBlog_Template_Exception('install of "' .
                $template . '" failed');
            }
        }
    }
}
?>
```

This is all we need to embed the PEAR installer, a mere 610 lines of code including extensive comments!

The MyBlog Post-Install Script

To wrap up the installation, we'll need a post-install script to initialize the environment. This time, let's see the code before we learn about it:

```
<?php
require_once 'MyBlog/Config.php';
require_once 'PEAR/Downloader.php';
```

```php
require_once 'PEAR/PackageFile/v2/rw.php';
/**
 * Post-installation script for the fake MyBlog blog.
 *
 * This script simply creates the templates/ subdirectory, if
 * not present, and makes it world-writeable
 * @version @package_version@
 */
class blogsetup_postinstall
{
    private $_where;
    /**
     * @var PEAR_Config
     */
    private $_config;

    function __construct(){
        $this->_where = '@php-dir@' . DIRECTORY_SEPARATOR .
        'MyBlog' . DIRECTORY_SEPARATOR . 'templates';
    }

    /**
     * Initialize the post-installation script
     *
     * @param PEAR_Config $config
     * @param PEAR_PackageFile_v2 $pkg
     * @param string|null $lastversion Last installed version.
     * Not used in this script
     * @return boolean success of initialization
     */
    function init(&$config, &$pkg, $lastversion){
        $this->_config = $config;
        return true;
    }

    /**
     * Run the script itself
     *
     * @param array $answers
     * @param string $phase
     */
    function run($answers, $phase){
        $ui = PEAR_Frontend::singleton();
        $blogconf = new MyBlog_Config;
```

```
$conf = $blogconf->getPearConfig();
$reg = $conf->getRegistry();
// we need the blog and template channels to be discovered
$conf->set('auto_discover', true);
if (!$reg->channelExists('pear.chiaraquartet.net/template',
            true)) {
    // make sure the registry directory exists, or this fails
    System::mkdir(array('-p', $conf->get('php_dir')));
    $dl = new PEAR_Downloader($ui, array(), $conf);
    $dl->discover('pear.chiaraquartet.net/template');
}
if (!$reg->channelExists('pear.chiaraquartet.net', true)) {
    // make sure the registry directory exists, or this fails
    System::mkdir(array('-p', $conf->get('php_dir')));
    $dl = new PEAR_Downloader($ui, array(), $conf);
    $dl->discover('pear.chiaraquartet.net');
}
// for dependency purposes fake the MyBlog package in
// our sub-install
$reg->deletePackage('MyBlog', 'pear.chiaraquartet.net');
$fake = new PEAR_PackageFile_v2_rw;
$fake->setPackage('MyBlog');
$fake->setChannel('pear.chiaraquartet.net');
$fake->setConfig($this->_config);
$fake->setPackageType('php');
$fake->setAPIStability('stable');
$fake->setReleaseStability('stable');
$fake->setAPIVersion('1.0.0');
$fake->setReleaseVersion('@package_version@');
$fake->setDate('2004-11-12');
$fake->setDescription('foo source');
$fake->setSummary('foo');
$fake->setLicense('BSD License');
$fake->clearContents();
$fake->addFile('', 'foor.php', array('role' => 'php'));
$fake->resetFilelist();
$fake->installedFile('foor.php', array('attribs' =>
                                array('role' => 'php')));
$fake->setInstalledAs('foor.php', 'foor.php');
$fake->addMaintainer('lead', 'cellog', 'Greg Beaver',
                                'cellog@php.net');
$fake->setNotes('blah');
$fake->setPearinstallerDep('1.4.3');
$fake->setPhpDep('5.0.0');
```

```
$reg->addPackage2($fake);

do {
    if (file_exists($this->_where)) {
        if (OS_UNIX) {
            if (!fileperms($this->_where) == 0777) {
                chmod($this->_where, 0777);
                $ui->outputData('set templates directory to
                be world-writeable');
                break;
            }
            $ui->outputData('templates directory already
            initialized');
            break;
        } else {
            $ui->outputData('templates directory ' .
            $this->_where . ' already created');
            break;
        }
    } else {
        $ui->outputData('creating template directory ' .
        $this->_where);
        System::mkdir(array('-p', $this->_where));
        chmod($this->_where, 0777);
    }
} while (false);
if (file_exists($this->_where . DIRECTORY_SEPARATOR .
    'default')) {
    System::rm(array('-rf', $this->_where .
                DIRECTORY_SEPARATOR . 'default'));
}
mkdir($this->_where . DIRECTORY_SEPARATOR . 'default');
copy('@php-dir@' . DIRECTORY_SEPARATOR . 'MyBlog' .
    DIRECTORY_SEPARATOR . 'Template' . DIRECTORY_SEPARATOR .
    'default' . DIRECTORY_SEPARATOR . 'body.tpl.php',
    $this->_where . DIRECTORY_SEPARATOR . 'default' .
    DIRECTORY_SEPARATOR . 'body.tpl.php');
copy('@php-dir@' . DIRECTORY_SEPARATOR . 'MyBlog' .
    DIRECTORY_SEPARATOR . 'Template' . DIRECTORY_SEPARATOR .
    'default' . DIRECTORY_SEPARATOR . 'head.tpl.php',
    $this->_where . DIRECTORY_SEPARATOR . 'default' .
     DIRECTORY_SEPARATOR . 'head.tpl.php');
$ui->outputData('default template copied');
return true;
```

```
        }
    }
    ?>
```

As with all post-installation scripts, this one has a class named according to the file name with DIRECTORY_SEPARATOR replaced by '_' in the class name, and _postinstall appended. In other words, since this is blogsetup.php and is in the root directory of our package.xml, our class name is blogsetup_postinstall. The script has required init() and run() methods.

This script is needed because we are going to set up a customized internal PEAR repository inside the working directory of the application. In other words, the templates will be installed in their own internal universe with a unique registry and configuration settings. As such, the directory structure will need to look like the following:

```
pear/
    .filemap
    .registry/
        pear.reg
        . . .
        . . .
         [global PEAR registry]
        .channel.pear.chiaraquartet.net/
            myblog.reg
    .channels/
        pear.chiaraquartet.net.reg
    MyBlog/
        templates/
            .filemap
            .registry/
            .channel.pear.chiaraquartet.net_template/
                .channels/
                    pear.chiaraquartet.net.reg
                    pear.chiaraquartet.net_template.reg
```

Registry files for installed templates will go in pear/MyBlog/templates/.registry/.channel.pear.chiaraquartet.net_template/.

In addition, in our design, the default template is copied over and is always available, so that the blog can work out of the box.

Although we did not implement this in the fake blog or the lister class, the `MyBlog_Template_Fetcher` class is also capable of installing local template files, which allows blog maintainers to design their own templates, or modify existing ones and install them directly. For a challenge, see if you can implement local listing of installed templates. Hint: check out code from the `PEAR_Registry` class found in `PEAR/Registry.php`, and how it is used by the `pear list` command in `PEAR/Command/Registry.php`.

The last new feature to look at is how we can retrieve and display the thumbnail images for each template. To do this, we'll set up a small file called `image.php`, and our `src` attributes in `<img>` tags will refer to it in order to grab images.

`image.php` simply takes a template name and version, and then grabs the remote thumbnail. It is important that a file of this nature is not in fact reading local files and displaying them, as it constitutes a severe security risk. For instance, if `image.php` simply read local files relative to the current path and displayed them, a few guesses later, something like this request would retrieve the `/etc/passwd` file:

```
image.php?i=../../../etc/passwd
```

In our case, if the requested template doesn't have a thumbnail on the remote server, it won't be displayed. Here is `image.php`:

```php
<?php
require_once 'MyBlog/Template/REST.php';
require_once 'MyBlog/Config.php';
$conf = new MyBlog_Config;
$a = new MyBlog_Template_REST($conf->getPearConfig());
$a->setTemplateChannel($conf->getTemplateChannel());
// sanitize input and retrieve a thumbnail image
// make certain that URL passed in fits on 1 line, so
// we don't magically send headers to the server by mistake
echo $a->getThumbnail(str_replace(array("\n", "\r"), array('', ''),
                $_GET['t']),
                str_replace(array("\n", "\r"), array('', ''),
                $_GET['v']));
?>
```

Again, note the highlighted security-conscious code. Security must always be a concern!

The Rest of the Fake MyBlog Package

At this point, we have examined all of the PEAR-specific code, so let's look at the fake MyBlog package (again, installable from `pear.chiaraquartet.net` as package `chiara/MyBlog`). First, let's see the code for the `MyBlog_Config` class, controlling basic configuration needs:

```php
<?php
/**
 * For MyBlog_Template_IConfig interface
 */
require_once 'MyBlog/Template/Interfaces.php';
require_once 'PEAR/Config.php';
// hard-coded "database" stuff for demonstration purposes.
// edit this code to try other stuff
if (!isset($_SESSION['template'])) {
    $_SESSION['template'] = '#default';
}
class MyBlog_Config implements MyBlog_Template_IConfig{
    function getTemplateChannel(){
        return 'pear.chiaraquartet.net/template';
    }

    function getCurrentTemplate(){
        return $_SESSION['template'];
    }

    /**
     * Get a customized PEAR_Config object for our blog
     * template system
     * @return PEAR_Config
     */
    function getPearConfig(){
        static $done = false;
        $config = PEAR_Config::singleton();
        if ($done) {
            return $config;
        }
        $config->set('php_dir', '@php-dir@' . DIRECTORY_SEPARATOR .
            'MyBlog' . DIRECTORY_SEPARATOR . 'templates');
        $config->set('data_dir', '@php-dir@' . DIRECTORY_SEPARATOR .
            'MyBlog' . DIRECTORY_SEPARATOR . 'templates');
        // restrict to the template channel
        $config->set('default_channel', $this->getTemplateChannel());
        return $config;
    }
}
```

Simplicity itself, eh? Next, we'll look at the main MyBlog class. To implement the MyBlog, I chose to use the excellent Savant3 package (installable from the `savant.pearified.com` channel at `http://savant.pearified.com`), a PHP template system that uses PHP as the templating language. For our fake blog, we will have two (or three) template files, one for the `<head>` element, another optional template for the attributes of the `<body>` tag, and a third for the contents of the blog. For our sample templates, we only use `head.tpl.php` and `body.tpl.php`. Here is the main blog file, `MyBlog_Main`:

```php
<?php
require_once 'Savant3.php';
class MyBlog_Main extends Savant3{
    /**
     * Output the <head> block
     */
    function doHead(){
        // output user-specific stuff
        $this->display('head.tpl.php');
        // output plugin-related stuff (dummy, but here
        // for example purposes)
        $this->displayPluginHead();
    }

    /**
     * Output any onload parameters, etc.
     */
    function doBodyTag(){
        try {
            $onload = $this->fetch('onload.tpl.php');
            if ($onload) {
                echo 'onload="' . $onload . '"';
            }
        } catch (Savant3_Exception $e) {
            // ignore
        }
    }

    /**
     * Display blog body
     *
     */
    function doBody(){
        $this->display('body.tpl.php');
    }

    function displayPluginHead(){
```

```
            return; // do nothing
        }
    }
?>
```

We have a few unused methods that are there just to show what could be done. Templates are actually displayed by `index.php`, which consists of this code:

```php
<?php
session_start();
require_once 'MyBlog/Main.php';
require_once 'MyBlog/Config.php';
$blog_config = new MyBlog_Config;
// default template is #default, so strip #
// other templates must be valid package names, and so
// can't contain #
$blog = new MyBlog_Main(array(
    'template_path' => '@php-dir@' . DIRECTORY_SEPARATOR . 'MyBlog' .
        DIRECTORY_SEPARATOR . 'templates' . DIRECTORY_SEPARATOR .
        str_replace('#', '', $blog_config->getCurrentTemplate()),
    'exceptions' => true));
$blog->title = 'Example MyBlog Blog';
$blog->content = 'blah blah blah here is my fake article';
?><!DOCTYPE HTML PUBLIC "-//W3C//DTD HTML 4.0 Transitional//EN">
<html>
  <head>
    <?php $blog->doHead(); ?>
  </head>
  <body <?php $blog->doBodyTag(); ?>>
    <?php $blog->doBody(); ?>
    <a href="admin.php">Administer Blog</a>
  </body>
</html>
```

The actual templates should be looked at for completeness, so here is `head.tpl.php` from one of the sample templates:

```php
<title><?php echo $this->title; ?></title>
  <link href="css.php/example1/index.css" type="text/css" />
```

And `body.tpl.php`:

```php
<div class="topbar">
<h1 id="pageTitle"><?php echo $this->title ?></h1>
</div>
<div class="leftbar">Left Bar
```

```
</div>
<div class="centerbar">Center Bar<br />
<?php echo $this->content; ?>
</div>
<div class="rightbar">Right Bar
</div>
```

Now I think it is clear why I keep referring to MyBlog as a fake blog! To demonstrate how the templates are installed, here is a `package.xml` file from the example1 template:

```
<?xml version="1.0" encoding="UTF-8"?>
<package packagerversion="1.4.11" version="2.0"
xmlns="http://pear.php.net/dtd/package-2.0"
xmlns:tasks="http://pear.php.net/dtd/tasks-1.0"
xmlns:xsi="http://www.w3.org/2001/XMLSchema-instance"
xsi:schemaLocation="http://pear.php.net/dtd/tasks-1.0
http://pear.php.net/dtd/tasks-1.0.xsd
http://pear.php.net/dtd/package-2.0
http://pear.php.net/dtd/package-2.0.xsd">
  <name>example1</name>
  <channel>pear.chiaraquartet.net/template</channel>
  <summary>fake MyBlog template example 1</summary>
  <description>fake MyBlog template example 1</description>
  <lead>
    <name>Greg Beaver</name>
    <user>cellog</user>
    <email>cellog@php.net</email>
    <active>yes</active>
  </lead>
  <date>2006-08-19</date>
  <time>13:14:58</time>
  <version>
    <release>2.0.0</release>
    <api>1.0.0</api>
  </version>
  <stability>
    <release>stable</release>
    <api>stable</api>
  </stability>
  <license uri="http://www.opensource.org/licenses/bsd-
                        license.php">BSD license</license>
  <notes>second release</notes>
  <contents>
    <dir baseinstalldir="example1" name="/">
```

```
      <file name="body.tpl.php" role="php" />
      <file name="head.tpl.php" role="php" />
   </dir> <!-- / -->
</contents>
<dependencies>
  <required>
    <php>
      <min>5.1.0</min>
    </php>
    <pearinstaller>
      <min>1.4.3</min>
    </pearinstaller>
    <package>
      <name>MyBlog</name>
      <channel>pear.chiaraquartet.net</channel>
      <min>0.2.0</min>
      <max>0.2.0</max>
    </package>
  </required>
</dependencies>
<phprelease />
<changelog>
  <release>
    <version>
      <release>0.1.0</release>
      <api>0.1.0</api>
    </version>
    <stability>
      <release>alpha</release>
      <api>beta</api>
    </stability>
    <date>2006-08-18</date>
   <license uri="http://www.opensource.org/licenses/bsd-
                      license.php">BSD license</license>
    <notes>first release</notes>
  </release>
  <release>
    <version>
      <release>1.0.0</release>
      <api>1.0.0</api>
    </version>
    <stability>
      <release>stable</release>
      <api>stable</api>
```

```
      </stability>
      <date>2006-08-18</date>
      <license uri="http://www.opensource.org/licenses/bsd-
                       license.php">BSD license</license>
      <notes>first release</notes>
    </release>
    <release>
      <version>
        <release>2.0.0</release>
        <api>1.0.0</api>
      </version>
      <stability>
        <release>stable</release>
        <api>stable</api>
      </stability>
      <date>2006-08-19</date>
      <license uri="http://www.opensource.org/licenses/bsd-
                       license.php">BSD license</license>
      <notes>second release</notes>
    </release>
  </changelog>
</package>
```

To conclude this final chapter, let's look at `admin.php`, the administrative control center, to see how all of these elements are brought together to display templates, download the right template versions, and install them:

```php
<?php
// silence potential notice
@session_start();
require_once 'MyBlog/Template/Lister.php';
require_once 'MyBlog/Config.php';
$blog_config = new MyBlog_Config;
$lister = new MyBlog_Template_Lister($blog_config->getPearConfig());
$lister->setConfigObject($blog_config);
if (isset($_GET['dodefault'])) {
    unset($_GET['dodefault']);
    $_SESSION['template'] = '#default';
}
if (isset($_GET['t']) && isset($_GET['v'])) {
    require_once 'MyBlog/Template/Fetcher.php';
    require_once 'MyBlog/Template/REST.php';
    $conf = new MyBlog_Config;
    $config = $conf->getPearConfig();
    $rest = new MyBlog_Template_REST($config, array());
```

```php
        $rest->setTemplateChannel($conf->getTemplateChannel());
        $fetch = MyBlog_Template_Fetcher::factory($rest, $config);
        try {
            $fetch->installTemplate($_GET['t'], $_GET['v']);
            $out = '';
            foreach ($fetch->log as $info) {
                if ($info[0] == 'log') {
                    $out .= '    ' .
                    htmlspecialchars($info[1]) . '<br />';
                } else {
                    $out .= htmlspecialchars($info[1]) . '<br />';
                }
            }
            // this is safe because installTemplate throws an exception
            // if the template or version are not valid PEAR
            // package/version
            // so input is validated by this point
            $_SESSION['template'] = $_GET['t'];
            define('MYBLOG_OUTPUT_INFO', $out);
        } catch (MyBlog_Template_Exception $e) {
            define('MYBLOG_OUTPUT_INFO', '<strong>ERROR:</strong> ' .
                $e->getMessage());
        }
    unset($_GET['t']);
    unset($_GET['v']);
}
?><!DOCTYPE HTML PUBLIC "-//W3C//DTD HTML 4.0 Transitional//EN">
<html>
  <head>
    <title>MyBlog Administration</title>
  </head>
  <body>
    <a href="index.php">Return to MyBlog</a><br />
    <h1>MyBlog Administration</h1>
    <?php
    // this is defined in install.php
    if (defined('MYBLOG_OUTPUT_INFO')): ?>
    <h2>Installation Information:</h2>
    <?php echo MYBLOG_OUTPUT_INFO; ?>
    <?php endif;
    ?>
    <h2>Choose a template</h2>
    <?php
      list($info, $pager) = $lister->listRemoteTemplates(1);
```

```
    $links = $pager->getLinks();
    echo $links['all'] . '<br />';
  ?>
  <?php if ($blog_config->getCurrentTemplate() == '#default'): ?>
  <span class="current_template">*</span>
  <?php endif; ?>[Default Template] <em>(Standard, ships with
                install)</em><a href="admin.php?dodefault=1">
                Choose Default Template</a><br />
  <?php
    foreach ($info as $template): ?>
    <?php if ($template['name'] ==
     $blog_config->getCurrentTemplate()): ?>
    <span class="current_template">*</span>
    <?php endif; ?>
    <img src="image.php?<?php echo 't=' .
     htmlspecialchars(urlencode($template['name'])) . '&amp;v=' .
     htmlspecialchars(urlencode($template['version'])); ?>"
     height="36" width="36" />
    <?php echo $template['name'] ?> <em>(<?php
        echo htmlspecialchars($template['summary']) ?>)</em>
    Version <?php echo $template['version'] ?><a
        href="admin.php?t=<?php
        echo htmlspecialchars(urlencode($template['name']))
        ?>&amp;v=<?php
            echo htmlspecialchars($template['version'])
            ?>">Install/Upgrade</a><br />
  <?php endforeach;
      echo '<br />' . $links['all'];
  ?>
 </body>
</html>
```

For experimentation purposes, there are two `package.xml` files available for the MyBlog package in the code included with this book. The first, `package1.xml`, describes itself as MyBlog version 0.1.0, and will display the templates example1 version 1.0.0 and example2 version 1.0.0 as being available for installation. After testing this, execute a from the MyBlog directory, a simple:

$ pear upgrade package.xml

You will be upgraded to MyBlog version 0.2.0. Immediately, you'll notice that only example1 version 2.0.0 is available for installation. This is based upon the fact that example1's `package1.xml` (version 1.0.0) has this required dependency in it:

```
<package>
 <name>MyBlog</name>
 <channel>pear.chiaraquartet.net</channel>
 <min>0.1.0</min>
 <max>0.1.0</max>
</package>
```

Whereas `package.xml` (version 2.0.0) has this required dependency in it:

```
<package>
 <name>MyBlog</name>
 <channel>pear.chiaraquartet.net</channel>
 <min>0.2.0</min>
 <max>0.2.0</max>
</package>
```

These dependencies ensure that the templates are only available for blog versions they are compatible with. As such, if you decide to adopt this model, you'll need to ensure that all templates are released with a `<max>` element in their dependency on the blog, defining the highest version they are known to work with. As new versions are released, the templates can be released with updated `<max>` tags, or modified and then released. In this way, working templates will always be available for the differing blog versions.

In short: complexity is all managed by the internals of the PEAR installer, freeing you to write great programs!

Improvements for the Ambitious

One of the vexing problems of all web-based plug-in installation systems involves security of directory permissions. In order to install something, the web server's user (nobody or apache are common web users) must have write access to the plug-in directory. This means that anyone with an account on the machine and a public web page can write and read from your application's plug-in directory, simply by creating a web page that does this.

In our sample MyBlog, I made the dubious assumption that you are the sole owner of the blog server and do not need to worry about such issues, and did not implement a system for this important security issue.

However, there is a simple solution that requires a bit of work, and is a wonderful exercise for the ambitious. The trick is to provide a link on the page that is a little lock. The user must unlock the directory prior to installation, and it must be locked after.

Locking the page consists of recursively iterating over the internal plug-in directory, and running this simple command:

```
chmod($file_or_dir, 0444);
```

Unlocking is its opposite, recursively iterating over the internal plug-in directory and running this simple command:

```
chmod($file_or_dir, 0777);
```

Why, you might ask, are there no blog or other applications performing this task? There are several answers. First of all, the same task can be accomplished quite easily using a shell script. In other words "let the user take care of their own dang security." Also, this particular security issue simply hasn't been on the radar because it requires a malicious hacker to already have access to the machine to take advantage of it — or so one would think.

The fact is, if the application happens to have a PHP code injection vulnerability, this would allow a malicious hacker to inject code that creates a malicious PHP script on the server, thereby gaining control over the server through the fact that the plug-in directory is writeable! Although it takes a very, very serious vulnerability to become a problem, having writeable directories can make the difference between having and losing control over a production server.

Keep this in mind as you develop — security is always an important task! Try to think like an evildoer as you design, and you will have (and cause) far fewer security vulnerabilities.

Summary

This chapter has been quite a ride. In it, we investigated common practice methods for embedding plug-ins into web applications. Specifically, we examined three examples — MDB2 (subpackages), Serendipity (Spartacus), Seagull (partially embedded PEAR installer). For each of these examples, we weighed the pros and cons of their respective approaches.

Having determined that there may be a better way to do things, we learned how to embed the PEAR installer most effectively, in order to create a plug-in manager.

For this purpose, we created a fake blog program in just under 1000 lines of code that provides the ability to seamlessly query a remote PEAR Channel server designed to distribute templates. Using the internal classes of the PEAR installer, our MyBlog web application can intelligently install and upgrade templates with all of the sophistication expected from the PEAR installer.

We took full advantage of the PEAR installer's built-in REST client to query the remote server, the PEAR installer's download capabilities, and its robust file installer complete with file transactions. In addition, we learned how to extend the remote server's REST code to include a thumbnail image, and instructed our MyBlog's administration page to display these thumbnail images.

Finally, I would like to thank you for reading this guide to the exciting and innovative PEAR installer, and I hope it will serve you well in your quest for the perfect website and developing environment!

Index

PUBLISHING

PHP Programming with PEAR

ISBN: 1-904811-79-5   Paperback: 250 pages

XML, Data, Dates, Web Services, and Web APIs

1. Maximize your productivity through the use of proven, powerful, reusable PHP components

2. In-depth coverage of a range of important PEAR packages

3. Many code examples provide a clear and practical guidance

Building Websites with Joomla!

ISBN: 1-904811-94-9   Paperback: 250 pages

A step by step tutorial to getting your Joomla! CMS website up fast

1. Walk through each step in a friendly and accessible way

2. Customize and extend your Joomla! site

3. Get your Joomla! website up fast

Please check **www.PacktPub.com** for information on our titles

PHPEclipse: A User Guide

ISBN: 1-904811-44-2   Paperback: 206 pages

Take advantage of the leading open source integrated development environment to develop, organize, and debug your PHP web development projects.

1. Compact guide to using Eclipse and PHPEclipse for web development

2. Slash development time by improving the efficiency of your PHP coding and organizing your projects in the PHPEclipse environment

3. Learn to use Eclipse for debugging PHP applications, interfacing with databases, and managing source code

4. No previous knowledge of Eclipse required

AJAX and PHP: Building Responsive Web Applications

ISBN: 1-904811-82-5   Paperback: 275 pages

Enhance the user experience of your PHP website using AJAX with this practical tutorial featuring detailed case studies.

1. Build a solid foundation for your next generation of web applications

2. Use better JavaScript code to enable powerful web features

3. Leverage the power of PHP and MySQL to create powerful back-end functionality and make it work in harmony with the smart AJAX client

4. Go through 8 case studies that demonstrate how to implement AJAX-enabled features in your site

Please check **www.PacktPub.com** for information on our titles

DATE DUE

Library Store #47-0108 Peel Off Pressure Sensitive

Printed in the United States
70253LV00004B/32